Earth, Love and Doom

(Mythico-Symbolic Dimensions of Sri Aurobindo's *Savitri*)

Earth, Love and Doom

(Mythico-Symbolic Dimensions of Sri Aurobindo's *Savitri*)

Nanda Kishore Mishra

AUTHORSPRESS

Worldwide Circulation through Authorspress Global Network
First Published 2007
by
Authorspress
E-35/103, Jawahar Park
Laxmi Nagar, Delhi-110 092
e-mail: authorspress@yahoo.com

Earth, Love and Doom
(Mythico-Symbolic Dimensions of Sri Aurobindo's Savitri)
ISBN 978-81-7273-383-4

Printed in India at Tarun Offset, Delhi.

All came back to her: Earth and Love and Doom,
The ancient disputants, encircled her
Like giant figures wrestling in the night:
The godheads from the dim Inconscient born
Awoke to struggle and the pang divine...

Savitri (Bk.I, Can.I)

Preface

My debts to various sources have been duly acknowledged in the endnotes. However, I would like to record with utmost candour my gratitude to the staff of the National Library, Kolkata, Sri Aurobindo Library, Pondicherry and Gangadhar Meher College, Sambalpur, Orissa, for allowing me access to their invaluable resources.

Many of the chapters form a significant part of a project I had carried out a little more than two decades ago. I acknowledge with gratitude to the University Grants Commission, New Delhi, for their financial help, enabling me to purchase books and journals for the said project.

I must express enormous debt I owe to the late Dr. P. K. Pati, former Professor and Head of the P.G. Department of English, Ravenshaw College, Cuttack and Sambalpur University, and former Vice-Chancellor of Sambalpur University, for his unfailing encouragement and wise counsel. I express my sense of deep gratitude to the late Prof. L. S. R. Krishna Sastry of Andhra University, who readily agreed to Dr. Pati's request and accepted me as a research scholar and thus aroused my deep love and interest for an intensive study of Sri Aurobindo's *Savitri.* He used to take care of my comfortable stay at Visakhapatnam during my several trips there. He graciously guided me at every stage of my research work. His love and affection have always remained a source of constant inspiration to me in moving forward in life.

It is with deep reverence that I acknowledge the enlightening guidance I received from Mr. K.D. Sethna, a close disciple of Sri Aurobindo, and a poet and critic of renown. I am most indebted, however, to my good friend, Ms Ashalata Dash of Pondicherry, for her cheers and jeers that kept my inspiration unabated.

I am really grateful to Prof. Uma Parameswaran of University of Winnipeg, Canada, and late (Prof.) Bidhubhushan Das, Former Director of Higher Education, Bhubaneswar, Orissa, for their insightful suggestions. The book has immensely profited from the constructive suggestions of Dr. Ashok K. Mohapatra, Rader, P.G. Department of English, Sambalpur University, who proposed changes and additions that have enhanced the quality of some chapters. I sincerely express my deep sense of gratitude to my wife, Dr. Sabita Tripathy, Reader, P.G. Department of English, Sambalpur University, to my daughter Ms Meerambika Mishra and to my son Sri Ashirbad Mishra who have so painstakingly adjusted with my time in the preparation of this book.

My sincere thanks are due to Kcherry Sudarshan, Managing Director of Authorspress, New Delhi, for the pains he has undertaken to publish this book. I also thank Dr. Nandini Sahu of IGNOU, New Delhi for giving inspiration to publish the book by Authorspress. Working in out-of-the-way places in Orissa, I had to face many difficulties in bringing this project to a satisfactory close. Were it not for the Grace of Sri Aurobindo and the Mother that sustained me through the hard days and enabled me to persevere in my endeavour, this work would not have seen the light of day. In all humility and with profound faith, I offer this modest work of mine at Their Lotus Feet.

N.K. Mishra

Contents

1

Sri Aurobindo: The Modern Vyasa

Sri Aurobindo is, indeed, one of those grand personalities who are cast in a colossal mould. It is difficult to present an accurate account of his early life as he has cautioned us: "No one can write about my life because it has not been on the surface for men to see."[1] Even from the surface point of view any attempt to write about Sri Aurobindo's life presents many difficulties due to his multidimensional personality. To recount them, he was a Professor of English and French, a scholar, a political leader, a journalist, a philosopher, a yogi, a mystic, a dramatist, an indologist, a psychologist, a literary critic, a poet, a translator, and an interpreter of the *Vedas,* the *Upanishads* and the *Bhagavad Gita.* K. D. Sethna, a staunch admirer and literary lieutenant of Sri Aurobindo, is awed by the latter's staggering personality and multi-form achievements:

> How shall we crown Sri Aurobindo? Is he greater as a *Yogi* than as a philosopher? Does the literary critic in him out-top the sociological thinker? Does he shine brighter as a politician or as a poet? It is difficult to decide. Everywhere Mount Everest seems to face Mount Everest. But when we study this Himalayas of various extremes of height, the first eminence that strikes us is Sri Aurobindo the poet.[2]

In keeping with the Indian traditional outlook, Robindranath Tagore and Romain Rolland have acclaimed Sri Aurobindo as the last of the great *Rishi,* an embodiment of a complete synthesis of the "genius of Asia and the genius of Europe." While eulogising Sri Aurobindo's overall achievements, *The Times Literary*

Supplement dated 8 July 1944 published under the editorship of D. L. Murray, records:

> He is not an arm-chair philosopher, but a man who, having led a life of intense activity, has retired to brood over it, if one may say so of a Hindu, in the dim light of a Gothic Cathedral. In fact, he is a new type of thinker, one who combines in his vision the alacrity of the West with the illumination of the East. To study his writings is to enlarge the boundaries of one's knowledge.

It is not easy to record the biography of such a great *Rishi* whose inner life is screened from his outer one as it is mysterious and unfathomable. Sri Aurobindo too issues a word of caution against any attempt to record the biography of a spiritual man:

> First of all, what matters in a spiritual man's life is not what he did or what he was outside to the view of the men of his time (that is what historicity and biography comes to... but what he was and did within; it is only that gives any value to his outer life at all. It is the inner life that gives to the outer any power it may have and the inner life of a spiritual man is something vast and dull and, at least in the great figures, so crowded and teeming with significant things that no biographer or historian could ever hope to seize it all or tell it.[3]

When one of his disciples once approached him to grant permission for writing his biography, Sri Aurobindo's curt reply was – "I do not want to be murdered by my own disciples in cold print."[4] It is partly true because he led an unobtrusive and shy life which he reveals in a letter dated 02 October 1934: "I was never ardent about fame even in my political days; I preferred to remain behind the curtain, push people without their knowing it and get things done."[5] In spite of all these forbidding, some attempts must be made here to assess Sri Aurobindo's personality as a seer poet.

Sri Aurobindo was born in the house of Barrister Mono Mohan Ghose in Calcutta, in the early morning of 15 August 1872. His father, Dr. Krishna Dhan Ghose, was a civil surgeon. When Dr. Ghose was 19 years old, he had married Swarnalata, the eldest daughter of Dr. Rajnarayan Bose according to the Adi Brahma Samaj rites. Dr. K. D. Ghose went to England in 1869 for further medical studies and returned in 1871 as an atheist being thoroughly Anglicised in his taste and preferences. As a consequence he subjected his children to a thoroughgoing process of Westernisation, a course of action favoured by many Bengali enlightened fathers at that time. After giving them initial education in an Irish nuns' school in Darjeeling, he sent them to England in 1879 and placed them under the charge of an English clerical couple, Mr. and Mrs. Drewett, with strict instructions to insulate their mind from Indian influence. Thus, Aurobindo and his brothers were brought up as Anglicised children. Mr. Drewett, being an accomplished Latin scholar, made Sri Aurobindo an avid learner of Latin. Moreover, the headmaster of St. Paul's School in London was so pleased with Sri Aurobindo's knowledge in Latin that he took personal care to teach him Greek and then promoted him rapidly into higher classes of his school.

Besides focusing his attention on his school-course, Sri Aurobindo used to spend most of his time at St. Paul reading English poetry, literature, fiction, and French literature, the history of ancient, medieval and modern Europe. He also showed a keen interest in learning Italian, some German and a little Spanish. To compose poems was a special passion with him even at a tender age. He secured the Butterworth Prize for literature and the Bedford Prize for history. This was the time of the greatest suffering and poverty. All three brothers, Benoy Bhushan, Mono-Mohan and Sri Aurobindo, were often in financial difficulties owing to irregular remittance from their father. Scholarship and stipend were the only source of money for their sustenance in London.

Sri Aurobindo successfully completed his school course at St. Paul obtaining senior classical scholarship. He then joined King's College at Cambridge where he studied for two years. He was awarded prizes in Greek and Latin verse in one year and passed the First Part of the Tripos, securing a first class from Cambridge. He would have got the degree, had he applied for it but a degree in England was only valuable if one wanted to take up an academic career. To respect the wishes of his father, he passed the open competition for the Indian Civil Service in 1890 securing high marks in Greek and Latin. But by certain manoeuvres he managed to get himself disqualified for horse riding without himself rejecting the service because he wanted to escape from the bondage of ICS service. Moreover, his family would not have allowed him to reject the offer.

Sri Aurobindo with his brothers became members of a society called "Lotus and Dagger" while at Cambridge. Then for some time he worked as the Secretary of the "Indian *Majlis*" and delivered many fiery and revolutionary speeches, which might have helped the authorities to exclude him from the Indian Civil Service; the failure in the riding test was merely a plea.

Having a great passion for reading, Sri Aurobindo was thoroughly acquainted with British along with other European thought and literature. His poetic ambitions were nurtured in 'the Edwardian romantic twilight' when the literary vogue was to experiment with blank verse poetic drama and write long poems. Most of his poetic creations project his implicit desire to excel in allegorical epic and mystical poetry, an ambition that seems to be redundant in the modern days. He remained unaffected by the modernist revolution brought in by Hopkins, W.B. Yeats, Ezra Pound, Eliot, etc, in modern poetry and dared to set his unique trend of a mystical age in poetry. No doubt his poetic trend has faced rough weather and received adverse criticism. H. M. Williams is very vocal in articulating the mordant criticism levelled against Sri Aurobindo's truncated literary fame and poetic achievement in the following way:

> Like his idol Milton, he erected a Chinese wall of English, using a highly abstract and abstruse literary style, almost a poetic jargon; recent Indo-Anglian poets have therefore have rejected him in favour of the idioms derived from Eliot and W.H. Auden preferring the 'colloquial' to the Aurobindonean 'mandarin'.[6]

If there was any intellectual and emotional attachment with any European land as a second country, it was not England but France, which he never saw in his lifetime. The irony of his life is that he took shelter in the French-dominated Pondicherry for more than 40 years in the later part of his life.

After being disqualified from the Indian Civil Service, Sri Aurobindo was introduced to the Gaekwad of Baroda, Sir Sayaji Rao who was then in London, by the brother of Sir Henry Cotton, and obtained an appointment in the Baroda State Service. Finally, he sailed in the *Carthage* to join the Baroda State Service in December 1892. The day he set his feet on the Indian soil, he had an ineffable spiritual experience at Apollo Bunder in Bombay. While recording his spiritual experience of that day, Sri Aurobindo felt as if his life was sent as a mission to earth for a divine purpose:

> Since I set foot on the Indian soil on the Apollo Bunder in Bombay, I began to have spiritual experiences, but these were not divorced from this world but had an inner and infinite bearing on it, such as a feeling of the Infinite pervading material space and the Immanent inhabiting material objects and bodies. At the same time I found myself entering supraphysical worlds and planes with influences and an effect from them upon the material plane, so I could make no sharp divorce or irreconcilable opposition between what I have called the two ends of existence and all that lies between them.[7]

Sri Aurobindo rendered valuable services to the Baroda state from 1893 to 1906 in various capacities. Initially, he was employed in the Land Settlement Department for a short time. Then he served the Central Revenue Office and the Secretariat and was a part-time Lecturer in French at Baroda College. Later on he was appointed Professor of English as well as French as soon as the post of Professor of English fell vacant. Subsequently, as years passed on he became the Vice-Principal of the college and then the acting Principal. He was called upon at times to draft memoranda, public speeches of the Maharaja and other work related to literary or educational matters which needed careful drafting. He often helped the Maharaja when he was invited to breakfast in carrying out his correspondence work with him. Once Sri Aurobindo was taken to Kashmir as the Secretary of the Maharaja, but there was much friction between him and the Maharaja, thereafter such a venture was never repeated with the Maharaja.

While in India he felt the dire necessity of learning some Indian languages. So he employed private tutors to learn Bengali (his mother tongue) and Sanskrit – a subject that has a rich literature. When he was in Baroda, it was easy for him to learn

Marathi and Gujurati; moreover, he studied the Hindu scriptures in Sanskrit. He made all efforts to assimilate the spirit of Indian culture and literature. Thus, at Baroda he reversed his father's process of Anglicisation by learning Indian languages and by rediscovering Indian religion, spirituality and philosophy. Besides teaching and administration he absorbed himself during this period in creative literature, political journalism and *yoga*. He evinced a keen interest to meet *yogis* and *sanyāsis* -such as, Swami Paramahamsa Maharaja, Indraswarup, Brahmananda, Madhardas and discussed spiritual matters with them to meet the curiosities of his agnostic mind.

Sri Aurobindo's intense patriotic love at last led him to choose the path of the life of a yogi. Let us analyse the political scene of those days in India that had attracted his total involvement. The British crown had taken over the administration of the country from the East India Company after the Sepoy Mutiny of 1857 (the first war of Indian Independence). Repressive measures were adopted by the British Government to subdue the patriotic zeal of the Indian people. The motive of colonial domination was economic exploitation during the British rule. The rulers looked upon India as a potential supplier of raw materials and a vast consumer in manufactured goods of England.

The birth of modern nationalism in Europe and America had brought about radical changes in the political arena of the world. Monarchy, feudalism, colonialism, autocracy and arbitrary rule received a serious jolt in some countries. The pioneers of nationalism became the role models of educated people in the colonised countries. Moreover, Western education had helped to arouse patriotic love and nationalistic fervour in the educated Indians. It has already been pointed out how Sri Aurobindo as a young man used to participate in the political debates during his leisure time in the "Indian Majlis" in London where he strongly advocated for liberation of India from British rule.

During the period of his Barodà service, Sri Aurobindo became more engrossed in the mission of political liberation of India. Lord Curzon's decision of the partition of Bengal provided him the immediate cause to give up his service at Baroda and came to Calcutta in 1906 to join as Principal of the newly founded Bengal National College. He was completely involved in intense political activities from 1902 to 1910, writing political pamphlets and journalistic articles. History can never forget that he played a key role in the Indian National Congress without projecting himself too much. The partition of Bengal provided an impetus to the rise of the extremist party and the nationalist movement gathered momentum. Sri Aurobindo took Barin's suggestion into confidence and wrote some inflammatory articles in the *Yugāntar* that advocated absolute denial of the British rule and incited the people for open revolt against the British Government. Spontaneously, the paper exerted tremendous influence on the mind of the people of Bengal for frenzied action.

As a sagacious thinker and writer on political freedom, Sri Aurobindo came to limelight by contributing articles to the *Indu Prakash* that was being published under the able editorship of K.G. Deshpande, his Cambridge friend. The nine articles he wrote under the caption "New Lamp for Old" vehemently denounced the then Congress "policy of prayer, petition and protest" and emphasized the need for a dynamic leadership and action. So he admired the role of Bal Gangadhar Tilak publicly as the only national dynamic leader to head a revolutionary party. Sri Aurobindo relentlessly pursued a unique police of giving encouragement to young men for propagation of the Swadeshi principle, which was in its infancy those days. He repeatedly reminded people through his fiery speeches and writings to shake off the economic yoke and develop Indian trade and industry as a necessary "Concomitant of the revolutionary endeavour."

So long as Sri Aurobindo continued in the Baroda Service, he refrained himself from taking active part openly in polities and preferred to remain behind the scene. After coming over to Calcutta, he became the working editor of an extremist newspaper, the *Bande Mataram*. The title of the daily newspaper was derived from the opening line of a famous Bengali novel, *Anand Math*, written by Bankim Chandra Chatterjee. The title of the novel became a battle cry, a potent *mantra* (to arouse patriotism) and political slogan. Sri Aurobindo's open involvement in politics lasted about three and a half years, from the middle of 1906 to February 1910. The action of the Government in prosecuting him as the editor of the *Bande Mataram* failed miserably. He was honourably acquitted of the charges levelled against him and people acknowledged him as a peerless national leader. Circumstances obliged him to take a leading part at Surat Congress held in December 1907.

The Calcutta session of the Indian National Congress in December 1906 gave an opportunity to act in unison with great nationalist leaders, such as, Lala Lajpat Rai, Lokamanya B.G. Tilak and others. By the time Sri Aurobindo withdrew from politics and came to Pondicherry, he had made an indelible mark; had done much to change the whole face of Indian politics. He had helped to awaken the supine spirit of people for political freedom as their cardinal goal, and had paved the way for non-cooperation and resistance. He was the first Indian to declare through the columns of the Bengali weekly *Yugantar* that the goal of India was to get completely free from British control in order to develop according to her own genius. *The Bande Mataram* was the first political journal that declared certain programmes of the nationalist party, such as non-cooperation, passive resistance, Swadeshi, boycott, national education, settlement of disputes in law by popular arbitration, etc. Sri Aurobindo engaged himself as a relentless warrior to declare persistently complete and absolute independence as the goal of political action through the pages of the journal. *The Bande Mataram* was unique in its journalistic endeavour to exert tremendous influence on the minds of the people to prepare them for broad-based revolutionary activities. As a sequel to his plunge into hectic political action, he had renounced all his personal comforts in all probability with a strong faith in the emancipation of his motherland. Such type of single-minded devotion to work was the imperative need of that time which Sri Aurobindo aptly gives voice to in one of his important short poems "A God's Labour":

> He who would bring the heavens here
> Must descend himself into clay
> And the burden of earthly nature bear
> And tread the dolorous way.[8]

On charges of sedition, Sri Aurobindo was arrested and detained in the Alipure Jail in connection with the Muzafarpore bomb case. The false charges framed against him were Govt's ploy to suppress his rebellious activities so his trial in the court room provoked nation-wide interest. Once again the prosecution failed and he was released on 6 May 1909. His confinement in jail for a year worsened the economic backbone of the *Bande Mataram*, and finally it was decided, "The journal should die a glorious death rather than perish by starvation."[9] The Government's ploy to stunt his political action got spoiled. He had earlier written the editorial articles so cleverly and skilfully that no legal action could be justified for his prosecution on the ground of sedition or libel.

To awaken the supine spirit of the people, it was necessary to provide the right kind of education to them. A system of National Education evolved by Sri Aurobindo was another programme that received his utmost attention. During his tenure as a teacher in Baroda College he had come to realise the pitfalls of the British system of education and its ineffectiveness in Indian condition as a waste and a yoke of servitude. Moreover, this system of education taught wrong intellectual habits, provided narrow information and mechanical instructions. The movement to provide an alternative system of education had made a good start. Many national schools were established wherein reputed and able men volunteered to teach. Sri Aurobindo had poured his heart in this programme, but his sudden departure from Bengal gave a serious jolt, a setback to the scheme; gradually most of the schools started tottering, either could not survive or fell far short of the expectation.

During his solitary confinement in Alipore jail Sri Aurobindo used to spent almost all his time in the study of the *Gita*, and at the same time practised yoga. C. R. Das, one of his national collaborators and a famous legal expert, had poured his heart and soul in the case to exonerate Sri Aurobindo from all seditious charges. The eloquent speech of Deshabandhu Chittaranjan Das delivered in defence of Sri Aurobindo in the courtroom presents the best estimate of Sri Aurobindo's personality against the backdrop of revolutionary political scene in those days:

> Long after this controversy is hushed in silence, long after this turmoil, this agitation ceases, long after he is dead and gone, Aurobindo will be looked upon as the poet of patriotism, as the prophet of nationalism and as the lover of humanity.... His words will be echoed and re-echoed not only in India but across distant seas and lands.[10]

Sri Aurobindo remained unperturbed in the proceedings of his case, as he had received an assurance from his inner self that he would be definitely acquitted of the charges levelled against him by the British Police. Thereafter his lifestyle changed drastically and he adopted yoga for divine guidance, to derive spiritual force and energy.

After Sri Aurobindo was acquitted of the Alipore Bomb Case, he found the then political atmosphere quite depressing. Most of the nationalist leaders were placed in confinement or in self-imposed exile. For the first time in his famous Uttarpara speech, he spoke publicly of his practice of yoga and his inner experiences. While he was working late up to night at the *Karmayogin* office, he received secret information about the Government's intention to search the office for his arrest. He too received a sudden command from within to abdicate his political role and to go to Chandernagore (then in French India). In response to the divine command, he became ready to leave Calcutta. Within a few minutes he reached the riverbank, crossed Hooghly in a boat. At Chandernagore, he stayed in a secret house and sent messages to Sister Nivedita to take up the editing work of the *Karmayogin* in his absence. At Chandernagore he was divinely directed to proceed incognito to Pondicherry. Finally, dissociating himself completely from hectic political activities, he reached Pondicherry, the "Cave of his *Tapasyā*" on April 4, 1910.

The first yogic experience he gained was the outcome of following the instructions of Vishnu Bhaskar Lele. They stayed together for three days. Sri Aurobindo wanted to develop spiritual powers to free India. He looked upon India as his own mother. His clarion call for sacrifice for the motherland became a new gospel. He wanted India to be completely free so as to spread spirituality to the world because he believed that India alone with her rich culture and a vast wealth of spiritual knowledge and experience was qualified among other countries to give a turn of spirituality to the modern the world.

Sri Aurobindo had a great mystic experience – Narayana darshan (*Vasudevah Sarvam*) : everything is Vasudeva – when he was confined to Alipore jail. This mystic experience effected a radical change in his outlook, which is reflected in his "Uttarpara Speech." He lent his inner voice through this famous speech to abjure active politics and made it explicitly clear that all great movements wait for their God-sent leader, "the willing channel of His Force." He came to realise that his personal intervention in politics was no longer necessary:

> As his vision of the future grew clearer, he saw that the eventual independence of India was assured by the march of forces of which he became aware, that Britain would be compelled by the pressure of Indian resistance and by the pressure of international events to concede independence and that she was already moving towards that eventuality with whatever opposition and reluctance.[11]

He lived in complete seclusion and practised silent yoga at Pondicherry. On receiving an inner divine command he changed the course of his life to set before him a vast magnitude of spiritual task that needed all his time and energy. His retirement from active politics did not cease his interest in the world affair or the fate of India. He continued to keep a close watch on all that was happening in and around India because "the very principle of his Yoga was not only to realise the Divine and attain to a complete spiritual consciousness, but also to take all life and all world activity into the scope of this spiritual consciousness and action and to base life on the Spirit and give it a spiritual meaning."[12]

As he concentrated his energy on *yogic sādhanā,* he came to possess a spiritual dynamic power. This spiritual power he used in a limited field of personal work but more on the development of the world. It is said that he had to apply his spiritual force behind the Allies from the moment of the incident at Dunkirk when the world was apprehending the fall of England vis-à-vis the triumph of Hitler. Sri Aurobindo did it deliberately because in his inward eye he saw Hitler and Nazism as dark *a-ssuric* forces. Their success would mean the enslavement of mankind to the course of evolution and especially to the spiritual evolution of the race. What is still worse is political enslavement does not allow the liberation of man's soul. Sri Aurobindo had sent a donation of Rs. 1,000 to the Secretary of the Viceroy of India for the War Fund as the token of his support to the cause of the Allies. Long back in 1906 the prophecy he made is being realised even today:

> A divine Power is behind the movement; the *Zeit-Geist*, the Time-Spirit, is at work to bring about a mighty movement of which the world at the present juncture has need. That movement is the resurgence of Asia, and the resurgence of India is not only a necessary part of the larger movement but its central need. India is the keystone of the arch, the chief inheritress of the common Asiatic destiny.... The idea of a free and united India has been born and grown to full stature in the land of the Rishis, and the spiritual force of a great civilisation of which the world has need, is gathering at its beck.[13]

From being an advocate of militant nationalism, he emerged through an inner guidance as the apostle of Indian spirituality and *yoga*. He became a great exponent of modern Indian Renaissance.

Yoga in Life and Literature

One's understanding of *Savitri* remains incomplete without a reference to Sri Aurobindo's Integral Yoga. From 1910 to 1950 Literature, yoga and spiritual *sādhanā* became the be-all and the end-all of his daily activities at Pondicherry. It is necessary to understand the importance of *Integral Yoga* as propounded by him that has got a direct bearing on his poetry and philosophical thoughts. His teaching is in tune with those of the ancient sages of India who have posited the view that behind the appearance there is the Reality of a Being and Consciousness, a Self of all things. All beings are united in that One Self but apparently divided by a separative consciousness, an ignorance of their true self. It is possible by a certain psychological discipline to remove this veil of separative consciousness and become aware of the true Self, the Divinity within man. Sri Aurobindo further explains that this one Being and Consciousness is involved in Matter. Evolution is the method by which it gradually and very slowly liberates itself. In the Inconscient there appears consciousness and by being self-impelled this dim consciousness grows higher and higher for developments towards greater perfection, towards Supermind. Formation of life is the first step of this release of consciousness and mind is the second stage. The next future step of the evolution will be the emergence of a higher state of consciousness in man which by nature will be spiritual and supramental. As per the hidden divine plan then full blossoming of consciousness will provide support to life to manifest itself perfectly on the earth. From the spiritual point of view man's life on earth can be considered incomplete, flawed and held in transition.

Man lives mostly in his surface mind, life and body; but there is an inner being within him with greater possibilities, which needs to be awakened. One has therefore to undergo the discipline of *Yoga* to open the vast ranges of this inner being. Then only can man govern his outer being by the light and force of his inner being. For perfection of life conquest of desire, attachment and a control over the body, its greed and instincts are inevitable. The whole being of man has to be trained so that it effectively responds to and gets transformed by the greater Light and Force of the Supreme. The main aim of Integral Yoga is an inner development so that each one can discover the One Self in all and transform himself to divinise human nature.

After intense practice of *sādhanā* and as the sequel of his spiritual realisations, Sri Aurobindo came to realise the imperative need of *yoga* in man's life. To him, "All life is yoga," and *Yoga* means the efforts towards self-perfection by uniting God and Nature with life. It blends man's mental make-up with his spiritual potentiality. Among all living beings man alone is perfectly made by God for higher mental spiritual work. So he is Nature's mould for future divine perfection. No other discipline except *yoga* can endow man with necessary equipments for self-perfection and liberation of the soul from the bondage of ignorance:

> The principle of Yoga is the turning of one or of all powers of human existence into a means of reaching the divine Being. In an ordinary Yoga one main power of being or one group of its powers is made the man's vehicle, path. In a synthetic Yoga all powers will be combined and included in the transmuting instrumentation.[14]

There are three aspects of a man's life — bodily life, mental life, and divine life. By the liberation and progress of the soul, we mean, God and Nature provide opportunities for man's ascent towards perfection. The body, the mind, the intellect, or the heart — any one of these could be improved for self-perfection. In *Hatha Yoga*, the body is the principal agent of transformation because the soul and the body are closely connected. The aim of a *Hathayogin* is to awaken the soul in the physical body. Through the practice of āsana and prāṇāyām – a systematic control of the limbs and breathing – a *Hathayogin* achieves control over his body's vital energy; emotions and links them with the universal energy. In *Rajayoga,* the control of mind leads to total mastery over man's consciousness. Besides these there are some more classical paths – *Karma Yoga, Jnāna Yoga,* and *Bhakti Yoga* which have been dealt with by many Indian sages. Even in the great Indian poem The Bhagavad *Gita* there is a reference to all these wings of *yogas* for perfection of man's body, mind and spirit. Sri Aurobindo synthesises all these multifarious *yogas* and Divises a scheme of *Purna Yoga, Integral Yoga.* In Integral Yoga as designed by him all aspects of life could be utilised to bring about the desired union with God vis-à-vis the desired transformation of man. A full treatise on *yoga* has been published under the title of the *Synthesis of Yoga* and another book *Letters on Yoga* is a compilation of the questions and answers put to Sri Aurobindo at various times by the seekers of spiritual life. During his later life he volunteered himself to answer the queries of the disciples, the sādhaks off and on. While expounding on the basic tenets of Integral *Yoga,* he reiterates his views that the Alpha and Omega of human existence should be to commune with the Divine Lord:

> The object of the yoga is to enter into and be possessed by the Divine presence and consciousness, to love the Divine for the Divine's sake alone, to be tuned in our nature into the nature of the Divine, and in our will and works and life to be the instrument of the Divine. Its object is not to be a great yogi or a Superman (although that may come) or to grab at the Divine for the sake of the ego's power, pride or pleasure. It is not for *Moksha* though liberation comes by it and all else may come, but these must not be our objects. The Divine alone is our object.[15]

Sri Aurobindo believes that the Absolute is the triune principle of Existence-Conscious Force-Bliss called "Satchidananda." The world of men and matter, i.e., the lowest field of ignorance is projected by Supermind and Overmind. Supermind is an expression of the Real-Idea and as the executive force of creative development. This state is the vision of the Absolute truth. Overmind is the link between Supermind and Mind. Supermind and Overmind are different phases of the Absolute developing the field of ignorance. Matter is the expression of the substance of the Absolute. Matter in its rudimentary state is inconscient, later in animals it becomes subconscient, and in man it is superconscient. All are finite centres of the Absolute limited by the action of Divine *Māyā*. *Māyā* is used in the sense of the faculty of the Absolute, which delimits Itself into finite centres. Life is the expression of the Conscious-Force of the Absolute. Mind is the mental expression of the Absolute. Soul is the expression of bliss of the Absolute and consists of two aspects: (a) the Surface Soul which is dominated by vital desires, and (b) the Psyching Being or growing individual moving from experience to experience.

The Absolute in a subtle invisible way ascends from matter upwards known as the evolutionary process. The knot of the matter is broken by man's growth into Supermind. 'Life- Divine' is the discipline, *sādhanā* to achieve the state of Supermind. When Sri Aurobindo uses the expression Divine *Māyā*, it does not mean illusion. It is, on the other hand, divine action developing multiple centres of the Absolute. Matter, life and mind are the veiled consciousness of the Absolute in seeming opposition. Some philosophers advance the hypothesis that matter is an illusion. If the material plane is an illusion, the individual along with the universe and the Absolute can be illusions. When man drops his ego-sense and enlarges his consciousness then only the true view will be revealed to him. Sri Aurobindo's philosophical thought pronounces that Matter, Life, Mind, and Supermind are stages of the Absolute which are to be accepted as equally real. As the Absolute is real, all its parts too are real. Human ego senses the cosmic Being as a dream or *Mā yā*, but this is false. Cosmic Being is the reality of the Absolute. So from the point of view of Sri Aurobindo's Integral *Yoga* the individual, the universe and the Transcendent are not contraries but complimentary states of the Absolute. In other words, the Absolute conceals itself in Matter, Life and Mind. The universe is the extension of the Absolute in time and space. From the point of view of Integral *Yoga* the world of pain, ignorance and death is the transitional stage of the Absolute leading to ultimate bliss. The ego and its dualities are the root cause of death, incapacity and suffering. It is when the ego gets transformed into Overmind or Supermind consciousness then only desire, incapacity and suffering of man can disappear.

Human aspiration to seek God, freedom, and immortality cannot be checked by the contradictions of his ordinary life, as these are his archetypal instincts. Matter, life and mind are the veiled consciousess of the Absolute in seeming oppositions in this world. These are the steps that point to the advancement of man into higher matter, higher life and higher mind. From the point of view of human ego, mind, matter and life are contraries but in the field of Integral Yoga these are complimentaries; hence, neither to be eliminated nor neglected. Divine action alone can liberate the individual soul from the bondage of the ego, ignorance. It is in this universe only that man can realise the Absolute. A spiritually liberated man realises a sense of impersonality by achieving universal consciousness. From the point of view of human ego the individual life ends in death; so the existence of God comes into question. When man's consciousness is supramentalised, the ego and its dualities disappear. Pain and pleasure are the intermediate stages from which the mental being makes advances. Mind is an intermediate phenomenon. It is not the creatrix of the world. It is an instrument of descending creation and an instrument of ascent to the Absolute.

As the individual and the universe are all appearances and not the separate states of the Absloute, Sri Aurobindo seeks to harmonise the two ends of existence, Spirit and Matter. Man's present existence in the material world is not a mistake or an illusion to be cast aside by the soul that aspires for *nirvānic* state. In the darkness and nescience is involved the presence and possibilities of the Divine. In the futuristic scheme of earthly evolution, Divine Consciousness in things will be manifested out of the Inconscience. We are still under the illusion that mind is a higher achievement man has got through the evolutionary process of Nature but it is not the last stage. A Supermind or the eternal Truth-Consciousness will blossom out in human mind, which has the self-determining light and power of Divine Knowledge. Mind is really in a state of ignorance which seeks after Truth, but Supermind is a self-existed knowledge which can bring out an overall perfection of man.

Sri Aurobindo's teaching starts from that of the ancient sages of India who reveal that behind the appearance of the universe there lies the "Reality of a Being and Consciousness, a Self" which is only one and eternal. All beings are united with that One Self and spirit but divided by their separative ego-mind, a sort of ignorance of their true Self and Reality. Sri Aurobindo contends that it is possible to remove the veil of separative consciousness by some psycho-spiritual discipline so that man can become aware of his true self.

Sri Aurobindo posits the view that in the universe the one Being and Consciousness is involved in matter. Evolution is the method that can liberate the involved Being: so that consciousness can appear in what seems to be inconscient. Expounding on the subtle process of the material and spiritual evolution that is taking place surreptitiously, he says:

> Life is the first step of this release of consciousness; mind is the second; but the evolution does not finish with mind, it awaits a release into something greater, a consciousness which is spiritual and supramental. The next step of the evolution must be towards the development of Supermind and Spirit as the dominant power in the conscious being. For only then will the involved Divinity in things release itself entirely and it become possible for life to manifest perfection.[16]

Nature has automatically released life in various forms down the ages. But the mental will in man does not go up the higher stages; it stops at a certain point and then moves in a circle. A breakthrough has to be made through a conscious participation in order to break the circle so that mind achieves higher consciousness. Ancient seers prescribed strict discipline and method in *Yoga* to raise ones consciousness. But the sages and disciples in the past were self-complacent and drew away from the world so as to remain content with higher principles, which would release the spiritual self out of the material world. When the spiritual self is aroused it drives away mind's ignorance, its very limited knowledge by a supramental Truth-Consciousness. Supramental consciousness enables the awakened being to discard his animal self and to grow into a divine being. His outward mind, life, and body govern man's life, but there is an inner being within with greater possibilities to which man is not awake. The first step of *Yoga* is therefore to open the ranges of this inner being, which can govern the outward life by its inner light and force to discover his true self. He has to live in his soul and purify it, and orientate the rest of his nature. There will follow a descent of a higher principle of the Being. Of course the mind has to pass through several ranges of consciousness between the ordinary mind and the supramental Truth-Consciousness. The process of this self-discipline, *sādhana* is therefore long and difficult, but not an impossibility. The type of self-discipline inevitable is a conquest of desire, attachment and a control over the body and its needs, greed and instincts.

This in short is Sri Aurobindo's teaching in *On Yoga* and its method of practice. It is wrong to suppose that he has enunciated a new religion. It must be emphasized that Integral Yoga aims at a conscious union with the Divine in the supermind and the transformation of human nature. It is a spiritual adventure, the odyssey of the soul. Other *yogas* emphasize the path to go straight from mind into some cosmic silence and disappear into the highest. But the object of Sri Aurobindo's Integral Yoga is to transcend mind and enter into the Divine Consciousness. To bring down the supramental consciousness upon earth is the aim of his yoga. It is a double movement of ascent and descent; one rises to the highest level of consciousness, at the same time brings down its power not only into mind and life, but also into the body. In the old *Yoga* those who seek the Self separate themselves from mind and life, abandon life for *Nirvānā* or some Heaven but Integral Yoga does not advocate abandonment of life. The cardinal task in Sri Aurobindo's yoga is to bring down the supramental power for transformation of terrestrial life and being. In this he does not agree with Shankar's Māyāvāda that the world is an illusion, *mithyā*. In the opinion of the former the Brahman is here as well as in the supracosmic Absolute. It is ignorance that makes man blind and prevents him from realising the Brahman in this world as well as beyond it. It can hardly be supposed that the Divine Reality employs its power or force only to create "a universal falsehood, a cosmic lie— *mithyā*."

People have a wrong notion that Sri Aurobindo's teaching is wholly based on the *Gita*. Whereas the *Gita* teaches cessation of birth in the world as the ultimate aim of its Yoga, it does not speak anything about spiritual evolution. Neither does it hint at the higher planes of consciousness and bringing down of the Supermind, the Supramental Truth Consciousness as the only means for transformation of earthly life. Even if the idea of the supermind is indicated in the *Rig Veda,* it does not appear in the Hindu tradition. The advancement of all these concepts constitutes the novelty of Sri Aurobindo's message in Integral Yoga. Moreover, the process of the awakened Kundalini rising through different centres and its action of ascent felt through the spine is absent in Integral Yoga. In Sri Aurobindo's yoga the centres open automatically by the descent of the Truth Conscious-Force. The aim of his yoga is to establish direct contact with the Divine above and bring down divine consciousness from above into all the centres. Spiritual realisation is of paramount importance in the life of a man. The object of Sri Aurobindo's *Yoga* is to transform life by bringing down into it Light, Power and Bliss of divine Truth. His is not the yoga of world-shunning asceticism but of divine life. The aim of his *yoga* is not a departure out of this world and life directed for heaven or *nirvānā,* but for a change of life and existence. The thing to be gained is the bringing in of a Power of Consciousness (the Supramental), which is not yet organised or active directly in earth-nature.

To discover one's true self, it is necessary to open to a greater divine consciousness and remain in constant touch with the Divine. To gain this knowledge on *yoga* Sri Aurobindo remained deeply involved in *sādhanā* throughout his 40 years' stay at Pondicherry to bring down the Supramental force for the transformation of mind and life. The November 24, 1926 is called Sri Aurobindo's *Siddhi Divas,* the Day of Realisation. Even after this *Siddhi* day of 1926, he worked relentlessly to perfect his inner *sādhanā* in order to bring down the Supramental Light and Power onto the earth. He came to realise that without the descent of the Supermind the problem of establishing the kingdom of Heaven on earth, which the seers and prophets in the past have visualised, would not be possible. As a *sādhak* got confused about the working of the supramental, Sri Aurobindo explained to him about the supramental power in a letter dated 14 January 1932:

> The Supramental is *not* grand, aloof, cold and austere; it is not something opposed to or inconsistent with a full vital and physical manifestation; on the contrary, it carries in it the only possibility of the full fullness of the vital force and

> the physical life on earth.... All other *Yogas* regard this life as an illusion or a passing phase; the supramental *Yoga* alone regards it as a thing created by the Divine for a progressive manifestation and takes the fulfilment of the life and the body for its object.[17]

According to Sri Aurobindo the Supramental is simply the Truth-Consciousness and what it brings in its descent is the full truth of life. Life and body would not remain forever imperfect, ignorant and impotent; "there has to be a change for fuller life-power, fuller body-power." In order to reach it one should rise to high summits. While explaining to the same disciple about supramental change which brings permanent bliss, Sri Aurobindo further records:

> The utmost Ānanda the body and life are now capable of is a brief excitement of the vital mind or the nerves or the cells which is limited, imperfect and soon passes: with the supramental change all the cells, nerves, vital forces, embodied mental forces can become filled with a thousand fold Ānanda, capable of an intensity of bliss which passes description and which need not fade away.[18]

In fact, throughout his 40 years' stay at Pondicherry, Sri Aurobindo devoted himself to *sādhanā,* and intensely worked to realise the aim of triple transformation of life for a possible liberation of mankind from ignorance, incapacity, desire and death so that divine life could be established. The establishment of divine life on the earth means evolving a new social order based upon peace, harmony, beauty, delight, knowledge and power of the spirit itself.

Sri Aurobindo avidly supported the scientific theory of the evolution. Originally all was matter, inert Matter; then out of this dead and inert Matter came Life. Life appeared in Matter because of an unforeseen factor. When life attained a certain level of growth and maturity, it became budded with Mind. No amount of mechanical or chemical operations can itself produce Mind out of Life. After Mind, the next grade of consciousness shall come by the same method and process. Neither Mind nor Life is the original creative power; like matter these are intermediaries, serried instruments of the evolutionary process. Sri Aurobindo elaborates the hidden aim of evolution:

> A spiritual evolution, an evolution of consciousness in Matter in a constant developing self-formation till the form can reveal the indwelling Spirit, is then the keynote, the central significant motive of the terrestrial existence. This significance is concealed at the outset by the involution of the Spirit, the Divine Reality, in a dense material Inconscience; a veil of Inconscience, a veil of insensibility of Matter hides the universal Consciousness-Force which works within it, so that the Energy which is the first form of the Force of creation assumes in the physical universe, appears to be itself inconscient and yet does the works of a vast occult Intelligence.[19]

Consciousness of man struggles towards knowledge. So "the mental man has still to evolve out of himself fully into conscious being, a divine manhood or a spiritual and supramental supermanhood" which is the next product of the evolution. Each type of life is a new step, and the manifestation of matter that in turn will manifest a new type of consciousness. Through evolutionary process matter in future will fully manifest the indwelling Spirit. There are at work invisible life forces and obscure psychological forces in Nature. Man, being the head of the earthly creation, has his own native law, limits - *svabhāva, svadharma*; but he does not exceed these limits. In order to become a superman, to put on the nature and capacities of a god, man has to exceed himself. If a supramental being is to appear in the terrestrial creation, it must be a new and independent manifestation of life. There is no reason to suppose that the whole race of human beings would develop perfection to become supermen. Such a line of reasoning has a considerable cogency.

As per the Hindu Scriptures, all exist here for the delight of existence, all is a game or *lilā*. Explaining the teleology of evolution, Sri Aurobindo records:

> A manifestation of the greater powers of Existence till the whole being itself is manifest in the material world in the terms of a higher, a spiritual creation, may be considered as the teleology of the evolution.[20]

A theory of spiritual evolution is different from the scientific theory of form-evolution and physical life-evolution. The scientific theory is concerned only with the outward process with the physical development of things in Matter. The natural process of evolution can be summed up in a simple way as: the better organised the form, the more it is capable of housing a complex, an able and developed Life and Consciousness. At first Matter, then life in Matter and then the evolution of Mind in living Matter. The ancient thought in India explains the existence of *avatārs* in the form of life in water, animal life and man. The *Upanishads* say that the self or Spirit after deciding on creation of life first formed animals like cow and horse. But the gods who are described in the *Upanishads* as the powers of Consciousness and Powers of Nature not being satisfied with the creation of animals created the form of man. Thus, the various theories of evolution support the creation of more and more developed form of beings that could be effectively capable of housing a higher consciousness.

With the march of science and technology man has rapidly developed new areas of knowledge and changed the form of environment. He has even established some control over them. It is not improbable on the part of man to help nature consciously in its spiritual and physical evolution and transformation. This means the secret indwelling spirit, the Daemon; the Godhead within is waiting for emergence. Man's urge for spirituality is the inner driving force of the spirit within him. The dynamic side of the spiritual urges points to a spiritual perfection of the being, a divinisation of mind, heart and body. If it can be achieved, the dream of the ancient sages of establishing a kingdom of God not only within us but outside would be achieved. Pointing out the goal of mankind on earth, Sri Aurobindo arrives at a conclusive observation:

> If a spiritual unfolding on earth is the hidden truth of our birth into Matter, if it is fundamentally an evolution of consciousness that has been taking place in Nature, then man as he is cannot be the last term of that evolution: he is too imperfect an expression of the Spirit, Mind itself a too limited form and instrumentation; Mind is only a middle term of consciousness, the mental being can only be a transitional being. [21]

The spiritual element is not a distinct or separate entity and cannot emerge independently. The mental being can only develop a spiritual interest. The spiritual tendency may become a predominant trend in some men just as some people have artistic trend.

At first the soul in man does not appear as something distinct from mind and from mentalised life. Human beings are ordinarily not aware of a soul in them screened from mind, life and body. Being detached and unrestrained the soul sees, controls and moulds man's actions only when an inner evolution proceeds. The liberation of the spiritual power in man from the bondage of ignorance is the decisive step of the spiritual evolution in Nature.

It is necessary that readers should have a fair idea about spirituality. According to Sri Aurobindo's opinion true spirituality is not a high intellectuality, not idealism, not an ethical turn of mind or moral purity and austerity, not religiosity or an ardent and exalted emotional fervour. Spiritual achievement does not mean a mental belief, creed or faith, an emotional aspiration, or a regulation of conduct. These things are of considerable value to spiritual evolution. While explaining the true nature of spirituality, Sri Aurobindo writes:

> Spirituality is in its essence an awakening to the inner reality of our being, to a spirit, self, soul which is other than our mind, life and body, an inner aspiration to know, to feel, to be that, to enter into contact with the greater Reality beyond and pervading the universe which inhabits also our own being, to be in communion with It and union with It, and a turning, a conversion, a transformation of our whole being as a result of the aspiration, the contact, the union, a growth or waking into a new becoming or new being, a new self, a new nature.[22]

The first object in the evolution of the spiritual man is the foundation of pure spiritual consciousness. The urge of that consciousness should be towards contact with the Reality, the self or the Divine Being. Usually there are four main ways to open up the inner being, these are religion, occultism, spiritual thought and an inner spiritual realisation and experience.

A spiritual seeker must know the hidden Power or Powers that control the world. If there is a Cosmic Self or Spirit or a Creator, he must be a universal Being, a supreme Spirit. The spiritual seeker must lift himself to his height out of his present imperfection and impotence. The purpose is to link the human with the Divine and admit the rule of the soul and spirit on his thought, life and flesh. Faith in the Divine is indispensable. Without faith man cannot proceed forward in his journey through the unknown. Faith should come as a free perception from his inner spirit. The real business of religion is to prepare man's mind, life and bodily existence for attainment of spiritual consciousness. Modern man stands at the crossroads and becomes confused. As he discovers the secrets and the process of physical Nature, his faith in occultism and religion goes on decreasing. Some still feel the need of spiritual factors in their lives. As the tendency towards intellectualisation increases, the occult elements of religion lose their significance. A day will dawn when there will be complete denial of religion, occultism and all that is supernatural. Instead people will be prompted to make self-discovery and inner seeking. Sri Aurobindo praises India where there have been persistent movements of evolutionary Nature, which he designates as the experimentations on all stages of spiritual evolution in man:

> For religion in India limited itself by no one creed or dogma; it not only admitted a vast number of different formulations, but contained successfully within itself all the elements that have grown up in the course of the evolution of religion and refused to ban or excise any: it developed occultism to its utmost limits, accepted spiritual philosophies of all kinds, followed to its highest, deepest or largest outcome every possible line of spiritual realisation, spiritual experience, spiritual self-discipline.[23]

This is not to denigrate the importance of religion in a society. It cannot be refuted that in disciplining man's thought, behaviour, attitude and ethical qualities, no doubt, religion has discharged an important role. Religion and occultism have produced saints, prophets or *Ṛishis*. Religion in India has taught us the ways of communion between man and God. Thus, through religion man's spiritual aspirations, spiritual experience is strengthened. Sri Aurobindo brings out the significance of religion and occult mysticism in the spiritual life of man in the following passage:

> Religion and its thought and ethics and occult mysticism in ancient times produced the priest and the mage, the man of piety, the just man, the man of wisdom, many high points of mental manhood; but it is only after spiritual experience

> through the heart and mind began that we see arise the saint, the prophet, the *Rishi*, the Yogi, the seer, the spiritual sage and the mystic, and it is the religions in which these types of spiritual manhood came into being that have endured, covered the globe and given mankind all its spiritual aspiration and culture.[24]

When spirituality in man puts on its distinctive character, there is spiritualisation of his natural activities, a spiritualised turn of thought with "uplifting illuminations" or a spiritualised turn of the emotional or the aesthetic being. An awareness comes to man of an inner light and guidance. A spiritually liberated man is one who has realised the Self and Spirit within him, entered into cosmic consciousness and possesses the experience of union with the Eternal. The sum total achievements in his life can be counted as a total liberation of his soul, mind, heart and action.

In Sri Aurobindo's opinion, a mystic does not detach himself from life even though he becomes an otherworldly ascetic or an isolated visionary. He possesses a sense of unity with all beings. So under the stress of universal love and compassion, he spends his energies for the good of all creatures. He emphasizes that the Buddhistic ideal of *Karunā*, universal compassion and sympathy, the Christian emphasis on love indicates the dynamic side of a spiritual being. The need of the contemporary world is the emergence of spiritual man. A pertinent question may be raised here : how can man prepare himself to achieve this goal in life? How can he turn his mundane or earthly attention to spiritual life?

To discover the spiritual being in oneself ought to be the central motive of man's terrestrial existence on earth. Hence, the true spiritual tendency is to look beyond life more than towards life. A spiritual change is always individual and not collective. In Sri Aurobindo's opinion the spiritual evolution of Nature still continues as a process, so it is incomplete. The secret aim of it is to develop a basis for spiritual consciousness and knowledge. Any premature attempt at large-scale collective spiritual life would expose it to vitiation because of the incompleteness of spiritual experience and knowledge. Spirituality illumines and at the same time liberates the inner being; it helps the mind to get rid of its limited thought and knowledge, and communicates with what is higher than itself. It also influences the outward nature of individual human being.

Sri Aurobindo's philosophico-metaphysical pronouncement can be enumerated as mind is not the last stage of evolution. From mental level man has to rise to the highest level of consciousness, which he calls Supermind. Man is evolving through the process of mind, body and matter. All these three states claim their sovereignty and are at strife. They all claim to lead the being to the Infinite. But being in finite state they cannot in separation and ignorance lead to the Infinite. In the Supermind they lose their separateness and become a unity. This reconciliation is Supermind, a state of perfect body; perfect mind and perfect existence to which all present conditions are evolving. Mental, vital and physical beings are imperfect formations. The evolution of supramental spiritual being is veiled in the movement of matter and mind. The supramental man will not be subjected to the material and mental limitations. He would possess a divine mind free from the bondage of matter. This is how Sri Aurobindo charts the course of Nature's evolution of the spiritual man from the mental being. Along with Teilhard de Chardin, Sri Aurobindo can be considered as a cosmic optimist. The pith and kernel of his message embodied in *The Life Divine* can be summed up in the words of H.M. Williams:

> The thesis of *The Life Divine* is that existence consists of two great movements of urges, one coming downwards, as it were, from a perfect Wholeness (God, Brahman) towards matter (disparate units of life), and the other moving upwards in a gradual ascent from matter mind and thence to the Supermind and finally to the Wholeness (God, Brahman). First Sri Aurobindo traces the way the Wholeness, also called Existence has split itself up into fragments of increasing minuteness as that proceed downwards, ultimately reaching ignorance and mere matter...In the second half of the treatise, Aurobindo traces the reverse process by which matter slowly ascends through mind and Supermind to the final goal of pure Existence (God). [25]

Sri Aurobindo hopes that a new race of human beings will inhabit the earth endowed with supramental consciousness. Then something supernormal to earth- life must be acquired as an individual achievement. Sri Aurobindo prophesies the inevitability of the coming of Supermind in future.

It must become the normal nature of a new type of being; as Mind is established here on a basis of Ignorance seeking for Knowledge and growing into Knowledge, so Supermind must be established here on a basis of Knowledge growing into its own greater Light.[26]

It is not easy to bridge the gap between Mind and Supermind as long as the spiritual-mental being has not blossomed fully into Supermind and brought down its powers into our terrestrial existence. This can be achieved, according to Sri Aurobindo, through triple transformation: there must be a psychic change, the conversion of our whole present nature so as to become an effective instrument of our soul; there must be a spiritual change, the descent of a higher Light, Knowledge, Power, Force, Bliss, and Purity into our whole being; there must take place an ascent into the Supermind. Mind, life and body are capable of divinity but they are by some means separated in consciousness from the divine Truth. If this separation can once be abrogated then their present functioning could be altered. In that case, not only would it be possible to manifest and maintain the divine consciousness in the human mind and body, but divine consciousness itself would remould mind, life and body and establish the kingdom of heaven upon earth, the glory and joy of God then be made to manifest upon earth.

Mind may divide, multiply, add or subtract; but it does not get beyond certain limits. The fundamental error of the Mind is that it conceives the individual soul as a separate entity instead of a part of Oneness. Mind makes itself the sovereign ruler of its own universe. From this fundamental error proceeds a limitation of consciousness and knowledge. It is conscious of things and knows them only as they present themselves to its individual mind; and it thus falls into an ignorance of the rest. Hence, there is an element of error in all-human knowledge. We can say that self-ignorance is the root of all perversity of our existence and egoism is the form taken by that self-ignorance, *avidyā*.

Sri Aurobindo discusses elaborately the transition of Mind to Supermind through Overmind; it is a passage from Nature into Supernature. Overmind, like the Mind is a dividing principle, so it achieves separate limited spiritual creations. A supramental transformation can only bring a complete change. Sri Aurobindo reasonably draws our attention to the impossibility of human conception of Supermind. As the summits of human mind are beyond animal perception, so the movements of Supermind are beyond the ordinary human mental conception. Only when we will have an intermediate higher consciousness then the supramental being can have a true meaning to our human intelligence. The being and powers of the Superconsciousness must descend into us and uplift us. There might be a race of mental beings who would possess intuitive mentality. The Supramental change does not admit of any premature descent of the highest Light. From the point of view of the ascent of consciousness from our mind upwards, there are four main ascents; such as Higher Mind, Illumined Mind, Intuitive Mind and Overmind. As our mental thought changes or passes towards supramental, there occurs a radical change of consciousness – our normal perception or imagination or formulation of things spiritual and mundane change dramatically. It is difficult for mental thought to understand or describe Supramental Nature. Mental thought and mental nature are based on a consciousness and power of the Infinite. Supramental nature sees everything from the standpoint of oneness. Mental nature thinks, sees, wills, feels and senses on the basis of division. The law of the Supermind generates unity fulfilled in diversity. A Supramental being or a Gnostic being would be the consummation of the spiritual man; his whole way of being, thinking, living, and action would be governed by the power of a vast universal spirituality. He would feel the presence of the Divine in every centre of his consciousness, in every cell of his body. He will be able to share the joy and grief of others. Sri Aurobindo points out the interrelation between the supramental being and the world in the following words:

> He will have the cosmic consciousness, sense, feeling, by which all objective life will become part of his subjective existence and by which he will realise, perceive, feel, see, hear the Divine in all forms; all forms and movements will be realised, sensed, seen, heard, felt as if taking place within his own vast self of being. The world will be connected not only with his outer but with his inner life... he will be inwardly in contact with the inner self of things and beings...[27]

The world we inhabit is observed ignorant, material and imperfect. It is in this world that we have to strive towards perfection, the perfection of our soul, mind, and body, even amidst pain and suffering. While expounding on pain and suffering, Sri Aurobindo says, "All delight, all pain, and suffering are a sign of imperfection, of incompleteness; they arise from a division of being, an incompleteness of the force of the being." To become complete in being and to achieve perfection in one's life is divine living. *The Life Divine*, the *magnum opus* of Sri Aurobindo's lifetime-achievement – a philosophico-metaphysical treatise written in the ancient spiritual tradition of India – bridges the gap of the two ends of existence: Matter and Spirit. V.K. Gokak sharply focuses his scholarly analyses on Sri Aurobindo's philosophico-metaphysical thoughts and yogic realisations:

> He mapped out a yogic discipline of spiritual ascent and descent which promotes the emergence of the Godhead involved in Matter and the bridging down of the Supramental Consciousness to transform mind, life and body. He spoke of the imperative need to shift the will from the instrumental self to the real inner person, the psyche, as the only cure for a war-stricken world.[28]

The grand synthesis Sri Aurobindo achieves in his writings does not only focus on individual liberation but also shows how the society can be uplifted by spiritualisation. Some of his books even map out the contours of the future spiritualised society. As a social thinker, his study of social development is cogently arranged in *The Study of Human Cycle*. This book describes the manner that the spiritual attitude of a spiritual seeker could be developed for the foundation of a new and everlasting social order. While presenting his prescient views on sociology, spirituality, economics and politics of the future society, the author records:

> A spiritualised society would live like its spiritual individuals, not in the ego, but in the spirit, not as the collective ego, but as the collective soul... A spiritualised society would treat in its sociology the individual, from the saint to the criminal, not as units of a social problem to be passed through some skilfully devised machinery and either flattened into the social mould or crushed out of it, but as souls suffering and entangled in a net and to be rescued, soul

> growing and to be encouraged to grow, souls grown and from whom help and power can be drawn by the lesser spirits who are not yet adult.[29]

In a spiritualised society each individual as a means of economic production would derive joy out of work, which can help one to grow inwardly. Politically these people could be regarded as not subjects but groups of souls in whom divinity is concealed, to be self-discovered in its human collectivities. They will grow hand in hand to help the whole race.

In *The Ideal of Human Unity,* another important work of Sri Aurobindo, he reasons out that human race has been groping towards human unity for centuries; it is not only possible but also inevitable. If only, Sri Aurobindo suggests, the leaders and statesmen upon who the destiny of the nation depends, could work for a unified spiritual evolution, the entire mankind can be shaped for an ideal of human unity. He professes a spiritual religion of humanity as the hope of the future. By religion of humanity, he means, the society should realise the presence of a secret Spirit, a divine Reality, in which all are one. The religion of humanity will create an awareness of spiritual oneness, which is the foundation for development of the human race. Sri Aurobindo's great concern for higher existence could be achieved through a free inner variation and a freely outer expression:

> A spiritual oneness which would create a psychological oneness not dependent upon any intellectual or outward uniformity and compel a oneness of life not bound up with its mechanical means of unification, but ready always to enrich its secure unity by a freer inner variation and a freely varied outer self-expression, this would be the basis for a higher type of human existence.[30]

Through *The Secrets of the Vedas, The Essays on the Gita, The Foundations of Indian Culture* and other writings on the *Upanishads,* he opens up new vistas for analysis of the ancient Indian texts from spiritual, philosophical and cultural points of view. Moreover, the effects of supramental transformation of human nature on the artistic life, poetic consciousness, techniques and forms of artistic expression have been cogently put forward in his *The Future Poetry and Letters.*

REFERENCES

1. Sri Aurobindo, *On Himself*, Pondicherry: Sri Aurobindo Ashram, 1972, p.II
2. K.D. Sethna, *The Poetic Genius of Sri Aurobindo*, p.1.
3. Quoted by A. B. Purani, *The Life of Sri Aurobindo*, p.vi.
4. Ibid., p.v.
5. Ibid.
6. H.M.Williams, *Indo-Anglian Literature 1800-1970: A Survey*, New Delhi: Orient Longman, 1976, p.33.
7. Sri Aurobindo, *On Himself*, Pondicherry: Sri Aurobindo Ashram, p.98.
8. *Collected Poems*, p.99.
9. Sri Aurobindo, *On Himself*, op.cit., p.30.
10. Quoted by R.R. Diwakar, *Mahayogi Sri Aurobindo*, Bombay: Bharatiya Vidya Bhavan, 1976, p. xi.
11. Sri Aurobindo, *On Himself*, op.cit., p.37.
12. Ibid., p.38.
13. R. Diwakar, *Mahayogic Sri Aurobindo*, p.x.
14. Sri Aurobindo, *The Synthesis of yoga*, p.695.
15. Sri Aurobindo, *On Yoga*, II, Tome One, p.477.
16. Sri Aurobindo, *On Himself*, op.cit., p.95.
17. Ibid., p.124.
18. Ibid., p.125.
19. Sri Aurobindo, *The Life Divine*, Pondicherry: Sri Aurobindo Ashram, Book II, Part II, 1977, p.824.
20. Ibid., pp.834-35.
21. Ibid., pp.846-7.
22. Ibid., p.857.
23. Ibid., p.872.
24. Ibid., p.881.
25. H.M. Williams, op.cit.
26. Ibid., p.890.
27. Ibid., p.979.

28. V. K. Gokak, *Sri Aurobindo: Seer and Poet,* Abinav Publications, New Delhi, 1973, p.3.
29. Sri Aurobindo, *The Human Cycle,* American Edition, 1950, pp. 284-6.
30. Sri Aurobindo, *The Ideal of Human Unity,* American edition, 1950, pp.322-23.

2

Overhead Aesthesis and Sri Aurobindo's Poetics: Poetry—The *Mantra* of the Real

In order to understand the poetic activity of Sri Aurobindo we need to focus our attention on his poetics. In his aesthetic speculations he views the totality of life. His poetic out put is closely linked with his inner life. Poetry, to him, forms a part of yogic *sādhanā,* "a means of contact with the Divine through inspiration." He holds the view that poetry opens in man by the power of the word the doors of the Spirit leading to the revelation of the inner sight.

Judging poetry as an aesthetic pleasure of the imagination, the intellect, the ear, or as a set of elevated pastime is to miss the essence of poetry. How does the poetic word differ from the ordinary speech sound? Ordinarily, speech is used for practical communication, such as for expression of ideas, feelings, sensations, experience, and attitudes useful to life. Words are used as conventional signs. But in Sri Aurbindo's opinion, words in ancient times had their own vivid life. Originally, the word 'wolf" (etimological derivation from Sanskrit -*Vrka)* means one who tears (tearer), expresses or conveys the sensational relation between wolf and man (the former's act of tearing the latter). In the primitive ages words had a power of their life — a concrete vigour, a natural force. Poetry down the ages has been trying to retrieve the suggestive force of the rhythmic sound. It associates with thought value - it is carrying up the power to express directly a higher reach of experience than the intellectual or vital sense.

Prose style associates words agreeably to please and clarify the intelligence accurately. Various figurative and rhetorical devices heighten the stress of its intellectual and emotional appeal.

The rhythmic word in poetry has a subtle immaterial element; its sound and sense value together constitute a soul value, a direct spiritual power. So its power soars beyond any law of mechanical construction. The perfection of the sound movement and style come spontaneously from the artist's soul. It is like the universal soul creating harmonies of the universe out of the power of the word, secret and eternal within him. This rhythmic word power of the poet, the supreme poetic utterance enables the expression of his self-vision or his world-vision. The poet through the inspired word, the supreme poetic utterance dives into the depth of sense; a power of infinite suggestion wells up directly from his spirit within. The rhythmic utterance while bringing out the intellectual value of the word, its power of emotion and sensation, its vital suggestion reaches out to its soul-suggestion. So poetry, in the opinion of Sri Aurobindo, dissipates the seeming definiteness of the meaning, beyond the determinate intellectual meaning of the poetic word. A comparative assessment could be attempted between this view and Derridean deconstructive method of displacement of meaning ('difference' and 'defferance').

Sri Aurobindo categorically disapproves the tendency of modern mind, which lays too much stress on the thought-value in poetry. This tendency has arisen because modern man is busy in depicting "the enigma of things, the cryptogram of the worlds" by the aid of his intellect. Instead of discharging the role of a supreme singer or an inspired seer, the present-day world demands the poet to become a philosopher, a prophet, a teacher, and sometimes, an ethical or religious preacher. If thought value in poetry is the canon of literary judgements for assessing the greatness of a poet, then probably there is more thought in a short essay of Francis Bacon than one can find in a whole play of William Shakespeare. A prophet may have a poet in him who often breaks out into rhythmic speech and sounds by revealing the image of the beauty of the Truth. There can be no denying of the fact that a true poet is different from that of a philosopher or a prophet:

> The prophet announces the Truth as the word of God or his command, he is the giver of the message; the poet shows us Truth in its power of beauty, in its symbol or image, or reveals it to us in the workings of Nature or in the workings of life; and when he has done that, his whole work is done; he need be its explicit spokesman.[1]

Sri Aurobindo pointedly remarks that the business of the philosopher is to discriminate Truth and arrange its parts into intellectual relation with each other. The prophet and the philosopher may have in them a poet who breaks out often into poetic utterance "to water the arid path of abstraction with some healing dew of poetry." There he ceases to be a philosophical thinker and becomes a poet-seer of Truth. The poet's creative experience must have gone into the making of the above discriminations and assigning them distinctive roles.

The phenomenological perspective and method could be used to analyse human consciousness and the experience (lived world) of the poet and the reader in the scheme of Sri Aurobindo's poetics. Consciousness is a unified intentional act and it is always directed to an object. Sight is the act of interiorisation of the consciousness of an object. It is a unique mode of the poet's awareness and imaginative feelings. The power of the poetic word is to make the reader see, become passively receptive and capable of achieving participation.

Sight is an essential poetic gift. To clothe poetry in a critical or philosophic idea of life is to the detriment of poetic vision. A spiritual excitement is caused by the vision of the soul. The vision may be anything in Nature or God or any living or non-living being. The outward seeing of the poet serves to excite the inner to its work. Sheer objectivity in production brings us down from art to photography. It is sufficient that the soul sees, the eye, the senses, heart and thinking-mind become the passive instrument of the soul. If the poetic expression is not purified or uplifted by a spiritual transmutation, what we get is inferior poetry from a lower level of the mind.

What counts much in becoming a powerful poet? Rejecting the Wordsworthean canon of the general nature of a poet, Sri Aurobindo pronounces that a poet is a man not speaking to *all* men. Poetry, according to him, addresses to man's inner senses which a very few readers can understand. Vision is the characteristic power of a poet. A poet is a seer and revealer of truth who awakens the inner senses of man. Neither the intelligence nor the imagination, nor the ear is the true recipients or creators of poetic delight. The true creator as well as the true hearer is the soul. Sri Aurobindo refers to the unique quality of *Mantra* in *The Future Poetry*. A *Mantra* is a highly refined artistic creation from Overmind the Vedic seers efficaciously designed to communicate the language of the Spirit. In Sri Aurobindo's conception *Mantra* is the incarnation or living vision of a great spiritual truth. It is a vision in living words that holds the highest intensities of rhythm, style and thought. *Mantric* utterance comes from the domain of Overmind inspiration and ensouls the mind with the sight of the self, the inmost reality of things, with its truth and with the divine soul-forms of it. *Mantric* poetry seizes hold up all that is finite and brings into each the light and voice of its own infinite. So sight is the essential poetic gift to compose *Mantra*. He says:

> The poetic vision of life is not a critical or intellectual or philosophic view of it, but a soul-view, a seizing by the inner sense; and the Mantra is not in its substance or form poetic enunciation of a philosophic truth, but the rhythmic revelation or intuition arising out of the soul's sight of God and Nature and the world and the inner truth – occult to the outward eye-of all that peoples it, the secrets of their life and being.[2]

In Sri Aurobindo's opinion, the native power of poetry is in its sight, not in its intellectual thought matter. In ancient times the connotation of the word *Kavi* was the seer and revealer of truth. He distinguishes a poet from that of a philosopher and a scientist on the basis of the quality of their thought, perception and vision:

> Vision is the characteristic power of the poet, as is discriminative thought the essential gift of the philosopher and analytic observation the natural genius of the scientist.[3]

Poetry appeals to the spirit of man through significant images. The essential power of poetry is to make us see, not make us feel or think. Thought and feeling should arise out of the sight. In Sri

Aurobindo's conception a poet should make the reader live in the soul and in the inner mind instead of appealing to the outer mind and the senses. As per the conception of the ancients the poet is a seer who sees beyond the sight of the surface mind and finds the revealing word, the inspired and the inevitable word. Sri Aurobindo defines the duty of an archetypal poet:

> The archetypal poet in a world of original ideas is, we may say, a Soul that sees in itself intimately this world and all the others and God and Nature and the life of beings and sets flowing from its centre a surge of creative rhythm and word-images which become the expressive body of the vision; and the great poets are those who repeat in some measure this ideal creation, *kāvāyāh satyaśrutāh*, seers and hearers of poetic truth and poetic word.[4]

Speaking about his own poetic creation, he points out in a letter that his great power over poetry and perfect expression was acquired not by reading others' poetry but from the heightening of his consciousness and the great inspiration that incessantly supported it. For him, poetry has been a means of spiritual expression that helps to open the consciousness of man. It is the expression of the great spiritual truth or vision in living words with the highest intensity of rhythm, style and thought. While taking a spiritual and syncretic view of art, he explains that it is the incarnation of the Real. Subjected to rigorous spiritual discipline, poetry can express and strengthen *yogic* consciousness. We should remember that it is not a substitute for *sādhanā*; it can be an accompaniment only. Poetry opens a channel between the external consciousness and the inner mind or vital; *sādhanā* helps in the opening up of the psychic and the inner mind and vital, the widening of the individual consciousness, the Self in all, the psychic and the spiritual transformation of human nature. For a *yogi* the expression in poetry keeps "flowing from a growing self within." Along with the growth of the inner self poetic power intensifies and strengthens. So poetry should be composed as a means of contact through inspiration with the Divine. Thus, literature can be made an instrument for divine life. Much of Sri Aurobindo's poetic creation is based on this theoretical premise which will be discussed in the subsequent chapters.

Overhead Aesthesis

Poetry is the rhythmic voice of life. But it is one of the inner and not the surface voices. Inspiration plays an important role in poetic composition. Sri Aurobindo draws our attention to the various sources of poetic inspiration and vision. In keeping with the ancient critical tradition, he says, the form of all great and high poetry is the outcome of "a supreme harmony of five external powers. Truth, Beauty, Delight, Life and the Spirit." [5] He names these as "the five greater ideal lamps or rather the five suns of poetry."[6] As our self-knowledge grows deeper, we come to realise that there is a greater life. It has already been pointed out earlier that a spirit brings a greater power of life. Poets and artists can effect "mediation between truth of the spirit and the truth of life." Poetic truth is infinitely wide. It has nothing to do with philosophical, religious or scientific truth. The function of poetry is not to teach truth of any particular kind, nor to pursue knowledge, nor to serve any religious or ethical aim, but to embody beauty and delight in living word. To reveal the delight of the soul, at any rate its function is to serve the spirit and to illumine and lead through poetry. The poetic vision of truth is different from all other type of perception. Sri Aurobindo analyses in the following passage a poet's way of perceiving truth which differs from other type of perceptions:

> The poet seer sees differently, thinks in another way, voices himself in quite another manner than the philosopher or the prophet. The prophet announces the Truth as the word of God or his command.... The philosopher's business is to discriminate Truth and put its parts and aspects into intellectual relation with each other; the poet's is to seize and embody aspects of Truth in their living relations.... [7]

There exists a close relation among truth, life, beauty and delight. The perceptions of modern man *per se* modern poet is intellectual and critical. A poet re-embodies in the beauty of word the infinite life-spirit and deals with the life of the soul.

Man can very well understand the infinity of life once he learns to look at life from a spiritual angle. The basic life is based on spirit of the soul. Physical, mental and vital lives are the expressive forms of the basic spiritual or eternal life. Sri

Aurobindo tries to reveal the joy of life in the spiritual sense when it is linked to poetry. In the spiritual sense all life becomes eternal life. So a poet should not get confined to physical life or outward life only; he should not get confined to an ideal life as imagined or fancied by the mind or even conceived by the intellectual imagination. The proper domain of poetry is man's inner life. That is the reason Sri Aurobindo views, "Poetry as the rhythmic voice of life." The more the poet reveals the inner life, the greater is his power of creation. Doubts may arise as to why should we turn to the spirit? Sri Aurobindo provides the answer to this important question in the following lines:

> The spirit gives us not only a greater light of truth and vision, but also the breath of a greater living; for the spirit is not only the self of our consciousness and knowledge, but also the great self of life.[8]

The poetry of Rabindranath Tagore, Carpenter, A.E. Houseman, W.B. Yeats and Whitman has succeeded in creating "a new and deeper manner of seeing life." The significant achievements of these poets lie in building "bridges of visioned light and rhythm between the infinite and eternal and the mind and soul and life of man." Our physical and material world is not the sole world of experience. With the unprecedented development in human knowledge our conception of life indeed must widen. Hence, Sri Aurobindo explains the poetic view of life as presented by the great poets of the world:

> What man sees and experiences of God and himself and his race and Nature and the spiritual, mental, psychic and material world in which he moves, his back looks upon the past, his sweep of vision over the present, his eye of aspiration and prophecy cast towards the future, his passion of self-finding and self-exceeding, his reach beyond and self-exceeding, his reach beyond the three times to the eternal and immutable, this is the life.[9]

A poet has the capacity to create a thing of beauty out of delight. In the absence of beauty and delight, poetry is bereft of the touch of immortality and perfection. The pleasure we derive from poetry can be raised and transmitted into the deeper delight of the soul. *Ānanda*, delight in the language of Indian aesthetics, is the essential joy, the Infinite feels in Itself and in Its creation. A seer poet creates divine *ānanda*. It is a delight interpretative, creative, revealing and formative. Such spiritual joy the soul of a poet feels that it succeeds in pouring it in equal measures into the mind or heart of all those who are prepared to receive it. The kindred souls of the poet and the hearer or reader enter into a bond of moved identity in establishing a direct contact through vision and touch of emotion.

Beauty and delight for man are instinctual aesthetic satisfaction. In other words, beauty and delight lie at the root of the impulse for aesthetic creation and enjoyment. Beauty, which the artist or the poet seeks, is not a mere physical or sensuous or even intellectual beauty but "the soul of beauty which is hidden from the ordinary eye, and the ordinary mind." It comes by a psychic or spiritual vision and inspiration. The same process holds good in the case of artistic delight.

What indeed is necessary to enkindle the right vision and intuitive response in the soul? In the words of Sri Aurobindo it can more elaborately be described as:

> It is, in truth, seeking, as in religion for the Divine, the all-Beautiful in man, in nature, in life, in thought, in art, for God is Beauty and Delight hidden in the variation of his mask and forms.... To find the highest beauty is to find God; to reveal, to embody, to create, as we say, highest beauty, is to bring out of our souls the living image and power of God.[10]

Modern man looks little into his deepest self and takes least interest in his soul. As a result, he is mostly concerned with his fragmented self, his bewildered mind and an array of conflicting emotions. Since the psychological and social environments have changed, our aesthetic attitude too has undergone a radical change. According to Sri Aurobindo our fine aesthetic sense and intelligence have become blunt, stripped off their finer qualities. The reasons are not very far to seek:

> Condemned to serve first and foremost our existential interest in life or our interest in thought or in troubled personality or the demand of the senses or passion and bidden to make them beautiful or vivid to us by an active aesthetic celebration and artistic manufacture of the word or a supply of carefully, apt or beautiful forms and measures.[11]

It is the deeper spiritual feeling which is the fountain of poetic delight and beauty. This feeling of *ānanda* springs from a supreme aesthetic sense, which is spiritual at the same time impersonal. Through spiritual and impersonal feeling the poet can transmute pain, sorrow, and the most tragic suffering into forms of beauty. A poet should be able to express the soul's universal delight in existence. In other word, poetic delight and beauty are born of a deeper rapture and not out of the enjoyment of surface life. Sri Aurobindo welcomes the modern mind that is opening to an "unprecedented largeness of vision of the wonders of the world, the self of man and the mystery of the spirit in him and the universe." With the help of this modernist trend, with this largeness of vision, future poetry will powerfully create a greater breadth of life. Foregrounding his futuristic vision for mankind, the seer poet records: "A greater era of man's living seems to be in promise." The age of intuitive poetry is dawning upon man's horizon: it will impel him to see "inmost in the inmost way."

Sri Aurobindo gives full breath in his poetic treatment to the problem of existence of God, Soul and Immortality, which are at the very root of life and reality. He presents his spiritual experiences in its variety, just as he has seen and realised them. He does not indulge in vague generalisations or colourful truisms in his poetic creation. While critically interpreting Sri Aurobindo's poetry, Nolini Kanta Gupta records how three terms of human consciousness forge a unity in Sri Aurobindo's treatment: "In him we find the three terms of human consciousness arriving at an absolute fusion and his poetry is a wonderful example of that fusion. The three terms are the spiritual, the intellectual or philosophical and the physical or sensational."[12] The intellectual or mental, as we know, is the intermediary, the Paraclete that bridges and negotiates with the others.

An imitable quality imbibed by a great poet is that he can go beyond the form of the thing he sees and not be limited by it. T.S. Eliot's seminal observation in the poet's mind is a medium. Sri Aurobindo supplements this procedure when he says that the personality of the poet is lost in the eternity of vision. For further study one can compare this view of Sri Aurobindo with that of T.S. Eliot's *Impersonal Theory of Art* to trace the lines of similarities and differences.

In the case of great poets, the originating source of inspiration is always a higher or a deeper plane of consciousness. Sri Aurobindo critically analyses these planes of inspiration that constitutes the theory and psychology of the creation of poetry and art. The various sources from which poetry could be written are: vital mind as in Kalidas and Shakespeare where vibrant play, delicate or vehement, of sensation, passion, emotion is directly expressed; intellectual mind (as in Vyāsa, Sophocles, Virgil, Dante and Milton) where the poetic vision markedly brings out thought-values of whatever is caught up from subjective or objective existence; subtle-physical mind (as in Homer and Chaucer, where the inner imaginative response is mostly to external gesture, movement and action). Sri Aurobindo categorises these sources as the Higher Mind, the Illumined Mind, the Intuitive Mind and Overmind.

In the poetry of the Higher Mind usually a certain spontaneous intensity of vision is marked. The poetry of the Higher Mind has a divine power, measure and dignity. The Illumined Mind has a greater intensity of spiritual light and comes forth with a direct vision of the fundamental realities. It discloses the true colour of Truth. Intuition deepens spiritual sight and spiritual insight. Directing our attention to an important characteristic of the Overhead Poetry, Sri Aurobindo says, "It draws into itself a fuller language of intuitive inspiration, illumination or the higher thinking and feeling."[13] Sri Aurobindo cites illustrations of some of the most powerful passages from Shakespeare, Virgil, Lucretius, the *Mahabharata*, the *Ramayana*, The *Bhagavad Gita*, the *Vedas* and the *Upanishads* to show various streaks of Overhead poetic inspiration. Making a spiritual analysis, he points out that in these passages "there comes down a supreme voice, the Overmind voice and the Overmind music and it is to be observed that the lines and passages where that happens rank amongst the greatest and most admired in all poetic literature."[14] These are obviously *Mantric* lines as they come out from the Overmind inspiration. Since the Overmind is a superhuman consciousness, when a poet writes from Overmind inspiration, he raises part of his mental level beyond the ordinary one. Unfortunately, poets, artists, and mystics have not spiritually advanced so far as to sustain the Overmind inspiration for long to remain in touch with it.

It is necessary to draw the attention of the readers to the distinction between truth and beauty in Overmental Poetry. Truth is not a dry statement of facts or ideas associated with the intellect; it can be "a splendid discovery, a rapturous revelation, and a thing of beauty that is a joy for ever". A poet can be a seeker of truth as well as a lover of beauty at the same time. The chief function of the Overmind is not only to separate the main powers of the consciousness but also to unite separate things and to reconcile the opposites. At that level truth and beauty become one involved in each other so that at that level "truth is beauty and beauty is truth." Their highest fusion takes place only in the Supermind. On that level truth itself is the highest poetry and appears utterly beautiful to the vision, the hearing, and the sensibility of the soul. Lines from the higher consciousness of the intuitive mind as well as those from the Overmind can have a *Mantric* character. The language used in a *Mantra* conveys more than the mere surface meaning of the words seems to indicate, a rhythm that means even more than the language. Sometimes, the Overmind inspiration comes down to an inferior consciousness so as to lift it to a higher level. Sri Aurobindo justifiably directs our attention to *Mantra,* which is defined as "a word of power and light that comes from the Overmind inspiration or from some very high plane of Intuition."[15] The *Mantra* is considered to be the Divine Word, the supreme revelatory speech of the Eternal.

It has already been discussed earlier that ordinary poetry is quite different from the Overhead Poetry. In ordinary poetry, the mind of the poet can play about, change, use one image or another; but in Overhead Poetry the technique is different because "it must be the right word and no other, in the right place and in no other, the right sounds and no others, in a design of sound that cannot be changed even a little."[16]

The Overmind is not a transcendental consciousness as Supermind. It is a cosmic consciousness. It is the source of all our mental, vital or physical actualities and possibilities. The Overhead poetry need not be mystic. Something behind the mental, or vital or physical consciousness has to be brought out in its own native tongue charged with deeper values. Overhead poetry makes an inevitable selection of words, which brings out a deeper meaning as in Shakespeare's: "And in this harsh world draw thy breath in pain. (*Hamlet*)." The combination of words is so arranged as to force on the mind of the reader an utter absoluteness of the difficulty and pain of living for the soul that has awakened to the misery of this world. Instances of overhead poetic utterance can be given from Wordsworth's: "Voyaging through strange seas of Thought, alone" and Milton's line: "Those thoughts that wander through eternity." Milton's choice of words such as "wander" to collocate with "through eternity" is apt; if he had chosen any other word, it no longer would have been an Overhead line.

The Higher Mind is the first plane where one becomes aware of the Self, the one everywhere. Sri Aurobindo quotes how Shakespeare's imagination at times is illumined by Overhead inspiration as the following lines upon sleep:

> Wilt thou upon the high and giddy mast
> Seal up the shipboy's eyes and rock his brains
> In cradle of the rude imperious surge?[17]

Keats' lines:

> ...solitary thinkings, such as dodge
> Conception to the very bourne of heaven,
> Then leave the naked brain.[18]

Vaughan's:

> I saw eternity the other night
> Like a great ring of pure and endless light,
> All calm as it was bright;
> And round beneath it, Time, in hours, days, years,
> Driven by the spheres,
> Like a vast shadow moved, in which the world
> And all her train were hurled.[19]

Sri Aurobindo cites a perfect example from Shelley's lines that is written with psychic inspiration:

> I can give not what men call love;
> But wilt thou accept not
> The worship the heart lifts above
> And the Heavens reject not –
> The desire of the moth for the star,
> Of the night for the morrow,

The devotion to something afar
From the sphere of our sorrow? [20]

We don't have plenty examples of Overhead utterance in any other language. We can mark here that Overhead poetry should not necessarily deal with the theme of the Divine or the Infinite or the transcendental. Overhead poetry can be written without any reference to the Transcendental as in Shakespeare's lines:

Absent thee from felicity awhile,
And in this harsh world draw thy breath in pain.[21]

The lines quoted above possess Overhead touch, rhythm and feeling. In fact each plane and its creation is beautiful and perfect. But the Overmind has a greater aesthesis; when it sees objects, sees in them what the mind cannot see, "so that the value it gives to them can be greater than any value that the mind can give."

The eye of the poet loves "to look on breathing acting life" in its perfected synthesis and rhythm, not on the dissected parts. The poet's inward gaze "seizes the soul of wonder of things, not the mechanical miracle." The mind of the poet sees by intuition, the aspect that thrills his heart is the living truth of the form, the supporting movement of the soul. A poet is a man of genius whose consciousness has attained higher power of conception and expression than ordinary men can hope to have. Sri Aurobindo points out: "Genius is the result of an intervention or influence from a higher consciousness than the ordinary human mental, a greater light, a greater force."[22]

Sometimes, the descent of higher consciousness comes in irregular and partial manner but usually these are not sustained for a long time, though they may produce high poetic utterance. It is very difficult for an ordinary mind to make these distinctions or understand them exactly.

Sri Aurobindo prefers Overhead poetry as it can open the door to the expression of new ranges of vision, experience and feelings. It can express spiritual and mystic themes with their inexhaustible perspectives. It can employ a new intensity of language and new rhythm. We have already noticed earlier that the great lines or passages in the world's literature bear Overmind touch or power. Sri Aurobindo reposes complete faith in the power of the Overmind while composing his great poem, *Savitri,* because it works entirely according to its own direction without any question or doubt:

> There is no invariable "how" – except that I receive from above my head and receive changes and corrections from above without any initiation by myself or labour of the brain. Even if I change a hundred times, the mind does not work at that, it only receives. Formerly it used not to be so, the mind was always labouring at the stuff of an unshaped formation.... The poems come as a stream beginning at the first line and ending at the last.[23]

Sri Aurobindo has given innumerable examples of Overhead touch in his own poetry. In fact, *Savitri* is the expression of a more sustained and constant expression of the Overhead inspiration in English poetic tradition. In the composition of *Savitri* Sri Aurobindo's mind acted only as a passive receptacle. From his letters to his disciples we come to know that he was used to reject inspiration that came from an inferior level, and patiently waited to recast the stuff from the lower level with a right one from higher level. Whenever he could detect any defect, he used to "appeal to headquarters" till the defect was removed and the proper and version came along.

A general Overhead inspiration prevails all through in *Savitri* touching one or the other higher level aiming at a lift towards the *mantra.* In order to express his new spiritual sensibility and realisation as it is found in "Rose of God", *Poems Past and Present, Last Poems,* much more he has done in *Savitri* employing the ancient rhythmical method, the traditional rhythmic mould to suit to his new needs. S. K. Prasad makes a pertinent observation about Sri Aurobindo's poetic creation that in his opinion is a blending of the human and divine power:

> But we shall be wrong to think that he became merely passive and inert, something like a merely mechanical recording instrument. No, it was a case of the fullest possible act of collaboration between, one may say, the human and the divine powers or souls, otherwise the idea or necessity of change or revision would not have arisen there at all.[24]

In order to receive Overhead inspiration, Sri Aurobindo had to labour hard at his poetical *Magnum Opus, Savitri,* for over more than four decades, revising and recasting the epic several times with an ardent desire not to allow the poem "to fall below the minimum height." He had to set his goal to make every line a "perfect perfection." He has himself described in a long passage how he was able to give a mystic touch to the poetic utterances that came spontaneously to him in *Savitri* from the highest level of Overmind inspiration:

> Oft inspiration with her lightning feet,
> A sudden messenger from the all-seeing tops,
> Traversed the soundless corridors of his mind
> Bringing her rhythmic sense of hidden things.
> A music spoke transcending mortal speech.
> As if from a golden phial of the All-Bliss,
> A joy of light, a joy of sudden sight,
> A rapture of the thrilled undying Word
> Poured into his heart as into an empty cup,
> A repetition of God's first delight
> Creating in a young and virgin Time.
> In a brief moment caught, a little space,
> All-Knowledge packed into great wordless thoughts
> Lodged in the expectant stillness of his depths
> A crystal of the ultimate Absolute,
> A portion of the inexpressible Truth
> Revealed by silence to the silent soul.
> The intense creatrix in his stillness wrought;
> Her power fallen speechless grew more intimate;
> She looked upon the seen and the unforeseen,
> Unguessed domains she made her native field.
>
> All-vision gathered into a single ray,
> As when the eyes stare at an invisible point
> Till through the intensity of one luminous spot
> An apocalypse of a world of images
> Enters into the kingdom of the seer.[25]

According to Sri Aurobindo's own critical estimate, the passage quoted above from *Savitri* is a superb example of his Overmind Intuition at work expressing its own rhythm and language. Though, of course, in a letter written in 1946, he had declared that ten years earlier, he was not in a position to command Overmind touch and inspiration. He could overcome such a sense of hesitation after he brought down the Supramental Force and Light to earth in 1936 and intensified his *yogic sādhanā*. A disciple wanted to know from Sri Aurobindo why he had to write and rewrite *Savitri* 10 or 12 times when he had all the inspiration at his command. In reply to the query Sri Aurobindo explained to him in another letter in 1936 that he had begun composing *Savitri* on a certain mental level and each time he reached a higher level he wrote from that level. Thus, he had to make several recast as he found the former stuff insufficient:

> The poem was originally written from a lower level, a mixture perhaps of the inner mind, psychic, poetic intelligence, sublimised vital, afterwards with the Higher Mind, often illumined and intuitivised, intervening.... Moreover, there have been made several successive revisions each trying to lift the general level higher and higher towards a possible Overmind poetry. As it now stands there is a general Overmind influence.[26]

In fact, Sri Aurobindo emphatically declares that *Savitri*, the *yogic* poetry must be regarded as "a field of experimentation to see how far poetry could be written from one's own yogic consciousness and how far that could be made creative."[27] Of course, this sort of experimentation had begun earlier and in other poems of Sri Aurobindo. The clues come to us as we have hints and occasional touches of various higher over mental planes such as in the following lines of his early poems:

1. O marvel bird with the burning wings of light and the unbarred lids that look beyond all space...[28]
2. Lost the titan winging of the thought...
   Arms taking to a voiceless supreme delight,
   Life that meets the Eternal with close breast,
   An unwalled mind dissolved in the Infinite,
   Force one with unimaginable rest...

   My consciousness climbed like a topless hill.[29]
3. He who from Time's dull motion escapes and thrills
   Rapt thoughtless, wordless into the Eternal's breast,
   Unrolls the form and sign of being,
   Seated above in the omniscient Silence.[30]
4. Calm faces of the gods on backgrounds vast
   Bringing the marvel of the infinitudes...[31]

5. A silent unnamed emptiness content
Either to fade in the Unknowable
Or thrill with the luminous seas of the Infinite[32]

6. Crossing power-swept silences rapture-stunned
Climbing high far ethers eternal- sunned. .[33]

7. I have drunk the Infinite like a giant's wine..
My soul unhorizoned widens to measureless sight
My body is God's happy living tool...[34]

8. Rose of God, like a blush of rapture on Eternity's face,
Rose of Love, ruby depth of all being, fire-passion of Grace!
Arise from the heart of the yearning that sobs in Nature's abyss:
Make earth the home of the Wonderful and life beatitude's kiss. [35]

When the lines quoted above from various poems were shown to Sri Aurobindo by a disciple, the former concurred with the observation that these bore the imprint of the Overhead inspiration.

The art of composing, identifying and critically appreciating Overhead Poetry is not an easy task on the part of a lay reader of poetry. Certainly, it is not even an ordinary poet's cup of tea, unless the poet has of course "the right intuitive keenness, receptivity", unless the poet has elevated his consciousness to an Overmind level and has become a true *yogi* in the Aurobindonean canon. Such a poet ought to have taken up composition of poetry as a means of spiritual discipline, *sādhanā*. While composing *Savitri*, Sri Aurobindo has categorically mentioned that he has made *Savitri* a means of ascension in attaining *yogic* consciousness. He used the composition of this spiritual epic as a field of experimentation to see how far poetry could be written from one's yogic consciousness.

Once we accept the hypothesis that Overhead inspiration is linked with *yogic* consciousness, then we should concur with the view that there exists a strong correlation between *yoga* and poetry. A *yogi* is not necessarily a literary man; at best he can be a fit channel and instrument of inspiration that comes from higher mental planes. In a letter dated September 11, 1934, Sri Aurobindo explains to a disciple the importance of "reading, poetic creation and yoga" in the life of a literary man and cites examples from his own life. He says, reading and painstaking labour is no more necessary for him as he has speeded up his *yogic sādhanā*:

As the Yoga increased, I read very little – for when all the ideas in the world come crowding in from within or from above, there is not much need for gathering mental food from outside sources... . What I wrote with some difficulty, often with great difficulty, I now write with ease. I am supposed to be a philosopher, but I never studied philosophy – everything I wrote came from Yogic experience, knowledge and inspiration. So too my greater power over poetry and perfect expression was acquired, in these last days not by reading and seeing how other people wrote, but from the heightening of my consciousness and the greater inspiration that came from the heightening.[36]

Sri Aurobindo's own experience as a great *yogi* and poet substantiated by his views that *yoga* intensifies poetic activity and creativity can be fully relied upon. Spirit and life are not incompatible; rather a greater power of the spirit brings a greater power of life. So poetry and art, of all other creative activities, help to drive this truth home. Mediation between the truth of the Spirit and the truth of life will be the chief function of poetry of the future. Life and Truth do not achieve perfection until they are suffused with Beauty and Delight. The aesthetic aim of poetry is to fill man's heart with delight. So poetry does not "water and feed upon human emotions and passions" by mere imitation; it creates a new order of sensation, helps in heightening one's vision, and revealing intuitive perception. The truth of poetry is not the truth of philosophy or truth of science, because it is a new way of self-expression of infinite Truth.

Poetry should express one's inner being and this can be achieved through one's contact with the Divine for right inspiration. The growth of the inner self is directly linked with the power of poetic expression. Finding oneself in the Infinite is a place of greater safety and surety. A *Rishi* can "drink of a deeper draught of Beauty and Delight" than the imagination of any ordinary poet can conceive of at its highest. A *rishi* is a disciplined man, one who sees or discovers the inner truth and expresses it in a self-expressive language, which is known as *Mantra*.[37]

As a practising poet and critic, Sri Aurobindo's critical output has an encyclopaedic range, same as the great poet Veda-Vyasa. While presenting an analysis of Sri Aurobindo's poetic theories and practice, V.K. Gokak makes the following scholarly observation:

> We hear in these writings a sovereign voice that chants a new poetry and teaches a new aesthetic. We behold the master at work as a literary critic of astonishing power and range of unsurpassed depth of insight, width of outlook and height of vision a seer who, moving with ease among the literature of the East and West, prepares us for a multitudinous, full-throated utterance that is going to be the *mantra* of a new civilisation.[38]

Like the great practising poet-critics of English poetry – Sir Phillip Sidney, John Dryden, Alexander Pope, William Wordsworth, S. T. Coleridge, P. B. Shelley, Matthew Arnold, T.S. Eliot, etc.,—who enunciated new theories, Sri Aurobindo too frames canons for the growth of a new taste and sensibility necessary for literary and critical appreciation and evaluation of poetic output. The more we get steeped in the Aurobindonean canon of taste and appreciation of poetry, the better we can hope to evaluate his poetic oeuvres.

As has already been pointed out Sri Aurobindo had a chequered career. He was called upon to play varied roles of a journalist, a philosopher, a yogin, a revolutionary, a playwright, a culture critic, etc. These diverse facets of his many-sided personalities were all of a piece to make him a prophet, a modern Rishi like Ved-Vyasa in the encyclopedic range of knowledge and experience. While recounting Sri Aurobindo's significant contributions to human thought and knowledge, K. R. Srinivas Iyengar observes that as a politician he has mapped the means and goal of our political movement in the pre-independence era. He has directed our attention to the goal of human civilisation towards the attainment of life divine, supermanhood, and has assiduously laboured to fashion the means to attain this noble purpose. As a poet and critic, he has carved out a niche among the great masters of our times because:

> ... his poetry was meant to bridge the present and the future, the self-divided present life and the Life Divine that is to be.

> The Seer has glimpsed the contours of ultimate possibility, the mystic poet has hymned his 'gloried fields of trance,' the philosopher has sought to interpret the Vision in terms of reason, while the Yogi has formulated a method, a multiform technique, for achieving the desired total change in consciousness; the sociologist has thrown out significant hints with regard to the organisation of tomorrow's world, while the creative critic has sensed the rhythms of the "Future Poetry" and described how the new poet will ride on the wings of an elemental spirituality and articulate the ineluctable rhythms of the Spirit.[39]

Sri Aurobindo's experience of a chequered career and his lifetime achievements have gone into the making of his spiritual epic. *Savitri,* spiritual in its theme, conception and execution, glorifies the all-inclusive inner change in human nature to effect a change in collective consciousness. In a symbolic way it paves the path through which an individual can change his consciousness, purify his outer self and realise a wider meaning of life in the context of the whole race. The epic challenge thrown to man is to exceed him, to realise that he is a transitional being in the cosmic drama moving towards a destined perfection by inner growth. This archetypal view of human destiny is embodied in this symbolic epic, *Savitri* which the present study seeks for a literary interpretation. Spirituality being the dominant trend, *Savitri* abounds in various symbols, images and mystic experiences, which are woven into the mystico-spiritual fabric of the epic. As the spiritual experience in *Savitri* is at once individual and collective, the poem has a symbolic and archetypal design.

Savitri's mystical experience by its very nature is untranslatable in terms of logical speculation; so it has to be conveyed in words, images and symbols as transcendental intimations, something springing up from the innermost psychic depths. Before a symbolic study of *Savitri* is attempted, the mind of the reader should be acquainted with the primary symbols Sri Aurobindo used in his early poetry and the mystical trend he set in with the mystic symbols he used in poetry.

References

1. Sri Aurobindo, *The Future Poetry*, Sri Aurobindo Ashram, 1972, p. 31.

2. Ibid., p. 34.
3. Ibid., p. 29.
4. Ibid., p. 30.
5. Ibid., p. 286.
6. Ibid.
7. Ibid., pp. 31-2.
8. Ibid., p. 321.
9. Ibid., p. 325.
10. Ibid., pp. 177-78.
11. Ibid., p. 337.
12. Nolini Kanta Gupta, *Poets and Mystics*, Madras: Sri Aurobindo Library, 1951, p.13.
13. Sri Aurobindo, *The Future poetry*, 1972, p.135.
14. Ibid., p. 135.
15. Ibid., p. 369.
16. Ibid., p. 368.
17. Ibid., p. 373.
18. Ibid., p. 377.
19. Henry Vaughan, "The World", in *The Winged Word*, ed. David Green, Delhi: Macmilan, ,1979, p.47.
20. Ibid., p. 365.
21. Ibid., p. 373.
22. Ibid., p. 386.
23. Sri Aurobindo, *Savitri*, 1977, p.728.
24. S. K. Prasad, *The Literary Criticism of Sri Aurobindo*, 1974, p.257.
25. Sri Aurobindo *Savitri*, p. 38.
26. Ibid., p. 729.
27. Ibid., pp. 727-8.
28. *Collected Poems*, "The Bird of Fire", p. 571.
29. Ibid., "The Life Heavens", pp. 574-5.
30. Ibid., "Jivanmukta", p. 576.
31. Ibid., "The Other Earths", p. 162.
32. Ibid, "Nirvana", p.161.
33. Ibid. "Thought the Paraclete", p.582.
34. Ibid., "Transformation", p.161.

35. Ibid., "Rose of God", p.584.
36. Sri Aurobindo, *The Future Poetry and Letters on Poetry Literature and Art*, 1972, p.503.
37. Ibid., p.517.
38. V.K. Gokak, *Sri Aurobindo: Seer and Poet*, p.152.
39. K.R. Srinivasa Iyengar, *Indian Writing in English*, rpt., 1984, p.153.

3

Symbolism in Sri Aurobindo's Poetry

Before attempting a symbolistic interpretation of *Savitri,* it is imperative that we should try to understand the word "symbolism" as used in literature *per se* poetry. The word 'symbol' carries various connotations. Indeed, our language itself is symbolic and every word we utter is a symbol. Not only in literature and religion but also in science symbols are used as non-verbal media such as graphs, models, mathematical formulae, etc. These media represent the relation between things. A symbol, although considered to be a sign, is in fact more than a sign. A lion, for example, is the symbol of courage; similarly a lamb represents mildness and innocence, and the Cross represents Christianity or church. Either in art or in religion, the term is applied to the various uses of language that has the aim of suggestion or insight rather than any direct or literal representation. Thus, we can define a symbol as something that stands for, represents or denotes something else. Not by exact resemblance or accident but by vague suggestion or conventional relation, a material object represents something immaterial, abstract or vice versa. *In Webster's Third New International Dictionary* a symbol is defined as:

> (a) Something that stands for or suggests something else by reason of relationship, convention, association or accidental but not intentional resemblance: especially a visible sign of something (as a concept or an institution) that is invisible...
> (b) An object or act that represents a repressed complex through unconscious association rather than through objective resemblance or conscious substitution.[1]

Thus, the primary function of a symbol may be representation, association or reference.

Wilbur Marshall Urban, while bringing out the differences between a sign and a symbol, lays down at the same time, in a convincing way, their function in his seminal work *Language and Reality*. In his accredited opinion, any datum may be a symbol if it means something or operates as a sign. Such data, we are further told, include conspicuous features of nature, "monuments, written or spoken words, small images or familiar objects easily duplicated or distributed. Any of these is a symbol provided it directs expectation or interest to something other than itself."[2] According to Urban all symbols are in a sense signs, but all signs are not symbols.

The study of symbolism provides us with an instrument of knowledge; and it is the most ancient method of articulation, which escapes other modes of expression. Symbols have magical power. Poetry is a special kind of knowledge. Through language, images and symbols, produced by the poet's creative imagination, the world of poetry becomes a reality. W.B. Yeats in an article "The Symbolism of Poetry" proclaims it as the most suitable form of expression:

> If I say 'white' or 'purple' in an ordinary line of poetry, they evoke emotions so exclusively that I cannot say why they move me, but if I say in the same mood in the same breath with such obvious intellectual symbols as a cross or a crown of thorns, I think of purity and sovereignty.[3]

A work of literature is symbolic form. Symbolistic, creative and critical writings formed a prominent movement in the nineteenth century in Europe. Edgar Allan Poe was a great exponent of the Symbolistic Theory. In his opinion a poet tries to secure a system of correspondence between things and thought. He achieves this feat by projecting a poem as a symbol. The poet through his imaginative faculty and intelligence organises words into specific literary structures. Thus we find that symbolism is a proven method to communicate unique personal feelings. While presenting an analysis of the Symbolist Movement in literature, Arthur Symons shows its significance:

> Without symbolism there can be no literature, indeed, not even language. What are words themselves but symbols, almost as arbitrary as the letters which compose them, mere sounds of voice to which we have agreed to give certain significations....[4]

The unique use of symbolism in literature is that it is a powerful instrument to reveal unseen reality apprehended by human consciousness.

Symbolism is an aid to spiritualise literature. J.E. Cirlot takes a philosophical view of the art of symbolism and quotes Landrit's words in support of his views:

> Symbolism is the science of the relations which unite the created world with God, the material world with the supernatural; the science of the harmonies existing between the diverse parts of the universe (correspondence analogy), operating within the process of involution, that is, of the materiality of all things.[5]

So symbolism is the study of the correspondence between the natural orders as a whole to the supernatural order. By virtue of this correspondence, the whole of Nature acts as a symbol of the supernatural or metaphysical truth. Thus, symbolism links together all orders of reality through the process of correspondence. A symbol may have both an esoteric and exoteric meaning. It has a dual function as it embraces the real and the unreal, truth and fiction. The way Sri Aurobindo has analysed the use of symbolism in the Vedic hymns, it can be said that the Vedic Ṛishis used "transcendental symbolism" in their hymns.

Their (the Vedic hymns) formulas and ceremonies are, overtly, the details of an outward ritual devised for the Pantheistic Nature-Worship which was then the common religion, covertly the sacred words, the effective symbols of a spiritual experience and knowledge and a psychological discipline of self-culture which were then the highest achievement of the human race.[6]

In the poetry of the Symbolist poets two types of symbolism are invariably traced out, one is "human symbolism" and the other "transcendental symbolism". Charles Chadwick points our attention towards the presence of personal note as a typical characteristic of "human symbolism". He continues to explain the other aspect of symbolism, known as "transcendental symbolism" in which "concrete images are used as symbols, not of particular thoughts and feelings or emotions within the poet, but of a vast and general ideal world of which the real world is merely an imperfect representation."[7] In his opinion, only through the medium of poetry this world is approachable. A poet's function is to prepare a ground within him or the reader into which the ideal forms of the infinite world will enter and stabilise there.

Sri Aurobindo uses fire, moon, dawn and solar symbolism to create a special type of consciousness in the reader. Fire or *Agni* is the divine power in man, the immortal element in mortal beings. In *Savitri*, fire symbolises power and light of the Divine Conscious-Force. Solar symbolism is used in *Savitri* to imply the outpouring of the Light and Knowledge, the Truth-force of the Divine Light.

The Symbolist poets used a different type of symbolism known as "human symbolism". Charles Chadwick shows us the presence of personal note as a typical characteristic of "human symbolism". While elaborating, he says, it is "the art of expressing ideas and emotions not by describing them directly nor by defining them through overt comparisons with concrete images, but by suggesting what these ideas and emotions are, by recreating them in the mind of the reader through the use of unexplained symbols."[8] Sri Aurobindo in "Rose of God" makes use of 'rose' as the symbol of God's grace, power and love. He attributes absolute Beauty, absolute Light, absolute Power, absolute Life and absolute Love to the Rose of God. Similarly, thought in "Thought the Paraclete" is presented as a poetic symbol of consciousness, which takes its flight from the mental level and *soars* towards the supramental region – Supermind. We find that symbolism is a potent instrument used for the expression of ineffable poetic vision. In this context Baudelaire's remark on "Notes Nouvelle Sur Edgar Poe" as recorded by Charles Chadwick runs as : "It is through and by means of poetry that the soul perceives the splendours lying beyond the grave."[9]

Thus is a reader transported to the other world through the medium of poetry. In fact in the "Book of the Divine Mother", Book III of *Savitri*, the reader is transported to an ethereal sphere and is presented with an ineffable vision.

At times a poet may evoke a symbol 'little by little' in a process of gradual revelation for enjoyment – "An object is evoked little by little so as to reveal a mood or conversely, the art of choosing an object, and extracting from it an 'e'tat d'ame,"[10] says Stephen Mallarme. The remarkable part of this definition is the evocation of an object 'little by little' because elsewhere Mallarme contends, "to name an object is to banish the major part of the enjoyment derived from a poem, since the enjoyment consists in a process of gradual revelation." [11]

Sri Aurobindo in "The Symbol Dawn" of *Savitri* while handling the major symbol gradually piles one suggestion upon another to present the picture of the appearance of dawn as a poetic symbol. Instead of presenting an accurate description of the earth half in darkness and half in light, he makes rapid changes of images so as to focus certain ideas and impressions "to form a symbol of a partial and temporary darkness of the soul and Nature which seems to be a temporary feeling of that which is caught in the Night as if it were universal and eternal."[12] In one part of the earth people lost in night does not think of the other half of the earth as full of light. The image of "the earth wheeling" is scientifically accurate because through rotation only the earth passes from darkness into light.

Let us analyse how Sri Aurobindo presents the dawn symbol in *Savitri*. First, there is a black quietude, then the persistent touch, then the first "beauty and wonder" leading to the "lucent corner". The next stage is the falling of darkness like "a falling cloak" suggesting the rapidity of change. What appeared as a rift then develops into a wide luminous gap. Next comes "a perpetual sign", the iridescences, then the blaze and finally the magnificent aura. The full import of "Symbol Dawn" will be discussed later on in a separate chapter.

Writers have attempted to classify symbols from their own points of view, though such a classification is based mainly on the function and nature of symbols. Wilbur Marshall Urban classifies these mainly into different classes: Extrinsic or Arbitrary Symbol; and Intrinsic or Descriptive Symbol. An Extrinsic Symbol has its origin from a process of "association congruity". We come across such symbols mostly in art and sciences. In Sri Aurobindo's poetry various colours, tree, rose, swan, bird, and flower are used as

Extrinsic Symbol. The Intrinsic or Descriptive Symbol is an associational link and is internal to the thing it symbolises. The symbolised thing carries identical characters of the intuitive object. For example, a lion as symbol stands for courage because it possesses the intrinsic qualities of strength and power. An Insight Symbol is deeply internal to the things it symbolises. Wilbur Urban shows its characteristics:

> The peculiar character of such symbols lies in the fact that they do not point to or lead to, but they lead into. They do not merely represent through partial coincidence, characters and relations; they are or at least supposed to be, a vehicle or medium of insight.[13]

It is the common feature of both the "Intrinsic" and "Insight" symbols that the images or ideas are from a limited sphere and applied in a more universal way because of the inherent pervasiveness and ideality. The only difference between these two categories of symbols is that whereas the Intrinsic Symbol represents, the Insight Symbol helps us to see through. Most of the Vedic symbols such as the sun, the moon, fire, and dawn used by Sri Aurobindo in his poetry are the instances of Insight Symbols.

The Symbolist method is supposed to be a powerful medium of expression of reality. The avowed aim of the Symbolist poets was to create in the mind of the reader a world outside the palpable reality. A poet's function is to estrange him from all contact with reality and to prepare a ground within himself into which the ideal forms of the infinite world will enter and stabilise there. To Baudelaire objects are not simply objects but are representative symbols of ideal forms lying behind them.

Another area, which is closely linked with symbolism, is mysticism. The whole literature of mystic experience is replete with symbols. Mysticism affects aesthetic experience of man as it brings more or less a direct communion with God. In the opinion of Edgar Elan Poe the special virtue which poetry possesses may be presumed to have its source in the power of mystical insight:

> Art does no more than reproduce the profounder vision of the seer. What the seer sees is variously described, though the formulae seldom move outside the repertoire of mystical

> tradition: it may be the 'essence of things' or ' the spirit of things' ... or alternately it may be the 'visible form of God' so recalling a tendency latent in Baudelaire but strongly encouraged in the works of Hegel and Schelling to treat art as in some way sacred, a quasi-religious rite, or at least on a par with religion as one of the absolute forms of mind...[14]

For Baudelaie the term 'symbol' is bound up with a theosophical view of the universe. All things are symbols of God or at least of a transcendental reality to which the artist has special access. Thus, the effect of symbolism is to spiritualise literature. A poem can be symbolic and mystic at the same time.

Mystic symbols, to Sri Aurobindo, are living things, not abstractions. Mystic poetry does not mean any thing exactly; it means things suggestively, things that are unknown, recondite.[15] He uses the word mystic in the sense of a certain kind of "inner seeing and feeling of things, a way which to the intellect would seem occult and visionary." In the more deeply symbolist and mystic poem mental explanation falls far short of the exact vision or things felt, seen or lived.

The Symbolist poets were deeply influenced by mysticism. In fact, some of the symbolist poets regarded poetry as an exercise in mystical account of reality that is hidden behind the appearance of the universe. A poet in this way is a potential discoverer who finds out unity in all created things and an overriding order in the universe. Sri Aurobindo shows the relation between "Symbolic and Mystic Poetry" in reply to a correspondent's query.

> It is when the thing seen is spiritually lived and has an independent vivid reality of its own which exceeds any conceptional significance it may have on the surface that it is mystic.... In the more deeply symbolist—still more in the mystic-poem the mind is submerged in the vividness of the reality and any mental explanation falls far short of what is felt and lived in the deeper vital or psychic response...Mystic poetry can strike still deeper - it can stir the inmost and subtlest recesses of the life-soul and the secret inner mind at the same time...[16]

From a technical point of view a mystic cannot wholly do away with symbol or allegory, for his experience must be communicated to stimulate the dormant intuition of a reader. An articulate mystic employs all kinds of symbolic languages. He has to convey in poetic language something that lies beyond the surface sense. To Sri Aurobindo mystic symbols are "living things, the inner truth or vision." In mystic poetry the symbol ought to be as much as possible "the natural body of the inner truth or vision, itself an intimate part of the experience."[17]

Some of Sri Aurobindo's short poems have a mystical base. In fact, *Savitri* is fundamentally mystical poetry, which is described by him as "a sort of poetic philosophy of the Spirit and of Life much profounder in its substance and vaster in its scope." Too much of metaphysical ideas and philosophical conceptions have gone into the making of *Savitri*. The poet apprehends that the general reader may find it hard to follow. He admits that if he had to write for the general reader, he could not have written *Savitri* at all. He further says:

> It is in fact for myself that I have written it and for those who can lend themselves to the subject matter, images, technique of mystic poetry . . . The mystic feels real and present, even ever present to his experience, intimate to his being, truths which to the ordinary reader are intellectual abstraction or metaphysical speculations.[18]

A mystic writes out of his direct experiences that are foreign to the ordinary mentality. To a mystic there is nothing called abstraction. Since *Savitri* is a new kind of poetry, it demands a new mentality in the recipient. It expresses truths that are unfamiliar to the ordinary mind or belong to an untrodden domain or field of occult experience. A mystic poet tries to express a vision, a spiritual contact or knowledge. The philosophy of *Savitri* tries to express a total vision or experience of all the planes of being. It expresses living truth or reality and not mere abstract ideas as some critics find it. The Overmind employs its native language and gives it supreme utterance. As it has already been pointed out, Overhead inspiration in *Savitri* brings some touch of a deeper power of vision.

The epic, Sri Aurobindo writes, is based on *Savitri-Satyavan* legend, which is in the nature of a myth and a prophecy. The communion of the human soul with the Divine is the theme, which is given poetic utterance. Spirituality is the dominant note of Sri Aurobindo's poetry. His spiritual imagination creates the archetypes of universal experience. The theme of *Savitri* offers him the mythic exploration of the *Mahābhāratā* legend, a *tour de force* of the soul's odyssey. *Savitri* is the record of Sri Aurobindo's visionary experiences, prophesizing the birth of a new world. R.K. Singh in his scholarly study, *Savitri: A Spiritual Epic* analyses the mythic mode of the epic:

> He (Sri Aurobindo) concerns himself with archetypal subjects like love and death in an archetypal situation which depicts the tension between the higher and the lower levels of consciousness in a person, the conflict of the male-female relationship, the search for the mother etc. *Savitri*, the heroine herself, is an archetypal character, a mythic image.[19]

Savitri's self-awareness is the glorification of the divinity of the soul. The poet recreates the legend as a universal symbol in which he discharges his role as a mythmaker. In the epic itself the symbol of the past acquires a new spiritual dimension and has relevance for the present as well as the future. Thus, man is symbolically elevated to a higher plane that is from human to divine, through spiritual transformation.

Having at length analysed the importance of symbolism in literature and the way the symbolist trend has evolved in European literary movement, it would be worthwhile to turn our attention towards a detailed analysis of the use of symbols in Sri Aurobindo's poetry. Some of the poetic symbols he used in his short poems have undergone a process of evolution in his early poetry and recur in *Savitri*. These symbols appear to have been used unconsciously in his poetry in marked contrast to what we find in the French Symbolist Poetry.

Fire or *Agni* is a powerful symbol in Sri Aurobindo's poetry. It is remarkable to observe how this symbol undergoes an evolution from the early poems to the later ones and culminates in *Savitri*, achieving a greater intensity and wider implications. "Bride of the Fire" is a poem addressed to the *Agni*- god. Having renounced his earthly desires, the poet requests the bride of the Fire to take him nearer to truth-consciousness. He yearns to be surrounded by divine knowledge where lies the real bliss. This bride of Fire is the voice of Infinity which has filled the heart of the poet with its rapturous bliss.

In the "Miracle of Birth" the soul is described as a spark of the eternal fire. In the "Flame Wind" the poet ardently desires to unite with the Divine. God-realisation comes like a flaming wind with power and force, and sets ablaze the mind and the body of the poet. The mind of the poet is enriched with divine knowledge. In a nutshell, the poem describes the power and force of a flame that symbolises truth and knowledge. At last he feels that the strength and power of the flame are too strong for him; so he rejects the flame in search of love "in silent ways". In other words, he wishes to achieve higher knowledge through love and divine compassion.

In "Death and the Traveller Fire" fire symbolises Truth-Consciousness, Light or Knowledge. Death's citadel in this poem is invaded by fire with the power of Light and Truth-Consciousness force. Death realises his own ignorance and seeks to rectify it by knowledge. Fire, which is the spark of the eternal, illumines the cavernous heart of Death.

The bird in "The Bird of Fire" is a symbol of man's ascending aspiration to transcend the limits of mortal life and mental plane. The bird is originally an Upanishadic symbol. The bird also symbolises the aspiring soul of man. The bird of fire is the bringer of divine knowledge and love to the heart of the poet. The bird of fire may also refer to the Vedic poet who brought *soma* to Indra. This symbol of the bird also recurs in *Savitri*.

The fire symbol is thus found in his various shorter-poems as the bringer of light, as the embodiment of divine consciousness, the messenger of the Eternal, the spark of the eternal and the guardian of truth. All these symbolic meanings of fire find expression in *Savitri* with wider dimension.

"The Bird of fire" is an important poem, considered in the light of the symbol fire. As has been discussed elsewhere, fire itself is a Vedic symbol. "The Blue Bird" after being liberated becomes the "Bird of Fire". Symbolically "The Bird of Fire" and "Thought the paraclete" are correlated. The theme of ascent which occurs in "Ahana" and "Urvasie", at last, finds consummation in *Savitri*.

The ascent of Aswapathy may be termed as an extension of "The Bird of Fire" through the regions of "Thought the Paraclete".

Let us analyse how "The Bird of Fire" implies a symbolic meaning in its theme of ascent. It is repeatedly said that the gods have established *Agni* as the immortal amidst mortals, the divine power in man, the energy through which they fulfil their work in him.

"The Bird of Fire" symbolises the ascending aspiration of a *sādhaka* that reaches the Timeless Divine and brings back to the material world a divine gift.

> Angel, here unto me
> Bringst thou for travailing earth a spirit silent and free or
> His crimson passion of love divine.[20]

The aspiration of the *sādhaka* can break the "barriers of mind" if the divine love is brought to his heart. In the last stanza, the Bird of Fire is invoked in these words:

> One strange leap of thy mystic stress breaking the barriers
> of mind and life, arrives at its Luminous term thy flight...[21]

This is the power of the Bird of Fire. So the poet invokes it to make his nature "wide, an intimate guest of his solitude." It is remarkable to note the colour symbolism in this poem. In *yogic* experiences, according to Sri Aurobindo, colours have symbolic significance. In *yoga* the colours are the symbols of different forces. "Gold-white" symbolises the divine consciousness, the light of the higher Truth. "White-rose" symbolises pure spiritual surrender. "Deep-red symbolises divine love in "The Bird of Fire". Each stanza of this poem reveals the power and nature of the bird. Sri Aurobindo's own general explanation of the symbolism reads as: "The Bird of Fire is the living vehicle of the gold fire of the Divine Light and the white fire of the divine Tapas and the crimson fire of Divine Love - and everything else of the Divine Consciousness."[22]

In the poem "Rose of God", rose is the central symbol. It is the symbol of beauty; so the Rose of God is the Divine Beauty. What is beauty? It is nothing but the perfection of form. That Form of the Divine is invoked in this poem to manifest itself in everything on earth. Rose is a favourite symbol of the great poets, particularly Dante and Yeats. This poem is written in the form of a prayer for the descent of the Rose of God's Grace, with its petals of Bliss, Light, Power, Life and Love. We have here a new experience of spiritual regeneration.

K.D. Sethna's opening remark on this poem is worth noting. He is all praise for the mystic touch, "Mysticism rising to a climax of the incantatory art – there we have that poem of Sri Aurobindo's 'Rose of God.' The most famous of mystical symbols he has steeped in the intensest inner light and lifted it on a metrical base of pure stress into an atmosphere of rhythmic ecstasy."[23]

The poem communicates the thrill of a poet's vision, which is vividly realised and intensely felt. The various secret aspects of the Divine Rose are revealed in this poem. The first two lines of each stanza are devoted to the adoration of Divine Glory while the second two lines depict the reality on earth. There is a slight alteration in this scheme in the last stanza. What blooms in the Divine Rose is invoked to manifest itself on the earth. The Rose of God is the embodiment of absolute Beauty, absolute Light, absolute Power, absolute Life and absolute Love as if these different aspects are each its petals.

There are touches of 'overhead' aesthesis in "Rose of God". Comparing "Rose of God" with "Thought the Paraclete", L.S.R. Krishna Sastry is of the opinion that the former poem traces the path of realisation through devout self-surrender and self-dedication – the *Bhakti-mārga;* while "Thought the paraclete" traces the *Jnāna-mārga* realisation through knowledge or Gnosis.[24]

In the first stanza the Rose of God is invoked as the Rose of Bliss to fill man's heart with creative delight. There are seven types of ecstasy that are blended in Bliss. The number seven bears a Vedic symbolism.

In the second stanza the Rose of God is invoked as the Rose of Light to manifest wisdom in the "mind of our earthhood", which is inert and rooted in nescience. Only through Thought and Knowledge can a man achieve Divine vision and Divine bliss. The Rose of Light is necessary to dispel the darkness, Ignorance.

In the third stanza, the Rose of God is described as the "damask force of Infinity" which is a "red icon of might". K.D.

Sethna draws our attention towards the damask texture. The damask colour might have been deliberately used to suggest the idea of a Damascus blade that can pierce through. So the "damask force of Infinity" has the piercing power of the Divine to penetrate the armour of Ignorance and inertia. The Rose of Power is invoked to form an "image of Immortality" for the "outbreak of Godhead in man" to make this earthly existence of man deathless. To work out this "divine desire" a strong will power is necessary.

In the fourth stanza such a Will Power is invoked. Our psychic being, which is in essence a spark of the Divine, enmeshed in material nature, keeps yearning for life's beatitude. When Divine love is enkindled in the bosom of man, he is ready to shed all "the down pull of earth" and keep yearning to redeem the earth from hatred, strife and suffering. The Divine alone can strengthen our will to "Bridge our earthhood and heavenhood", to "make earth the home of the Wonderful and life beatitude's kiss." As we see, the Rose symbol in this poem is self-explanatory.

P.B. Shelley in *The Revolt of Islam* presents a similar vision and points out that human will is a directive force in human history. He refers to "that intertexture of good and evil with which Nature seems to have clothed every form of individual existence." Cythna's counsel in the poem to the mariners is that they have to observe natural and social evils and how the destructive forces are everywhere at work. So men ought to cast out hatred and infuse love and joy, which can make "the foulest breast a paradise of flowers." In fact, Love, Justice, Truth and Joy are the only powers, which can guide man out of the present labyrinth of falsehood. Cythna disagrees with the teacher who asserts that man by nature is "weak and sinful, frail and blind." Virtue and hope and love surround the world, and man must become their instrument.

An interesting thing to mark in the fourth stanza of "Rose of God" is the poet's use of words, such as "colour's lyre" which means the Divine Beauty that not only manifests through visions but also becomes the sound-power. Artistic visions are expressed through sounds. Another remarkable word is "ruby":

> Rose of God, like a blush of rapture on Eternity's face,
> Rose of Love, ruby depth of all being, Fire passion of Grace![25]

The use of the words "ruby depth" is very symbolic. It is not only used for its symbolic colour but for its availability in the underground earth. Like this the Divine Love is felt to be present even in the deep abyss of the human heart. As in Sri Aurobindo's poems, the rose symbol appears frequently in W.B. Yeats's poems also. The lady in "The Binding of the Hair" is "the Rose of my Desire, the Lily of my peace." The pagan saint in "Where There Is Nothing, There Is God" stirs up an odour of rose miraculously. The Quixotic Knight in "Out of the Rose" prays to the Divine Rose of Intellectual Flame. The ladies of "The Heart of the Spring" symbolically crown themselves either with roses or lilies according to whether they choose love or purity. In "Of Costello the Proud", the moon "glimmered in the distance like a great white rose" and the women of the Shee rush "together in the shape of a great silvery rose." The magical power of the rose is prominent in "The Vision of the Hanrahan the Red". At the climax of "Rose Alchmia" there is a pagan ceremony in which the cross and the rose are joined. The cover of *The Secret Rose* (1897) has at its centre a four-petalled rose joined to a cross occupying a place just below the middle of a tree. Like the rose symbolism in Sri Aurobindo's "Rose of God", the four petals of *The Secret Rose* are chiefly the four elements. The conjunction of rose and cross is the central myth of Rosicrucianism and the conjunction is often referred to as a "mystic marriage". The cross symbolises struggle and opposition while the rose blossoms with love, harmony, and beauty. The masculine principle, the cross, merges with the feminine principle, the rose.

Not only W.B.Yeats, but also Dante and T.S. Eliot have made use of the rose-symbol in their poetry. T.S. Eliot at the close of his *Four Quartets* writes, 'At the end the fire and the rose are one.' Beatrice leads Dante in the *Divine Comedy* to Paradise. He is raised into the empyrean and his sight is strengthened by her aid; then he sees around a multitude of angels and souls of the blessed. The poet elaborates this vision in the following lines with the help of a rose symbol:

> So now, displayed before me as a rose
> Of snow-white purity, the sacred might
> I saw, whom with His blood Christ made His spouse . .
> As bees ply back and forth, now in the flowers
> Busying themselves, and now intent to wend

Where all their toil is turned to sweetest stores
So did the host of Angles now descend
Amid the flower of the countless leaves,
Now rise to where their love dwells without end.[26]

In Sri Aurobindo's poem 'Ascent' we come across the symbol of swan. "Swan", says the poet "is the Indian symbol of individual soul, the central being, the divine part which is turned towards the Divine, descending from there and ascending to it."[27] Swan is also a favourite symbol used by W.B. Yeats.

The poem "Ascent" invokes the "Spirit immortal" to shed all earthly connections and rise up. This "Spirit immortal" is addressed as "Swan of the supreme and spaceless ether", which symbolises the "spiritual being", the "unsullied soul". The soul of man in "Ascent" is invoked to "Rise with the World" to "exceed life's boundaries", so as to "surpass the universe" and become:

One with the Eternal, live in his infinity,
Drowned in the absolute, found in the Gothead.[28]

Thus, the theme of the ascent of man's soul in "Ascent" is symbolically projected in the larger framework of Aswapathy's epic journey in consciousness to achieve perfection and meet the Divine Mother in *Savitri*. The swan-image also suggests Divine perfection.

Most of the symbols, Sri Aurobindo employs in his poetry have specific spiritual significance in the discipline of *Yoga*. His images and symbols are inherent in his visions, which for this reason are esoteric in nature and sometimes obscure. He reveals a world of realities that he saw and knew, but to our minds they appear supernormal. To appreciate his poetry, our minds should be free from the shackles of old ideas and conventions.

The central theme in "Thought the Paraclete" is the experience of the poet's consciousness soaring towards the supramental region and beyond it. It is an esoteric experience, and is a bright example of Sri Aurobindo's 'overhead poetry'. Poetic experience is put forth with symbols and visions taken from spiritual planes.

The colour scheme in "Thought the Paraclete" has symbolic significances from the *yogic* point of views. The title of the poem connotes Christian symbolism. Paraclete, the Holy Ghost in Christian theology is the mediator between the Divine and the human being. "Thought in this poem is a symbol and as a poetic symbol it becomes the 'instrument of consciousness.' The poet's thought takes flight from the mental level towards the Supermind - the supramental region." S. Krishna Sarma points out, The progress of consciousness from Mind to Supermind as analysed by Sri Aurobindo in Chapter – 'Ascent towards Supermid' (in his *Life Divine*) is given a poetic utterance in this poem.[29]

In the first stage of its flight the "Thought" leaves the "long green crests of the seas of life" like some archangel in a dream. Green colour is the symbol of "vital force" in Sri Aurobindo's *yoga*. Orange symbolises the desire for union with the Divine. The mystic mind of the poet leaves earth–consciousness and yearns for a union with the Divine.

> Sleepless wide great glimmering wings of wind
> Bore the gold-red seeking of feet that trod
> Space and Time's mute vanishing ends. [30]

In the lines above the expression "wings of wind" symbolises the soaring aspiration of the poet. The two words "wide" and "great" signify the heightening and widening of the consciousness of the poet before it takes a flight. In Sri Aurobindo's scheme of mystic colour symbolism the "gold-red" colour symbolises the aspiration of the divine consciousness to ascend towards higher planes.

"Hippogriff" is a mythological animal, like a griffin, with the body and hindquarters of a horse. Horse itself is a Vedic symbol, which symbolises life force. The "pale blue" symbolises light of higher knowledge.

> Crimson-white mooned oceans of pauseless bliss
> Drew its vague heart-yearning with voices sweet.[31]

This is the stage in which the poet's own consciousness is no more capable of taking "self direction", so the divine consciousness with its "voices sweet" intervenes and pulls the poet's consciousness to its higher plane. "Crimson-white" symbolises divine consciousness. This is one of the characteristics of the consciousness when it rises higher up to the "overmind" stage.

In the last movement the "thought" moves from "Overmind" towards the Supermind state, and is hungry for the final union with the Infinite. When the consciousness of the poet reaches the supramental region, it experiences bliss, *ānanda*. At this stage the Self is "alone", nude, as it has shed all its dross. Thus, one can mark how the "Thought" of the poet passes through two significant regions, "green crest of the seas" and "the orange sky" to shed its earthly impurities and to experience divine bliss in the union with the Infinite.

In its theme and symbolic treatment "Soul, my Soul" can be considered a continuation of "Thought the Paraclete".

"The Sea", although a small poem, has also symbolic overtones. The sea is the symbol of earthly consciousness. In the beginning of the poem the sea is presented in its fiery image. This fierceness of the sea is not in vain; so the poet cries looking at the dreadful sea: "Thou hast a message". What is this message that the poet has discovered? It is the message to face heroically danger, difficulties, pain and suffering and to go on advancing on the path of *sādhanā*. To one who is initiated into practice of *Yoga*, it is a challenge to his ordinary consciousness like the "gray wide-sea" to overcome the difficulties, pain and suffering; and to rise up in one's consciousness. Thunder and storm, avail us not in vain, but with a purpose. The purpose is explicitly stated in the following lines:

> The cloud He informs
> With thunder and assails us with His storms,
> That man may grow
> King over pain and victor of o'erthrow
> Matching his great
> Unconquerable soul with adverse Fate.[32]

Doesn't *The Holy Bible* reverberate with similar thoughts? It is mentioned in *The Book of Job* that "he fills His hands with lighting, and commands it to strike its mark... God's voice thunders in marvelous ways; he does great things which we cannot comprehend. He seals the hand of every man, so that all men he has made may know his work."[33] (*The Book of Job* 36:32, 37:57).

Elsewhere, *The Book of Job* emphatically underlines that God, the Almighty fashions man's life through adverse fate, pain and suffering as in:

> For God does speak . . . Or a man may be chastened on a bed of pain with constant distress in his bone . . . His souls draws near to the pit, and his life to the messengers of death . . . 'God does all these things to a man – twice, even three times – to turn back his soul from the pit, that the light of life may shine on him.[34] (Job 33:14,19, 22-29, 30.)

The indomitable spirit that the poet gained in his yogic experience has prompted him to meet the challenge, as he says, "To measure my enormous self with thee." Because,

> To linger is to lose what god has planned
> For man's wide soul,
> Who set eternal godhead for goal.[35]

The sea stands for eternal existence. As is said in the Poem man's goal is to achieve godhead — the Divine Consciousness. In the poem the river of human mind seeks to merge into the ocean of Divine consciousness.

"Symbol Moon" is another poem which rings with symbolic notes. Moon, as Sri Aurobindo says, symbolises spiritual consciousness. The opening line of the poem is very symbolic.

> Once again thou hast climbed, o moon,
> Like a white fire on the glimmering edge...[36]

"White-fire" symbolises the fire of aspiration, aspiration for the Divine. The 'climb' indicates the *ascent* of divine aspiration. As the moon glimmers in the sky, it dispels the darkness of the "Night" like a 'fiery torch'. Symbolically explained, it means when the aspiration for union with the Infinite is enkindled, all ignorant and earthly desire are burnt out. "Night" always symbolises ignorance, *avidya;* when this happens the "inconscient gulfs stir and are vaguely thrilled."

The "wonder light" in the poem symbolises divine light. The "unheard cry "of the deep heart is heard by the Divine, and so the divine light descends to "unlock with a wizard rod of fire the dumb recesses of the sleep."

In the second stanza, the symbol moon is addressed as the "ship of the gods". It is through our spiritual consciousness that our "self" can sail towards the state of God-consciousness. This spiritual consciousness is the "very bliss that floats in opaline air over heaven's golden roads", to "capture our human lives like a nectar face of light." The symbolic meaning of the moon is made more explicit in the line", "O icon and chalice of spiritual light whose spots are like Nature's shadow stains on a white and immaculate soul."

If in Sri Aurobindo's poem the 'Symbol Moon' symbolises man's spiritual consciousness, Shelley employs the same symbol to suggest human reason. Shelly believes in Plato's theory that the soul of man is divided into three parts. First, the immortal part which is seated in brain, is alone divine and akin to the soul of the universe. Secondly, there is the higher mortal soul which takes the side of human reason. The third part receives the commands of the immortal part which Shelley calls appetitive soul. In the Moon-episode in Shelley's *Epipsychidion,* the soul is rescued from "false imagination by the cold chaste Moon" of Reason, which "warms not but illumines."

One can find a symbolic note in the poem "Dream Boat". It symbolises a psychic opening that soon vanishes away. The opening of the psyche is as temporary as a dream. It is the sense of loss and nostalgia to which the poet has given poetic utterance in this poem. To such a call of the divine most of us do not usually respond. The experience of the psychic opening is expressed as something shuddering in one's heart:

> Hidden in the recesses of the heart something shuddered,
> It recalled all that life's joy cherished,
> Imaged the felicity it must leave lost for ever,
> And the boat passed and the gold god vanished.[37]

The "Gold God" referred in the line above is a god who comes from the supramental region. The horror of an irreparable inner loss is conveyed in the last stanza:

> Now within the hollowness of the world's breast inhabits–
> For the love died and the old joy ended –
> Void of a felicity that has fled, gone for ever,
> And the gold god and the dream boat come not.[38]

It is a loss that man has deliberately incurred. It is very difficult to make compensation for such a loss. Francis Thompson handles a similar theme in his poem "The Hound of Heaven" where man knowingly refuses God's grace, "for I knew His love who followed", the clasp of "His hand outstretched chasingly" and thus misses a providential opportunity:

> I fled Him, down the arches of the years,
> I fled Him, down the labyrinthine ways
> Of my own mind; and in the mist of tears
> I hid from Him, and under running laughter...
> Adown Titanic glooms of chasmed fears
> From those strong Feet that followed, followed after.[39]

In the sonnet "The Pilgrim of the Night", Sri Aurobindo describes his experience of journeying in the region of Ignorance, *avidyā*. Armed with *yogic* experience and supramental knowledge, the poet at once plunges into the abyss of "Night". The heart of the "Night" is pitch dark and dangerous. The poet's "weary journey knows no end", he moves on and on. He fails to find its boundary, as it is boundless. His bitter experience is more aptly conveyed in the following lines:

> And travelled through a vastness dim and blind
> To the grey shore where her ignorant waters roll.
>
> I walk by the chill wave through the dull slime
> And still that weary journeying knows no end;
> Lost is the lustrous godhead beyond Time,
> There comes no voice of the celestial Friend...[40]

The region described in the poem is obviously undivine because godhead is lost here beyond Time. The word 'grey' implies the colour of smoke that screens one's conscience and conveys a sense of gloom and invisibility.

Dawn is a dominant symbol in Sri Aurobindo's poetry. While elaborating the symbolic functions of the divine Dawn, Usha in his *The Secret of the Veda*, Sri Aurobindo observes:

> The Rishis hymn the divine Dawn, daughter of Heaven, as the bringer of Truth, the bliss, of vision, maker, follower, leader of the paths of Truth, remover of the darkness, the eternal and ever youthful goddess of our godward journeying.[41]

In "Urvasie" king Pururavas after his victory over the Titans while coming back from heaven gazes at the emerging dawn:

> Nearer it drew now to him and he saw
> Out of the widening glory move a face
> Of dawn, a body fresh from mystery,
> Enveloped with a prophecy of light
> More rich than perfect splendours. It was she,
> The golden virgin, Usha, mother of life.[42]

But dawn in "Ilion" suggests a completely different approach. She appears with a suggestion of the imminent destruction of the city of Troy. The following lines are highly symbolic:

> Out of the sun and its spaces she came, pausing tranquil and fatal,
> And, at a distance followed by the golden herds of the sun-god,
> Carried the burden of Light and its riddle and danger to Hellas.[43]

The opening of "Ahana" announces the advent of dawn. The hunters of joy, the seekers after knowledge, and the climbers of power cheer her. As soon as the dawn smiles at men, the latter are transformed and divinised. So in a deeper way "Ahana" foretells the coming of Savitri. The dawn symbol thus evolves through many of Sri Aurobindo's poems and gets its luminosity and intensity in *Savitri*. In it *Savitri* brings a hope and nectarean assurance to mankind.

In the poem "Tree" man's aspiring soul rising towards heaven is symbolically presented through the tree. Sri Aurobindo prophesies the coming of peaceful days in "The Tiger and the Deer" to put an end to the chaotic and violent ways of the world. We can contrast Sri Aurobindo's prophecy with the one presented by W.B. Yeats. Yeats in "A Galway Race" is elated at the prospect of the whole of earth changing its tune. But in one of his most important poems, "The Second Coming", he makes a prophecy of the coming of a new destructive god in the form of a sphinx-like beast that will wreak havoc on mankind. Significantly enough Yeats points out in this poem how "The ceremony of innocence is drowned." And at the same time he sums up "the growing murderousness of the world." The sphinx-like beast symbolises the coming of a new destructive god. Whereas W.B. Yeats projects a pessimistic vision, Sri Aurobindo being a Rishi, gives us an optimistic vision of the future world. In Sri Aurobindo's poem, the ferocious beast - the tiger is the symbol of violent, wild and mighty forces. On the other hand, the deer represents simplicity, innocence, beauty and peace. Stretching to another limit, we can say that Savitri who represents beauty, love, peace and bliss puts an end to the violent, mighty ways of the Lord of Death on earth and brings an assurance of the coming of a new race of man, a New Age. The prophecy given in the short poem "The Tiger and the Deer" bears fruit in *Savitri*.

In the poem entitled "Evolution" Sri Aurobindo traces the evolution of the human soul and its ascent towards God's bliss. It describes the adventure of man's consciousness, which achieves greater depth, expansion and richness in the journey of Aswapathy in *Savitri*. With such a comparison we can clearly see how Sri Aurobindo's poetic vision gradually widens, achieves greater depth and richness.

Sri Aurobindo takes various characters from Indian mythology, the *Puranas*, and ancient history, and symbolically interprets them with the help of his spiritual vision. In "The Triumph Song of Trishuncou" he describes the indomitable spirit of Trishuncou who refuses to accept defeat even at the cost of his mortal body. His unyielding spirit acquires a greater symbolic meaning in *Savitri*. She refuses to yield to the God of Death. Trishuncou is a symbol of man's endless quest for victory over death. In a visionary way the poet shows man's victory over death in *Savitri*. It is through this mythical character that Sri Aurobindo conveys his vision symbolically as a redeemer of the world, the vanquisher of God of Death.

The journey of Pururavas described in "Urvasie" is quite different from the journey Aswapathy makes. So the latter's journey assumes greater spiritual and symbolic significance. As a mythical character Pururavas's role is glorified by the elimination of his weaknesses. He is presented as a perfect symbol of man's aspiring soul, the forerunner of mankind in the character of Aswapathy. Exploring the various dimensions and symbolic significance of the Puranic and mythological characters like

Trishuncou, Pururavas, and Markendeya, the poet has at last presented in Aswapathy the perfect seeker of the Divine.

Sri Aurobindo uses most of his symbols to convey his spiritual experiences. As stated earlier, he could see realities beyond this world, but to our sense perception these are supernormal. It was necessary for him to employ poetic symbols to convey his mystic and spiritual experience, realisation and visions. Who could more aptly convey such spiritual visions and realisation in better symbols than those conjured up by a seer-poet like Sri Aurobindo? We find the full blossoming of some of these symbols in his marvellous epic, *Savitri*.

Thus, we see that in Sri Aurobindo's employment of poetic symbols a distinct trend emerges focusing on the mystic vision in his poetic out put. His integral philosophy of the worldview reveals that he is a nature mystic. As he is a seer (*drstā*) of an eternal truth and possesses impersonal knowledge, he tries to reveal the secrets of Nature through the employment of nature symbols such as the sun, the moon, dawn, night, fire, tree, swan, rose, etc., which lend expression to esoteric, revelatory knowledge and vision. These objects of nature embody powerful mystic visions as well as spiritual realisations and can be projected with symbolic suggestions. By their esoteric qualities these mystic symbols forge a perfect synthesis of the external and the internal, material and spiritual, concrete and abstract, thought vision, etc. The mystic vision of the poet reveals various psychological planes of consciousness. To Sri Aurobindo spiritual experiences were like vivid realities, which he interprets in a symbolic way. The spiritual truth Sri Aurobindo realised is incomprehensible to ordinary mentality. For instance physical light as a poetic symbol in his poetry symbolises divine knowledge.

Poetry expresses spiritual reality and mystic experience through a symbolic language. In ancient times the symbolic and the mystic way of the Vedic singers and the unique utterances of the Vedic seers were couched in a symbolic form using the wealth of poetical suggestions. Their symbols suggest a glimpse of the truth behind the self, Nature and things behind the emotional and the vital perceptions of the seers.

As has already been discussed earlier by the force of his yogic *sādhanā* Sri Aurobindo achieved higher planes of consciousness and was at times an inhabitant of the other worlds. He had the first hand knowledge of spiritual reality. Through yogic realisations his mystic mind could envisage the self, the spirit of the universe and Nature in communion with each other because everything on this earth is indirectly a veiled expression of the Absolute, the Omnipotent Reality. He was able to visualise in a mystic way man, God and Nature as One and the Many, unity in Multiplicity. Divine is ultimately self-revealed in both man and universe. An individual is a part of the cosmic Being. Man's knowledge of God and Nature are only helps towards self-knowledge. *Yoga* is the right discipline to seek self-knowledge. In the course of one's progress in yoga, one gradually discovers step by step the union of man, God and Nature. The Self, the Absolute is veiled in Nature. A unity behind diversity, discord or disharmony is the secret of self-knowledge, indeed of world-knowledge. The diverse external forms of Nature internalise the psychological planes of consciousness and reveal occult truth. In tune with Wordsworthian view of man and Nature, Sri Aurobindo too professes a distinct and intimate communion with Nature. Nature is an inalienable part of his philosophy of the yoking together of Matter and Spirit.

References

1. Webster's *Third International Dictionary*, Chicago: Encyclopedia Inc., Vol.III, 1976, p.2316.
2. Wilbur Marshall Urban, *Language and Reality: The Philosophy of Language and the Principles of Symbolism*, part III, London: George Allen & Unwin Ltd., 1951, p.404.
3. David Lodge, ed., *20th Century Literacy Criticism*, 1972, p.32.
4. Arthur Symons, *The Symbolist Movement in Literature*,1908, p.1.
5. J. E. Cirlot, *A Dictionary of Symbols*, p.xxx.
6. Sri Aurobindo, *The Secret of the Vedas*, Pondicherry: Sri Aurobindo Ashram Press, 1971, p.6.
7. Charles Chadwick, *Symbolism*, London: Methuen and Co., Ltd., 1971, pp.2-3.
8. Ibid., p.3.

9. Ibid.
10. Charles Chadwick, *op.cit.*, p.3.
11. Ibid., pp.2-3.
12. Sri Aurobindo, *Savitri*, pp.733-34.
13. Quoted by A.G. Lehman, *The Symbolist Aesthetic in France* (1885-1895), p.105.
14. A.G.Legman, *The Symbolic Aesthetics in France*, p.105.
15. Sri Aurobindo, *The Future Poetry*, 1972, pp.355-56.
16. Ibid., pp.355-56.
17. Ibid, p.361.
18. Sri Aurobindo, *Savitri*, op.cit., p.735.
19. R.K. Singh, *Savitri: A Spiritual Epic*, 1984, p.16.
20. Sri Aurobindo, *Collected Poems*, p.571.
21. Ibid., p.571.
22. Ibid., p.578.
23. K.D. Sethna, *Sri Aurobindo - The Poet*, 1970, p.264.
24. L.S.R. Krishna Sastry, "Two Poems of Sri Aurlbindo", *Banasthali Patrika*, July, 1969, p.20.
25. Sri Aurobindo, *Collected Poems*, op.cit., p.584.
26. Dante Alighieri, *The Divine Comedy-3*, Tr. Dorothy L. Sayers and Barbara Reynolds, Penguin Books, 1976, p.327.
27. Sri Aurobindo, *Letters on Yoga*, Part Two and Three, 1971 p.976.
28. Sri Aurobindo, *Collected Poems*, op.cit., p.568.
29. S. Krishna Sarma, *Seed of Grandeur*, 1972, p.11.
30. Sri Aurobindo, *Collected Poems*, op.cit., p.582.
31. Ibid., p.582.
32. Sri Aurobindo, *Collected Poems*, op.cit., p.45.
33. *The Holy Bible* (W), *International Bible Society*, New Jersey, U.S.A., 1984, p.379.
34. Ibid., p.379.
35. Sri Aurobindo, *Collected Poems*, op.cit., p.45.
36. Ibid., p.593.
37. Ibid., p.561.
38. Ibid.
39. Francis Thompson, "The Hound of Heaven", *The Winged Word*, ed. David Green, Madras: Macmillan, rpt.1979, pp.163-63.

40. Sri Aurobindo, *Collected poems*, op.cit., p.132.
41. Sri Aurobindo, *The Secret of the Veda*, op.cit., p.527.
42. Sri Aurobindo, *Collected poems*, op.cit., p.189.
43. Ibid., p.392.

4

Savitri—A Mythicised Romance with Symbolic Overtones

Even though society has developed technologically, mythical thinking and mythmaking has not disappeared; these emerge in subtler forms, one of which is literature. Freud's discovery of the connection between myth and dream, his efforts to transform metaphysics into meta-psychology, have led to a wide acceptance of myth as an expression of the unconscious drives and wishes. Moreover, myth provides a clue to the psychic history of the human species. It carries centuries of accumulated connotations. Instincts are mythical because they are the "archaic heritage" of civilisation. Freud's approach to myth reveals an explicit statement and concrete example of it as the expression of human instincts. He posits the view that in a legend human desire is transformed into a divine privilege. Essentially, the significance of Freud's contribution lies in the understanding of the relation between myth and dreams, his conception of unconscious feelings, drives and instincts as mythical in their universality and continuity. He opened pathways for further scientific studies of myth and its poetic applications.

There is a basic difference between Freud and C.J. Jung's exploration of the significance of myth. Jung assumes in all men a conflict between the 'natural instincts' and the 'spirit', both of which are powerful forces whose exact nature man does not know. Religion, in his opinion, has a "positive value" because it provides a means of "dealing with the forces of the inner life." Without a spiritual base man's life becomes bewildered, chaotic and at times, neurotic. Jung's writings indicate man's yearning for some spiritual meaning in life - some direction from a supernatural force. He is of the view that poets in general are in touch with the reality beyond human perception because they are able to discover "the spirits, demons, and gods." Poets know that "a purposiveness out-reaching human ends is the life giving secret of man."[1] According to Jung's view, psychic truth is actually a step forward to spiritual fulfilment, and it can be used as an instrument to forge a union between the unconscious and the supernatural. For this purpose he uses the term "archetypes of the collective unconscious," which he considers as universal patterns of human behaviour expressed in mythical mode.

Of course, a mythical expression of archetypal experience opens an avenue through which man can perceive an older but a deeper level of reality. Jung regards myth, religion, and unconscious psychological forces "essentially inseparable" because religion, he believes, both releases and channels unconscious experience of man. He considers God-image as a "psychic organ" intrinsic to the nature of man deeply imbedded in his being for which man receives instinctual force. Among Jung's chief archetypes are "the *shadow*", the "*wise old man*", the "*child*", and the" *mother*" ("Primordial Mother" and "Earth Mother") as supraordinate personality. Thus, Freud and Jung are at one with the view that myth discloses unconscious feelings and desires for powers beyond those of limited mortals. Both these protean scholars are the pathfinders of how myth can be creatively used as a new and potent symbolic language.

Mythical and legendary stories have served as allegories, allusion, and metaphors, sometime as intrinsic expression, and at other times an elaborate and pretentious decoration. Myth reveals the internal qualities of man to fight with falsehood. One of the strange qualities of myth is that it is both false and true at the same time. What he discloses about himself can be expressed in no other way. Myth opens up the boundless reaches of man's vision. In the opinion of Lillian Fedder:

> The revival of myth in the present time indicates, of course, that in his desire for order, for belief in some standard beyond lies individual reaction, man turns back to traditional symbols, which evoke an emotional, if not spiritual, sense of permanence, recurrence and stability.[2]

Claude Levi-Strauss has been credited with the discovery of structural basis for myth. He has found out its 'constituent units', which he calls 'mythemes', the combinations of elements of myths. His points of view are essentially anthropological. In studying the reappearance of ancient myth in modern poetry it is possible to glean the way unconscious drives convert experience into a mythical pattern because the narrative structure of myth is profitably suitable for endless adaptation. Lillian Fedder points out that it has evolved like the language to the needs of contemporary society:

> There is more empirical evidence to support a structural theory of myth when that theory is based on the assumption that the unconscious contains repressed instinctual drives and memories which express themselves in mythical forms and constructions, and can in turn be depicted consciously in mythical narrative.[3]

In *Civilisation and Discontents,* Freud discusses ancient man's projection of his inner desire for 'omniscience and omnipotence' on gods who personified his ideals of these qualities. While making an oblique remark, Freud says that man has become "a kind of prosthetic God." Lillian Fedder draws our attention to the traditional myths that have been steeped in modern language projecting the tension between man's supposed superiority and helplessness against the gods within, his instinctual drive is more powerful than any prostheses. A significant theme of contemporary poetry is the spiritual sterility of the "prosthetic God who is suspicious of his own superiority."

Myths in the modern poetry provide many valuable indications to contemporary thought, to poetic techniques and new themes. Even in an age where intellectual endeavours have been guided by science and technology, myth continues to function powerfully "recording and interpreting the personal and universal history of man's inner life." Myth like superstition expresses "conscious ignorance and unconscious knowledge." The basic nature of classical myths demonstrates similar human problems; dilemmas encountered by man from antiquity to modern times though somewhat in an altered form. The repeated return to classical myth in literature as the store-house of symbols, structures, themes, allusions, etc., should not be misconstrued as lack of creative imagination in artists and writers. On the other hand, artists have intended to illumine the present reality through myths of the past in order to project a heightened significance to the sterility and ugliness of contemporary life in comparison to the heroic grandeur of man portrayed in many of the myths. In critical crisis of the world, the mythical heritage for many writers presents eternal models. The timeless values and profound universal truth embodied in classical myths make it possible to reinterpret them over and over again and to adopt them to contemporary experience and problems. The mythic characters have served as role models for human endeavour and conduct. Whether in the hands of the Marxists, Existentialists or traditionalists, classical myths in literature continue to reveal an amazing source of adaptation to man's changing conditions. W.B. Yeats has rightly called myths "the builders of my soul."

W.B. Yeats, T.S. Eliot, Ezra Pound, W.H. Auden, Rainer Maria Rilke and other modern poets project a new awareness of the use of myth as a guide to and an instrument of expression of unconscious feelings and instincts. For Yeats and Eliot myth offers the promise of a light beyond the enlightment of self, a hope for eternity. Eliot views the potency of myth to exert control, to establish order when man feels threatened by universal anarchy.

Indian tradition, steeped in myths and legendary tales, has left its indelible imprint on Indian Literature even of the modern technological age. There is something immensely significant in these legendary tales that has ever gripped the imagination of poets down the ages. Poets and writers have ever found a surer stay for the free play of their imagination in these tales. The messages of the *Puranic* and mythological stories reveal that great artistic possibilities lie in them and provide constant delight to the common readers. Like the legends of other great civilisations of the world, Indian legends either deal with man ascending to the level of godhead or the gods descending on earth to participate in earthly life lured by its irresistible fascination. It is a world that goes back to an undated past. The superhuman status is a remarkable feature of Indian mythology. Marian W. Smith applauds the importance of these legendary tales and parables in the following words:

> India may be largely illiterate but it is definitely articulate. Love stories, fairy stories, animal stories, parables, and tales of the gods are used as media for expressing new feelings and thoughts which must be assimilated to the old traditions and ways of life. These heroic tales may follow an ancient pattern while they tell the trials of real men in a shifting political and economic scene. They are, as always, among the most popular of oral accounts. Though India is rich in tradition, its long literacy and oral heritage shows no signs of abating.[4]

In these mythological stories there is a perceptible struggle between the forces of light and darkness, good and evil. J.M. Macfie is eloquent about the moral teaching through these stories. He observes:

> They tell us of their thoughts and fears, their joys and sorrows, their speculations about this life and the hereafter. They show us what was taught about meekness and temperance, about kindness to man and beast, about patience and self-control. They dwell on the dangers of anger, pride: on the beauty of truth and purity... But God fulfills himself in many ways, and India has heard God speaking to her soul, with the result that there has been expressed for her in living parable and legend that wonderful variety of moral teaching which has helped to make the people what they are.[5]

It is not a surprise that Sri Aurobindo turned his attention towards this invaluable wealth of Indian mythology and legends for literary exploration. Being himself a versatile scholar of the *Vedas*, the *Upanishads* and the epics, he made full use of these mythological and legendary stories for creative purposes in his writings. Not only Indian mythology and legends, but also the European, Greek and Roman mythologies have been profitably utilised in his writings. He realised that legends and tales give variety, subtlety and flexibility to the writer's creative imagination. These are a veritable gallery for a poet's ready reference and use. An eerie atmosphere pervades these tales and absorbs the reader's attention. These legends and tales can be moulded to any form by the skill and the vibrating breath of a poet's imagination. What is paradoxical and extraordinary is taken by the readers to be no less real. The superhuman feats of the legendary heroes suspend the disbelief of the Indian readers, as these tales are full of religious doctrines and messages. These legendary tales present life of those human beings whose souls are fully awakened, whose truthfulness and pious life ever places an ideal before the suffering humanity. Some of these heroes and heroines, as it seems, are the masters of spiritual forces and dear to the Divine.

Some of these legendary tales serve as the storehouse for Sri Aurobindo's poetic themes. His poetic imagination hovers around them giving them symbolic twists and subtle shapes to suit the modern taste. Rich in poetic imagery and varied in style, they appear before the reader as if they are the original stories. The two great epics of India, the *Mahābhārata* and the *Rāmāyana*, are remarkable for a number of such tales woven into them, in which even the common people find profound interest. These tales are quite absorbing and are integrated into the main theme of the topic. In many of his poems Sri Aurobindo adopts some of the legends to give a greater breadth and depth for his poetic creation.

The poet must have seriously considered what he should adopt for the theme of his *magnum opus*. Very appropriately he selected the legend of Satyavan-Savitri from Veda Vyasa's the *Mahābhārata*. The poetic genius of Vyasa captured the heart of Sri Aurobindo more than that of any other ancient epic poet of India. Sri Aurobindo considers him the most masculine of writers. The *Mahābhārata* abounds in innumerable tales woven by his deft hand. Here in these tales one comes across the morning twilight of Vyasa's genius. Sri Aurobindo's symbolic casting of the tale of Savitri and Satyavan has its roots in his ingrained impression of Vyasa's lofty genius and his depth of insight into the human life. He superbly eulogises the creation of Savitri and Satyavan by Vyasa in the following cogent words:

> Savitri is a maturer and nobler work, perfect and restrained in detail, but it has still some glow of the same youth and grace over it. This then is the rare charm... that we find there the soul pale and marble Rishi, the philosopher, the great statesman, the strong and stern poet of war and empire, when it was yet in its radiant morning, far from the turmoil of courts and cities and the roar of the battlefield and had not yet scaled the mountain tops of thought.[6]

Another source of potential attraction for the poet is the theme of *Shakti* (the power) - the mother spirit that is one of the abiding concerns of Sri Aurobindo's creative genius. It is interesting to observe the extent to which the worship of *Shakti* has influenced the Hindus down the ages. The popular image of goddess Durga haunts the Hindus mind as the Woman Saviour of men and gods. As the legend goes, she is an immortal creation of the gods to extirpate the *dānava* (giant), Mahishasura, who had plagued the kingdom of heaven, the dwelling place of immortal gods. To the Hindus the image of Durga is a symbolic potent force for dispelling evil and darkness. Attempts have been made by various scholars to trace the exact beginning of the cult of "*Shakti*" worship (*Shakti upāshanā*). One such version runs as:

> ... the doctrine of Devi as the female side of Siva has enabled Brahmanism to accept as part of its creed the widespread worship of Mother Earth... The worship of this "Shakti", the personification of female aspect of Siva's nature, is the chief development of Saivite cult, and it forms the subject of the new literary species, which comes into prominence after the tenth century of the Christian era.[7]

At a particular phase of ancient Indian history, the *Shakti* worship reached its zenith and people were more and more drawn towards this famous cult. Besides Durga, Lakshmi, Saraswati, Parvati, and Kali, etc., are the other prominent goddesses who are invariably worshipped by the Hindus in some form or other throughout India. The concept of the Woman Saviour is not alien to the West. Christianity accepts Virgin Mary as the Woman Saviour.

An analysis of Sri Aurobindo's various writings reveals his staunch faith in the concept of "Shakti", the feminine genius that can bring errant marvels. He posits strong faith in the doctrine of feminine Incarnation. He has composed a magnificent prayer in praise of Durga—*Durga Stotra*. The theme of *Savitri* is prophetically based on the mystic vision of the woman as saviour. Savitri is an emanation of the eternal Mother to save the suffering humanity from the grip of ignorance and death. It is not only *Savitri* but in other long poems and plays, Sri Aurobindo projects the feminine genius as the embodiment of power and perfection.

Sri Aurobindo reminds us of Shakespeare in the close delineation of female characters. In an amazing scale we come across the varied aspects of feminine power such as the supreme compassion of Andromeda, the angelic beauty, enduring love and single-minded devotion of Rodogune, the uncompromising love for country of Vidula, the belligerent spirit of Chitrangada and Penthesilea, etc. These characters in his plays and long poems are among the eternal creations of Sri Aurobindo. Among these characters Savitri's love and her victory over death fascinates his poetic imagination because she in her love sacrifices nothing, rather achieves everything. Unlike the desperate pairs of lovers in "Urvasie" and "Love and Death", the reunited lovers, Savitri and Satyavan victoriously return home. This aspect must have greatly fascinated Sri Aurobindo who structurally gave the legend a spiritual base and a symbolic twist in his epic.

Savitri as per the poet's estimate is a mythicised romance. The epic embodies most of the characteristics of a romance. Like his dramatic romances Sri Aurobindo too wrote a number of poetic romances which primarily deal with a love-story. Each poetic romance centres on love and the various ways of lovemaking in an environment of typical romance tradition. It is subtilised by a mystical and platonic notion. Love is treated as a passion and not an erotic desire. The poet delineates the physical beauty of the beloved as an image of Heavenly beauty. Chastity is a prerequisite virtue in the theme of lovemaking. Love and courtship lead to marriage. Usually, the lady is not a married one. Unlike the Western tradition marriage is transformed from a mundane social institution into a spiritual union of two souls. This changed attitude to love is perfectly in conformity with the Hindu philosophy and tradition. Humility of the lover remains a cardinal virtue and the active form of courtesy is observed. The poet's treatment of romance slightly deviates from the Western tradition. The poet does not at all follow the Western tradition of adultery. Nowhere does Sri Aurobindo follow the Cult of Dejection – the lady being scornful of the lover's approach and adamantly hard to be wooed. In other words, the lady is never cruel, proud and disdainful to the lover. Occasional touches of the marvellous – the dreams, celestial beings, demons, supernatural beings — inhabit the poet's world of romance. This inherent extravagance of the narrative heightens the romantic effects. The narrative keeps faithfully to the romantic conventions of poetic justice. Events are so manipulated by amidst misery and sufferings that the conclusion is on the whole a happy one, with the good and the virtuous being triumphant and the evil discomfited; villainy is persistently foiled. The lovers emerge from their trials that deepen love. The characters are actuated by impossible motives, grouped in rigid categories of good and bad. Characters are personifications of abstract qualities. The plot is deliberately far-fetched, astounding and artificial. Faithful love is put to grievous and abnormal strain.

In the "Book of Love" Sri Aurbindo foregrounds the destined meeting place of Savitri and Satyavan. We have an excellent presentation of love at first sight and an efflorescence of passion. The poet creates another Garden of Eden, the right theatre for enactment of love - union of two pure hearts and the communion of souls awakened and eternal. The wedding of the Eternal Lord and the Spouse is solemnised by Nature. Characters in the epic are not personified qualities but incarnations or emanations of living conscious forces. These characters help man and show him the way form his mortal state to a divine consciousness immortal life.

Explaining the symbolic meaning of the legend, Sri Aurobindo mentions that Satyavan is the symbol of the soul of Truth that was caught up by Death and Ignorance in its descent into the atmosphere of earth. Savitri is the Divine Light that released the soul of Truth from the grip of Death and Ignorance. Similarly, Aswapathy and his father, Dyumatsena have symbolic significance in this ancient legend. It is now clear why Sri Aurobindo chooses this legend for a symbolic treatment. He gives a lucid treatment to the need for an inevitable change in man's nature and earth's destiny in *The Life Divine* and in other treatises. He discusses the concerted discipline necessary for an integral change. Yet he was not satisfied with the prosaic treatment he gave in that massive book and Srinivasa Iyengar has pointed this out:

> ... a visual or dramatic presentation of the whole adventure of a break through into a new world, a new power of consciousness, a new destiny — would not *that* serve the cause, help to accelerate the pace of change and

> transformation, more surely than even such a masterpiece as *The Life Divine* which was but metaphysics in the form of a prose symphony? Perhaps Sri Aurobindo thought that he should try to render the Savitri legend in such a way that the decreed change would be actually *seen* happening, the reader becoming a spectator of the birth of the new world – a spectator and perhaps a participant as well.[8]

Most probably these were the grounds which Sri Aurobindo found the legend preeminently suitable for epic as well as symbolic treatment. The personality of Savitri by far must have been the greatest attraction for the poet. In her invincible wifely devotion (*pativratā*), her inner strength and power to encounter the Lord of Death, and in her total achievements she excels the lady protagonist of any other legend. She is the creatrix of a new higher life on earth.

Indian literatures are packed with the legends about the wifely chastity, as in the stories of Sita, Draupadi, Damayanti, Gandhari, Shakuntala, Ahalya, etc., but none is placed as high as to vanquish the Lord of Death and to restore to life one's deceased husband, to revive her dead love. While analysing the life of these chaste women, K.R. Srinivasa Iyengar, is of the opinion that these heroines were dejected, abandoned, gambled away, or deceived to stand the test of their true love. Savitri is the only heroine who is the mistress of all circumstances, who in turn rescues her dead husband without losing anything in life. She has absolute trust in the "hymeneal purity of her love." Her love transcends her mortal limitations.

Giving symbolic treatment to such an age-old theme, Sri Aurobindo infuses into it his own philosophy and yoga and heightens it with a symbolic significance of universal relevance. While he was in Baroda, he had already drafted the poem in two parts ('Earth and Beyond'). This original poem, as the poet confesses, would have been merely a legend and not a symbol, a *magnum opus* at all if it were not recast.[1] After a lapse of many years, he made deliberate attempts to revive the first draft to put his *yogic* knowledge and experience to poetic test in giving it a symbolic form. Within these years he had led a varied life: as a secret revolutionary, politician, journalist, seer, a mystic, a philosopher and a *yogi*. His realisation and his experience of ascending the stairs of Mind to Supermind enabled him to invest the legend with symbolic significance. Amidst his hectic life schedule, he busied himself scrupulously recasting the earlier draft in Pondicherry for nearly more than 20 years as if this piece of work was his life's last mission. His failing eyesight necessitated the help of Nordbaran to take down dictation from him. In fact, in the new form, *Savitri* is "a sort of poetic philosophy of the Spirit and of Life much profounder in its substance and vaster in its scope than was intended in the original poem."[9]

Explaining the symbolic dimension of the legend, Sri Aurobindo separates the elements of romance from the epic structure and observes that the characters are not mere abstractions:

> Satyavan is the soul carrying the divine truth of being within itself but descended into the grip of the death and ignorance; Savitri is the Divine word, daughter of the Sun, goddess of the supreme Truth who comes down and is born to save; Aswapathy, the Lord of Tapasya, the concentrated energy of spiritual endeavour that helps us to rise from the mortal to immortal planes; Dyumatsena, Lord of the shinning Hosts, father of Satyavan, is the Divine Mind here fallen blind, losing its celestial kingdom of vision, and through that loss its kingdom of glory. Still this is not a mere allegory, the characters are not personified qualities, but incarnations or emanations of living and Conscious Forces with whom we can enter into concrete touch and they take human bodies in order to help man and show him the way from his mortal state to a divine consciousness and immortal life.[10]

Like any other great Indian artist, Sri Aurobindo symbolically presents in this cosmic epic a spiritual reality modelled on an ideal prototype envisioned by the great seers existing in a state of supranormal consciousness, the example could be found in the *Vedas,* which in the critical estimate of Sri Aurobindo, is the archetype of "imaged spiritual intuition and psychological and religious experience." The reflective and poetic mind of the great poets like Dante, Milton, Pound and Sri Aurobino and others symbolically harp upon the spiritual and inward urge to explore man's destiny that is aligned with eternity, the Absolute or God. In Milton's epic the Son is the protagonist. The poet tries to regain symbolically the paradise within that man has lost due to his disobedience to God. *The Divine Comedy* of Dante orchestrates the journey of human soul after death. The life of Gilgamesh is a quest leading to the destiny of man to suffer and die – a search for immortality that is never achieved. *The Prelude* of Wordsworth is the odyssey of human mind in its proximity to Nature – a bounteous manifestation of divine secret. Ezra Pound in the *Cantos* makes a dialectical play of the forces of good as opposed to forces of darkness in our materialistic money-driven world.

Sri Aurobindo too presents a historical vision of spirituality in this materialistic world. *The Rāmāyana,,* in Sri Aurobindo's opinion, portrays ideal manhood and a "divine beauty of virtue and ethical order a civilisation founded on *Dharma,* the ideal law of conduct." At a symbolic level an exalted moral ideal is projected against a wild, anarchic violence and superman egoism and self-ill. These two powers of mental nature are brought into conflict in the embodiment of the characters of Rama and Ravana. Like wise the *Mahābhāraṭa* embodies "a humanity aggrandised and half uplifted to super humanity yet always true to human motive, idea and feeling." Thus, we see that the mythopoeic imagination of the great epic poets of the world is invariably steeped in spiritual perspective.

Spiritual sensibility is not unfamiliar to Indian poets. Indian artists believe that art can express eternal truth. Sri Aurobindo draws readers' attention to spirituality in art in the following passage:

> Spirituality is a wider thing than formal religion and it is in the service of spirituality that Art reaches its highest self-expression. Spirituality in a single word expressive of three lines of human aspiration towards divine knowledge, divine love and joy, and divine strength, and that will be highest and most perfect Arts which, while satisfying the physical requirements of the aesthetic sense, the laws of formal beauty, the emotional demand of humanity, the portrayal of life and outward reality, as the best European Art satisfies these requirements, reaches beyond them and expresses inner spiritual truth, the deeper not obvious reality of things, the joy of God in the world and its beauty and desirableness and the manifestation of the divine force and energy in phenomenal creation.[11]

An over importance given in this chapter to spirituality may inevitably raise the eyebrow of an ordinary reader. A question may creep in one's mind as to the role of spirit in human life. Should men in a materialistic world run after the spirit which is obviously invisible and at times unknown and elusive to rational mind? Why should man aspire for divine love and joy, which are elusive and mysterious in nature? To all such types of query Sri Aurobindo provides the justifiable answers in the following extract:

> The spirit is that in which all the rest of the human being reposes, towards which it returns and the final self-revelation of which is the goal of humanity. Man becomes God, and all human activity reaches its highest and noblest when it succeeds in bringing body, heart and mind into touch with the spirit... The great truths of religion, science, metaphysics, life, development, become, concrete, emotional, universally intelligible and convincing in the hands of the master of plastic Art, and the soul of man, in the stage when it is rising from emotion to intellect, looks, receives, the suggestion and is uplifted towards a higher development, a diviner knowledge.[12]

The loftiest function and spiritual utility of Art is to gradually mould the finite into the image of the infinite. *Savitri* is not merely spiritual poetry but it is mystic poetry cast into a symbolic form. A new extension of consciousness and aesthesis demands the understanding of the technique of mystic poetry. Nolini Kanta Gupta draws the line of distinction between spiritual and mystic poetry. When the spirit speaks its own language, it is spiritual poetry but when it chooses to speak an alien language we get mystic poetry:

> If, however, the Spirit speaks — from choice or necessity — an alien language and manner, e.g., that of a profane consciousness, or of the consciousness of another domain, idealistic or philosophical or even, puts on or imitates spirit's language and manner, we have mystic poetry.[13]

A certain freedom of the mind freed from the shackles of age-old convention is necessary to appreciate the poem in its right perspective.

The opening canto of *Savitri* is a 'key beginning' and makes a crucial announcement that unlocks the doors of the vast realms of Sri Aurobindo's spiritual vision and mystical insight. It makes a symbolic reference to dawn and ends with an explicit reference to a 'greater dawn'. The passage from night to day is described in the first movement of the opening canto. Like the physical dawn, the passage from night to day, there is also a symbolic dawn. The night described in the first few lines is immobile, dense, and silent and foreboding, which lies across the 'divine event'. The full implication of this symbolism however, has been discussed separately.

In the first few lines the poet presents a fitting background for the action to take place. Srinivasa Iyengar sums up the whole theme of the epic *Savitri* in the following terms:

> The death of Satyavan... means the defeat of truth, the eclipse of light through the invasion of darkness and Savitri is the light of love that defeats the darkness and achieves the recovery of Truth... Savitri also encompasses the recovery of soul and Nature from partial and temporary darkness that have overtaken them.[14]

The cosmic epic *Savitri* begins with the line, "It was the hour before the Gods awoke." The time of action of the poem is called dawn (*Usha*) in the Hindu tradition. The epic speaks of the time when the gods who preside over various functions of this cosmos are not awake to initiate their work. Sri Aurobindo posits the view that gods are executive powers of light, the supreme Godhead. It is believed that the gods awake in the dawn for the sacrifice.

The first line refers to the condition of the cosmos before the gods were born. Explaining the symbolic significance of these lines, The Mother of Sri Aurobindo Ashram, Pondicherry draws our attention to an ancient belief, according to which the universe was created by the first emanation of the supreme Mother who sent four emanations to the earth. In the execution of their powers these emanations cut off their link from their origin and became independent. As a result of such separation, they entered into darkness and got transformed. The first one that was consciousness in light turned into unconsciousness. The second, Bliss turned into suffering. The third was truth that turned into falsehood. The fourth one was life that turned into death. This happened after they came down into the vital level. When this happened it was decided that some second emanations would descend to rectify the mistake of the first one. The second emanations were gods. The Mother is of the opinion that the result of this separation between the first emanation and their origin, the creation by these first emanations became obscure and inconscient. The "divine Event" in the second line of the first canto refers to the creation that will go on and on in eternity.

In this canto the line, "It wrote the lines of a significant myth..." refers to the story of Savitri. It was the time of the first contact of the emanation from the Divine with the atmosphere of the earth that the story of Savitri was written with "Sky for page" in a brilliant code. This is the day on which the divine manifestation was disclosed. The Mother Divine manifested her form on the earth. We can say that it is the descending of Savitri on earth as an Emanation of the Divine Mother. Her appearance is a "lonely splendour from the invisible goal."

The universal Divine Mother is the "Ambassadress twixt eternity and change" who regulates the journeying of the stars, sees that the spaces are favourable for her full manifestation. This is what the poet refers to the leaning downward of the Divine Love and Grace when Dawn made her novel appearance.

Unfortunately, this "prostrate soil" of ours remained indifferent to this "awakening ray". The "divine afflatus" which we may call the ray of light changed here into 'prophetic gleam' and common meaningless shapes were transformed into miracles. But it was unwillingly received. So it "spent, withdrew" and faded from mortal's range. No proper response was found for it. So the "divine afflatus" left behind her a "Sacred yearning". Such a "Sacred yearning" is the "prescience of a marvellous birth to come" on earth. This "marvellous birth" is the birth of life divine on earth. But this birth is delayed, for it is "too perfect to be held by death-bound hearts." This birth, however, will turn the smallest things into living miracles. Indeed, this is the message of Sri Aurobindo's *The Life Divine* and *Savitri* to the suffering humanity.

The second part of this canto describes the appearance of Savitri. She also awoke in such a dawn to join the "summoner's chant". Here the "summoner's chant" is the message of omniscient power. In the opinion of A.B. Purani: "The appearance of Savitri, after the withdrawal of the Divine Goddess almost suggests the continuity of the work begun by the Goddess Dawn and the Imperishable ambassadress, Omniscient power of the Divine."[15] This statement of Purani is quite convincing as Sri Aurobindo says that Savitri is the incarnation of the Divine Mother.

In the subsequent lines Sri Aurobindo goes on to describe the nature of Savitri. Her inner divinity in mortal frame makes no response to the din and bustle of human life. So great is her love that she consents to her doom, to suffer in a human body for the love of humanity. In one of his early poems, "God's Labour", the poet expresses the same idea:

> He who would bring the heavens here
> Must descend himself into clay
> And the burden of earthly nature bear
> And tread the dolorous way.[16]

The first canto of Book One serves as the prologue to the whole poem. The main crisis of the poem is clearly stated in this canto. It also raises many a problem in the mind of the reader like the determinism of Nature, The Fate of Man, the purpose of Divine Incarnation (*Avatār*), etc. Some of the important ideas that this canto imparts to its reader pertain to the creation of earth, and the creation of human beings, Nature and Gods. In his conception of the creation of the Universe, the seer poet has made his unique contribution, which is of eternal significance, though in his treatment he does not follow any scientific theory or hypothesis. The whole poem is a revelation of the seer's inner experience. The quest for the Infinite is clearly indicated in the very first canto.

In the original *Mahābhārata* story, Aswapathy's role is very insignificant. Not much is said about him except that by performing *tapasyā* for 18 years, he is blessed with a daughter named Savitri. Sri Aurobindo found it necessary to enlarge Aswapathy's role and present him as a symbolic figure. He often revised this portion to devote a considerable part of his poem to Aswapathy's psycho-spiritual epic journey. The latter is not only a king, but also a forerunner of human beings. The king performing "*tapasyā*" has been dexterously transmuted by the poet into a symbol of human soul striving to acquire knowledge of the world and the worlds beyond. Aswapathy delves into the depths of human consciousness. The whole of Book Two deals with his symbolic journey, which will be discussed under a separate heading.

Through his consciousness, Aswapathy reaches the Absolute Silence where he meets the Divine Mother. She is the Mother of all godheads and all strength. She is the mediatrix who binds earth to the Supreme. This episode is absent in the original story. Standing before her with supplication, Aswapathy requests her to extirpate suffering from the world. The Divine Mother considers the present condition of the world not ripe to accept the celestial light from heaven, because Death is still unconquered on earth. Although man aspires for freedom, he prefers to live in bondage. Man has some inherent defects for which he cannot attain higher light and complete perfection. Weighing these various problems the Divne Mother in the poem admonishes Aswapathy with the following words:

> Only one boon, to greaten thy spirit, demand;
> Only one joy, to raise thy kind, desire.
> Above blind fate and the antagonist powers
> Moveless there stands a high unchanging Will;
> To its omnipotence leave thy work's result.
> All things shall change in God's transfiguring hour.[17]

The last line is in contrast to the line "All things can be done if the God touch is there" of Book One-Canto One. The undaunted spirit of Aswapathy does not remain content with a single boon to heighten his spirit. As the forerunner of human race, he has achieved universal consciousness. So he apprises the age long grief of humanity to the Divine Mother in these magnificent words:

> How long shall our spirits battle with the Night
> And bear defeat and the brute yoke of Death...[18]

With the passage of time many changes occur and we hear only "the feet of passing gods." God descends to earth in human form to help human beings. The poet discusses the principles of Divine Incarnation in a long passage. Not remaining content Aswapathy prays further to the Divine Mother with the ardent desire:

> Mission to earth some living form of thee.
> One moment fill with thy eternity,
> Let thy infinity in one body live,
> All-Knowledge wrap one mind in seas of light.
> All-Love throb single in one human heart.[19]

The entire passage is more a picturesque way of presenting the process of the Divine Incarnation on earth, than what appears in the *Bhagavad Gita*. A highly philosophical subject has been expressed in a lucid way.

At last, the Divine Mother grants Aswapathy's earnest appeal. She condescends to descend to earth and gives Aswapathy a nectarean assurance:

> O strong forerunner, I have heard thy cry.
> One shall descend and break the iron Law,
> Change Nature's doom by the lone Spirit's power.
> A limitless Mind that can contain the world,
> A sweet and violent heart of ardent calms
> Moved by the passions of the gods shall come.[20]

Such is the Divine promise to mankind and the passage describes the incarnation to come in sublime words. The Divine Mother further assures:

> A seed shall be sown in Death's tremendous hour,
> A branch of heaven transplant to human soil;
> Nature shall overleap her mortal step;
> Fate shall be changed by an unchanging will.[21]

The doctrine of *Avatārhood* is the poetic theme of *Savitri*. This is how a symbolic twist is given to the original legend.

Symbolically Aswapathy represents man's growth from mental consciousness through various intermediate stages to the Supreme Divine consciousness. Savitri, too, comes to the world to wrestle with Death and to confront "life's brief struggle in dumb Matter's night." The problem before her here on this earth is:

Whether to bear with Ignorance and Death
Or hew the ways of Immortality,
To win or lose the godlike game for man,
Was her soul's issue thrown with Destiny's dice.[22]

All the characters of the epic are symbolic representations of different shades of consciousness. Focusing his attention on the symbolic character of Savitri, Nolini Kanta Gupta makes an editorial comment in *The Advent* that Savitri is the Divine Grace upon earth-

> The Divine consciousness has abandoned its own supreme transcendental status to enter into the human consciousness and partake of the earthly life; it has taken up a mortal frame, to live and dwell here below. Only thus can she transform the lower nature into the divine nature; raise man to godhead; make of earth heaven itself.[23]

From tradition we come to know that the Divine incarnation descends alone to earth companionless to face the human problem. Similarly, in her superhuman task Savitri, too, is companionless in her fight against Death. In the legend she is purely a human being; but Sri Aurobindo delineates her character in a symbolic way making her half-divine, a divine incarnate as a human being. He portrays her ideal love which is expressive of a universal harmony. The poet describes her love in the following words, which is unparallel:

A wide self-giving was her native act;
A magnanimity as of sea or sky
Enveloped with its greatness all that came
And gave a sense as of a greatened world...
Love in her was wider than the universe,
The whole world could take refuge in her single heart.[24]

Sri Aurobindo does not deviate from the legend in reporting the growth of Savitri from childhood to youth, her journey in search of a life-partner, her amorous meeting with Satyavan, and return to her parents, and later on the meeting with Narad. It is to this meeting with the divine sage, Narad that the poet has given a new dimension. In Hindu Mythology the character of Narad is an enigmatic one but his discourse in the poem has a symbolic significance.

In Indian mythology the character of Narad is of great interest. He is the divine sage who takes pleasure in creating internecine strife and family quarrels. He is always painted as a sincere devotee of Lord Narayana (One of the Trinity). In Sri Aurobindo's epic Narad symbolically represents godward love, knowledge and wisdom. He is omniscient and a denizen of heaven. In Book Six–Canto One of the epic Narad descends from Paradise to the "mortal's plane" by crossing a wide expanse of brilliant peace, chanting the Lord's praises. He passes from the realm of Mind to Matter. With his descent to the material world his chanting also assumes a symbolic deterioration. A change comes to his voice and to the theme of his song:

> A rapture and a pathos moved his voice;
> He sang no more of light that never wanes,
> And oneness and pure everlasting bliss...[25]

And it changes :

> He sang the Inconscient and its secret self,
> Its power omnipotent knowing not what it does,
> All shaping without will or thought or sense,
> Its blind unerring occult mystery,
> And darkness yearning towards the eternal Light.[26]

Narad's chanting symbolises the stairs of consciousness that a divine being has to descend to touch the material world from heaven. It also expresses the poet's philosophy of Ascent and Descent. Narad sings how Love has been denigrated in this terrestrial life. He comes down to earth as "Man Divine", and enters the palace of Aswapathy of Madra. The king and the queen reverentially welcome the divine sage. The royal couple sits for an hour listening to the venerable saint's "high and rhythmic voice." He speaks to them about "the toils of men and what the gods strive for" and joy that " throbs behind the marvel and mystery of pain." His song in a symbolic way foretells that the "lotus-heart of love" shall one day bloom "in the garden of spouse" once she weds her discovered lord.

While Narad thus enraptures the royal couple with his divine song, Savitri's radiant tread glimmers across the floor. She has just returned from the forest after meeting and choosing Satyavan as her life's partner. Now she appears no more the same Savitri. Narad is able to see the divine aura in the face of Savitri and her heavenly gaze. Her luminous figure and the description of her beauty reconcile both the divine and the human:

> A happy wonder in her fathomless gaze,
> Changed by the halo of her love she came;
> Her eyes rich with a shining mist of joy
> As one who comes from a heavenly embassy
> Discharging the proud mission of her heart,
> One carrying the sanction of the gods
> To her love and its luminous eternity.[27]

Savitri notices a fiery sweetness in the son of Heaven. Narad sees at a glance the transformation that has taken place in Savitri after meeting with Satyavan as if love has alchemised her human body. He can see the past, the present and the future, as he is a divine sage and nothing remains veiled from him. Srinivasa Iyengar describes:

> Narad as "...a gifted seer and heaven's minstrel, the messenger of the gods and the paraclete between present actuality and future becoming."[27]

Casting a divine glance at her marvellous beauty, Narad understands everything but naively enquires –

> Who is this that comes, the bride,
> The flame-born, and round her illumined head
> Pouring their lights her hymeneal pomps
> Move flashing about her? From what green glimmer of glades
> Retreating into dewy silences
> Or half-seen verge of waters moon-betrayed
> Bringst thou this glory of enchanted eyes? [29]

This passage is one of the exquisite poetic passages with such sensuous evocation as is found in the poetry of Spenser and Tennyson. The symbolic beauty of Savitri is heightened by such a marvellous description. Singing of Savitri's divine sports and her divine melody, the divine sage, Narad continues:

> Assailed by trooping voices of delight
> And seized mid a sunlit glamour of the boughs

In faery woods, led down the gleaming slopes
Of Gundhamadan where the Apsaras roam,
Thy limbs have shared the sports which none has seen...[30]

Up to her present age Savitri has never experienced suffering or pain. To her, life is a piece of music. Her earthly body is lovely to the eyes, and she is akin in joy to heaven's sons. Narad thus praises Savitri in eulogistic superlatives, and deliberately holds back his seer knowledge about the trials and tribulations awaiting her future life. But it fails to elude Aswapathy's observation, who marks the dubious speech and discovers "An ominous shadow felt behind the words". Aswapathy humbly speaks out with guarded speech that he has been led to suppose, Savitri would lead a divine life on earth, as she is the paragon of earthly virtues. He makes a philosophical statement about life. Although in our human life we have some brief and perfect hours in which we catch a glimpse of the eternity behind the tread of the mechanical Time, such moments are very rare.

We then find Aswapathy requesting Narad to take note in Savitri an image cast by light and love. Her young virgin life is unstained by the drops of tears of suffering. With parental prescient hopes for his daughter, Aswapathy invokes the grace and blessings of Narad on Savitri. He is not only concerned with the bright future of his daughter but also prophesies how she shall remove death and suffering from the tortured breast of earth. His concern for the whole of humanity is a marked deviation from the original legend. Disclosing his vision of the future, he says, Savitri is born as "a flame of radiant happiness" and surely she will set the earth alight with that flame and "Doom surely will see her pass and say no word."

Narad looks into "the unseen with seeing eyes" and "knowing that words are vain and Fate is lord" evades a direct answer. He changes the topic to enquire about the high mission on which Savitri had gone and has come back with glory in her heart. Replying to Narad's question, Aswapathy explains that Savitri was on a mission to find out the lord of her heart. Now she has returned and her lips hold the secret treasure with an air of quiet happiness. He directs Savitri to reveal the name of the chosen lord of her heart. She replies in a calm voice. She says that she has obeyed her heart in choosing her life's partner. In the wild forest's lonely verge she has met Satyavan, the son of Dyumatsena. Once Dyumatsena was a mighty king but now dwells in a thatched hermitage, blind, exiled and an outcast.

After listening to Savitri's choice all sit silent and astonished for a while. But the seer king, Aswapathy could see in his *yogic* vision:

> A heavy shadow float above the name
> Chased by a sudden and stupendous light... [31]

The floating of "a heavy shadow" portends something ominous. And he could further visualise that a sudden and amazingly bright light chasing the heavy shadow. In his seer vision he sees the wisdom of Savitri's choice:

> Well hast thou done and I approve thy choice...
> Whether it seem good or evil to men's eyes,
> Only for good the secret Will can work.
> Our destiny is written in double terms:
> Through Nature's contraries we draw near God;
> Out of the darkness we still grow to light.
> Death is our road to immortality.[32]

This speech of Aswapathy is quite prophetic and in a symbolic way presents the whole theme of the epic. At this stage Narad looks as if he would disclose the long hidden secret; but wise Aswapathy hastily intervenes and prevents him. In these marvellous speeches, the seerhood of Aswapathy is indisputably established. He utters solemnly:

> O singer of the ultimate ecstasy,
> Lend not a dangerous vision to the blind,
> Because by native right thou hast seen clear.
> Impose not on the mortal's tremulous breast
> The dire ordeal that foreknowledge brings.[33]

Aswapathy's queen as a general human being fails to grasp the precise meanings of Narad's symbolic speech and remains so long silent, intervenes now in their conversation. Her character is symbolic of earthly wisdom devoid of divine prescience. Her knowledge does not go beyond what she sees and her mind shapes. She is a representative of the common lot. She is alarmed at the prophetic speech of her husband, who is a seer king. Breaking her silence, she impatiently requests Narad:

> Then let the speech benign of griefless spheres
> Confirm this blithe conjunction of two stars
> And sanction joy with thy celestial voice.
> Here drag not in the peril of our thoughts,
> Let not our words create the doom they fear. [34]

In the original story of the *Mahābhārata* the queen mother is assigned a very insignificant role. But in *Savitri* Sri Aurobindo deliberately introduces the character of the Queen Mother to present a human level of consciousness. Both Narad and king Aswapathy are seers and cannot stoop to human folly of viewing things in an arational and prejudiced way. To such a request Narad replies to the Queen philosophically commenting on man's craze for foreknowledge. He speaks in a Miltonic tone:

> What help is in prevision to the driven?
> Safe doors cry opening near, the doomed pass on.
> A future knowledge is an added pain,
> A torturing burden and a fruitless light
> On the enormous scene that Fate has built. [35]

To soothe the worrying heart of the Queen, Narad says that the cosmic mind of the eternal poet has written down each line of his "imperial act." Man is a puppet in the hand of Fate, "He knows not even what his lips shall speak." In his every action there is a mysterious power that compels his every step. The words of Narad pierces into the bosom of the Queen like a shaft.

The Queen has always aspired to grow into the consciousness of gods; her mind has always been preoccupied by mighty thoughts. She impulsively opens "her doors to grief" which is the typical nature of human beings. Being grief-stricken, she complains of the inflexible Law of the Supreme God and of the injustice imposed on mankind. She represents the common worldly woman whose consciousness is still shut up within the walls of ego and ignorance. Her judgment, naturally, is conditioned by her limitations and she accuses the Immanent One of perversity and partiality. The poet shows here how readily the mortal men erringly break down under the load of adversity instead of displaying a tranquil spirit, and encountering the evil forces with courage. Like the queen, man accuses the imperturbable will of the Supreme Being working behind this world.

Not only does man fail to understand the working will of the Absolute One but he loses faith in Him; suspicion lurks in his heart: his faith yielding place to disbelief. The Queen suspects that some stealthy doom has crept in from the "dark forest's sullen heart" and has cast its evil shadow on Savitri's path. Her misconstruing mind does not spare Satyavan, the Shalwa prince, whom Savitri has chosen as her partner. The following lines reveal the Queen's mind is assailed by superstitious belief:

> Perhaps he came an enemy from her past
> Armed with a hidden force of ancient wrongs,
> Himself unknowing, and seized her unknown... [36]

Savitri's mother analyses the nature of our evil days. Our days are linked with the past, present and future events. The old cruelties and our past deeds, which we might have forgotten in course of time, come back unrecognised in hideous forms. The gods make use of our forgotten deeds to avenge the old cruelties. She vaunts – we are the masters of our fate; it is our mind that shapes and moulds our destiny. We learn nothing from our valuable past experiences and go on repeating "Our stark misuse of self and others' selves." Explaining the ever poignant misery in the world, the Queen further adds, the dreadful angel visits his quivering prey and forces him "to cling enamoured to his grip" as if he is in love with his agony. This is not the only source of misery in our world; there are other lassoes of grief - "Our sympathies become our tortures." The Queen is perplexed by the sorrow that scourges the helpless creatures on earth. We mortals are not like gods who do not experience sorrow and grief. Man is so sympathetic that even the misery described in an ancient tale moves him to tears, "We are shaken by the sight of human pain." The Queen assigns in her speech a higher position to man compared to gods.

Viewed in this perspective *Savitri* is a song of Life. The speech of the Queen Mother explains Sri Aurobindo's concept of human consciousness. To be in suspense is worse than suffering itself; so the Queen Mother requests Narad to disclose the nature of the impending doom, "To know is best, however hard to bear."

Being ardently requested by the Queen mother, Narad assures her that Satyavan, chosen by Savitri as her life's partner, is a marvel in whom the earth and heaven meet. He is a representative figure of Nature's evolutionary march and "His single being excels the works of Time," all other products of Time's creation are inferior to him. His is a delightful soul like "A sapphire cutting from the sleep of heaven."

It is remarkable to see to what extent Sri Aurobindo heightens the character of Satyavan. Narad draws Satyavan's character even superior to that of the gods in heaven. In the opinion of the former gods, who are happy in their ethereal world, possess heart, which is not more sweet and true than that of Satyavan's. The speech of Satyavan is couched in the light of inner truth. There is also a strong will in him to rise high. It will be a great loss if Satyavan breathes his last before he has spread his sweetness in the world. He is a rare being of divine cast. But this sovereign glory, regrets Narad, has only one brief year to sojourn on earth and then the 'splendour of his life' will vanish from the mortal sky. With the return of the same day after twelve months Satyavan must die. This prophetic sentence comes from Narad like the stroke of lightning. Being shocked beyond her imagination and perturbed, the queen mother raises a startling cry:

> Vain then can be Heaven's grace!
> Heaven mocks us with the brilliance of its gifts,
> For Death is a cupbearer of the wine
> Of too brief joy held up to mortal lips
> For a passionate moment by the careless gods. [37]

The Queen mother tries her best to persuade Savitri to change her mind and admonishes her to ride her car and travel at once through the peopled lands once again to choose her Lord. She warns Savitri not to plead for her first choice "For death has made it vain." A less rare choice may bring a happier fate." But Savitri remains unperturbed and replies with a determined voice:

> Once my heart chose and chooses not again.
> The word I have spoken can never be erased,
> It is written in the record book of God. [38]

Savitri is resolved not to alter her decision and reveals her will power and firm stand:

> My heart has sealed its troth to Satyavan:
> Its signature adverse Fate cannot efface,
> Its seal not Fate nor Death nor Time dissolve...
> Death's grip can break our bodies, not our souls;
> If death takes him, I too know how to die. [39]

After listening to Savitri's speech of tremendous self-confidence, there ensues a parley of sealed silence. Breaking the icy silence of the place, the Queen raises her voice to question the inexorable fate and its rigidity. She becomes inquisitive to know: how did the mystery of grief and pain arise in this twi-natured life? Indeed, it is a fatal seed that was sown in the beginning of life on this earth when evil was conjoined with good on this soil. The discourse on pain is highly philosophical and original.

The poet analyses in a few lines human predicament and makes succinct remarks - at every step of our life's journey a snare is set. Our actions originate from darkness, which is alien to reason and contrary to spirit's light. Our actions have deep roots penetrating ignorance and nescience. Although man has ample freedom to make choice, in practice he flounders while making a proper choice and walks unknowingly into the trap of hell. In fact man is his own worst enemy. The poet disapproves of the tremendous progress modern science has achieved and sarcastically remarks that science is the "artificer of mortal's doom." More than any formidable animal, man ransacks the earth for weapons to destroy his fellow beings. In such an ominous attempt he mars his own happiness and cripples the good of others. He takes no lesson from Time and its history. War, plunder, ruin and massacre are still the pastimes of belligerent tribes. An idiotic and whimsical hour destroys what man has taken centuries to make. The only truth of search for man's soul is wide and unending, but every time it ends in dismal failure.

The Queen truly voices a pessimistic view of life. By nature the master poet is neither a pessimist nor a nihilist. The questions that trouble the Queen's mind are often those that come to common men filled with despair. To balance this pessimism, the seer poet presents an optimistic view also; otherwise the poem would not have been a song of the divine life. The poet presents shades of doubt that lurk in her mind:

> Why is it all and wherefore are we here?
> If to some being of eternal bliss
> It is our spirit's destiny to return
> Or some still impersonal height of endless calm,
> Since That we are and out of That we came,
> Whence rose the strange and sterile interlude
> Lasting in vain through interminable Time?
> Whence rose the call for sorrow and for pain? [40]

The divine sage, Narad expresses an optimistic view of life. He says, man is not far away from God as the Eternal lives hidden in the chamber of the soul. The divine Guest is screened from our vision by an intermediary darkness as a result of which we are not able to hear or feel his immanent presence. In this context the seer poet has skilfully provided a suitable background to analyse the emergence of pain on this earth. Such philosophical discourse heightens the symbolic dimensions of the epic.

In the poet's opinion, it is due to such dissociation from the Immortal-domain of bliss that there arose the need for an intruding Dark God. This Dark God is a dreadful teacher who is the creator of pain in this world. He has intruded into this earth for teaching mortals to strive for the higher truths of life amidst the formidable forces of pain and suffering. The poet philosophically views the emergence of suffering: "Where Ignorance is, there suffering too must come." It comes to break the shell of Ignorance. The poet treads on a philosophical discourse to provide a didactic lesson.

While probing deep into the problem, Narad further points out that Inconscience is the dumb original base of mortal body. Out of the Inconscience pain was the first-born child. The absence of consciousness is the origin of pain. Unconsciousness alienates us from the higher truths of life and forces us to writhe under the treading feet of pain and suffering. The dreadful rigour of pain emerged from one caul with joy like a twin. First manifests pain to hew the path of material joy in life. It first breaks up the hard crust of Inconscience and stirs life in the subliminal deep to awake from the hidden Matters' trance. Pain acts like a hammer of the gods to break a dread resistance in the mortal's heart and makes possible man's ascension to divine heights.

In his prophetic vision the poet sees the earth undergoing the throes of endless birth to deliver the godhead. Though centuries have passed vainly, the godhead is yet to be born. The ancient Mother Earth willingly faces all birth pangs with joy, "For with pain and labour all creation comes." This internecine struggle is between the forces of Darkness and Ignorance on the one hand and the powers of Knowledge and Light on the other. In this struggle "Men die that man may live and God be born" and "the silence of the spirit profound" watches the awful passage of tragic time. Nature works upon an unwilling humanity with a deliberate cruelty but with a lofty goal.

In the opinion of the divine sage one who leads humanity has to share the pains of all. An individual who strives for self-liberation lives alone in calmness; but a saviour of human race who is moved by noble urges has to lead a life of struggle and stress. Narad then refers to the role of the leaders of humanity and the saviours of the human race in a poetic way that echo one of Sri Aurobindo's short poems, "A God's Labour."

> The great who came to save this suffering world
> And rescue out of Time's shadow and the Law,
> Must pass beneath the yoke of grief and pain:
> They are caught by the Wheel that they had hoped to
> break,
> On their shoulders they must bear man's load of fate. [41]

Among the many saviours of human race, the poet cites the case of Jesus Christ, the Son of God who took birth as the son of man. To save humanity he had to drink the bitter cup of earthly suffering and death. "The Eternal suffers in a human form" and through His suffering salvation to all is assured. So it is not only the leaders of men but also Gods who undergo suffering to raise the human race to a supernal height. When God's messenger comes to help the world he has to bear the pang that he would heal. Otherwise, how shall he cure the ills he never felt? The immortal chooses to lead a mortal life so that "the world may be new-born and live." Only by a hard sacrifice Heaven can be appeased. The poet's famous theory of incarnation, the *Avatārhood* rings in these lines. A dark hostility is hidden in the depths of human beings, which persistently opposes any spiritual change, and is bent upon marring God's work. Narad analyses the pervading evil of the universe.

The poet deviates from the original legend by introducing, Narad's discourse on the theory of pain, his prophecy of the coming of the world's redeemer and the function of Titan in this universe. It is not Narad but the seer poet himself who explains his own philosophy in lucid poetic terms. The poem can be regarded as a study of Life and the world and in treatment it is psycho-spiritual.

Aswapathy listens with rapt attention to the philosophical discourse of Narad. It is strange that even Savitri who is armed with divine power is also subjected to Fate. According to Narad she is not an ordinary woman. For an ordinary man or woman everything is determined from above. If human thought could echo divine thoughts, man would become omnipotent. Paradoxically Narad assures the Queen that even though the hour is fixed for Satyavan's death, Savitri has the power to change Fate. She alone is equal to her mighty task. It is Narad who first foretells the death of Satyavan and now it is he who assures her of the inner strength of Savitri to face the great ordeal. He advises them not to intervene in this struggle that is "too deep for mortal thought to sound." He assures them of a day to come when she will stand unaccompanied "on a dangerous brink of the world's doom" carrying the world's future on her lonely breast. Alone she will either conquer or fall and no human help can reach her in that momentous hour; not even God shall stand by her. She can alone save herself and the world because:

> The great are strongest when they stand-alone.
> A God-given might of being is their force...[42]

Savitri has taken birth on earth to fulfil a great mission. Her inner strength will rescue her to meet the inevitable danger. It is this momentous hour that will be a trial of Savitri's spiritual strength. Narad admonishes the Queen to hush her doubts:

> O queen, stand back from that stupendous scene,
> Come not between her and her hour of Fate.

> Her hour must come and none can intervene:
> Thou hast no place in that tremendous strife;
> Thy love and longing are not arbiters there,
> Leave the world's fate and her to God's sole guard.[43]

After clearing all doubts of the Queen, Narad leaves for his heavenly abode. Sri Aurobindo thus moulds the legend and offers it in a symbolic way so as to make it a vehicle of his philosophical thoughts.

Another episode that is fraught with symbolic significance is Savitri's *yoga*. At the time of crisis in her life, she seems to be very bitter against the Forces of Heaven for not helping her lover. In such a desperate moment a mighty Voice calls from her true Being. Savitri voices forth her inner grief and expresses her readiness to submit to "earth's unyielding laws" and "follow close behind" her "lover's steps" to the world beyond. The Voice replies, "What shall thy soul say when it wakes and knows" that the work is left undone for which you have come to this earth? Then the Voice advises Savitri to find out her soul, to recover her hid self. Savitri follows the instructions of the Voice. From the outward consciousness, she enters into her deep consciousness. In her journey towards her soul she separates herself from the body and looks at the inner depth of her being. The "Serpent of the threshold" guarding the entrance of the "inner worlds" starts hissing at her. Having no fear, she enters the inner worlds. She finds it a region of vague Inconscient. She crosses this region and comes to a sense world. Even in this world "all was still confused." Then she faces the "physical mind" where she finds the surging of opposite powers.

Savitri then begins the ascent towards her soul. She comes across a Woman, the Mother of Seven sorrows. She narrates to Savitri the various forms in which she works in human life, in the life of animals, in fact, in the life of all living beings. Savitri gives assurance to the Madonna of Suffering that misery shall pass abolished from earth giving place to a reign of peace and joy forever.

As Savitri advances "in her upward route," she meets the Mother of Might. The latter works to help the unfortunate ones, saves the doomed and topples down the reign of the tyrant kings.

Suddenly, Savitri hears the voice of the Dwarf-Titan, the Ego of this great world of desire who claims earth and the wide heavens for the use of man. It is the aspect of man's thinking animal. Savitri listens to the voice of this power and does not say anything. But to the Madonna of Might she gives assurance, "One day I will return, a bringer of light," to liberate you.

Savitri ascends higher and meets another Woman who has lustre in her eyes, a sunlit-face and moonbeam feet. She says that she alleviates the pangs of earth and brings peace to people's heart. Her agony is that the human mind still clings to its ignorance; hence she does not succeed in her work. Savitri, on the other hand, hears the "voice of the sense shackled human mind" whose knowledge is incomplete. This mind says that when mind progresses; all its knowledge is contradicted. Savitri assures the Woman that when she returns with the Divine Life everything will attain perfection.

As Savitri advances further she finds a dark region, where there is no mind, no light, no heart and knowledge. She finds the great figures of gods. These gods are the "executive figures of Cosmic Self," who come from the Infinite *Sat, Chit* and *Ananda*. Then she passes through a tunnel and comes to a place where shines a deathless Sun, "a house all made of flame." This is the deepest truth of the individual. Here Savitri's human personality meets her true being. They become one. She sits in the "deep lotus home," "calling the mighty Mother of the worlds" to descend on her to make her earthly flesh her house. The divine Mother descends in her heart and a mighty transformation takes place in Savitri. A flaming serpent rises in her released from sleep. The centre of her being is surcharged with Supernal Light and Bliss. In her occurs a high celestial change, "powers and divinities burst flaming forth." Every act of her then becomes an act of God. Thus she escapes into infinity. Her soul is now the Cosmic Soul which is beyond Time and Space and yet omnipresent in Time and Space. In order to seek her soul, Savitri passes through various layers of consciousness to attain that sensitivity which may help her to respond to the Intangible.

The *yoga* of Savitri like Aswapathy is symbolic and has immense significance in rousing her slumbering spirit. It is the "yoga of transformation".

On the fateful day, Savitri accompanies Satyavan to the forest. The poet follows the original legend in narrating what happens in the forest. While Satyavan lays his head on the lap of Savitri and before his life passes away, he cries out in despair to get a kiss from her lips. Savitri kisses him as if she could persuade his soul to come with her kiss. Near her she feels the presence of a shadow. An awful hush pervades the place. She knows that Death is standing near her and Satyavan is no more alive. In such a trying circumstance, Savitri rends not "with tears the marble seals of pain." A sudden unexpected change comes over her. She finds herself being supported by an immortal Power. Her heart is filled with divine strength. Her grief vanishes and her mind becomes still.

The Lord of Death tells Savitri to unclasp the body of Satyavan, and to return to earth. But she does not move. As Death leans over to touch the body of Satyavan, she sees "another luminous Satyavan", "forsaking the poor mould of that dead clay" and standing between Savitri and Death. Later on he noiselessly follows the tread of Death. She too follows the eternal Death and travels through 'the perilous silence.' She frees her true Being from the atmosphere of earth and it breathes a "deep and unfamiliar air." As her physical body falls into a trance her spirit separates itself from the body and follows the shadow. Savitri and the Lord of Death come to a place where they must part. The three travellers pause "on the chill dreadful edge of Night." Her flame-bright spirit starts burning like a torch. Armed with light she steps into a dreadful land. Her steps pick up mysterious speed. The poet vividly describes Savitri's experience in this symbolic land in the following words:

> In the smothering stress of this stupendous Nought
> Mind could not think, breath could not breathe, the soul
> Could not remember or feel itself; it seemed
> A hollow gulf of sterile emptiness,
> A zero oblivious of the sum it closed,
> An abnegation of the Maker's joy
> Saved by no wide repose, no depth of peace. [44]

Death reminds her that the ancient goddess can give nothing to her. He speaks disparagingly about the efforts of man who is nothing but a "fragile miracle of thinking clay." "God", "heaven" is the imagination of man. Death mocks at the gods who lead men on and make him vainglorious about the future. Death is himself the symbol of emptiness, void, and negation. It is natural that Death satirises the action of Gods. He gives an account of how the gods have made man a puppet in their hands. They have given to humanity nothing but grief.

With such discouraging words Death thinks that Savitri would be dissuaded from her determined path and would return to her house. He again reminds her that she should not expect Satyavan to come back to her. Moreover, he offers her gifts to soothe her wounded life. Her reply to Death is that she has come to his gate "not as a suppliant" but as "a Victor spirit." She asserts in bold words that hers is the "labour of battling gods." She demands from Death whatever Satyavan had desired from his childhood but had failed to achieve in his beautiful life. Death bows his head indicating his scornful cold assent to Savitri's demand. In a raised voice he says, "I yield," to his father his "Kingdom and power and friends and greatness lost" and eyesight to the blind king. He then advises Savitri to return to her cottage. But she emphatically says that she is born equal in spirit with Death and is immortal in her mortality. She expresses her desire to follow Satyavan, "earth's path that leads to god." She expresses her preparedness to pursue wherever he would lead Satyavan's soul. Death reminds her about his absolute powers. But her undaunted spirit is not to be terrified by the bullying words of Death.

They advance silently in the trackless land. Death finds that neither gift nor threat could produce any change in Savitri. So he decides to follow the path of logic and convinces her that her hopes and quest are unreal as a mere mirage. To create fear in her heart, Death then reveals his almighty power, describing himself as even greater than the gods. He discloses that he is the shapeless formidable Vast, and the emptiness that men call Space. He says, "I, Death, am He; there is no other God." All from His depths are born; all to His depths return. He has made man a toy by His inconscient Force.

Then, he speaks to Savitri that if she desires immortality she should live by herself and forget the man she loves. It is the One, which is only permanent. That One being contains no love. There is no Time or Space. It is nameless and formless. But Savitri asserts her immortal self by saying, "I am, I love, I see, I act, I will." She tells Death that her coming to the world is a ripple from the omniscient. Her love cannot be understood by Death's reasoning mind.

The journey of Savitri, Death and Satyavan is symbolic. The death of Satyavan takes place in a forest. Traditionally 'forest' symbolises riddles and confusion. The riddle here is about the establishment of a Life Divine. One wonders whether Satyavan's life can be recovered or not. In the event of Savitri conquering Death, Love shall triumph over Death. Death shall be transformed from an enemy to a friend of Life.

The three travellers come to a land, which is described by the poet in the "Dream Twilight of the Ideal". This sphere symbolises the ideal, which Savitri pursues - the victory of Love over Death is perceived as a twilight stage, a stage where the ideal or the light is hoped. Such a materialisation is only possible when the divine life will be established on the earth; and that will be the consummation of Savitri's long-sought ideal; the fructification of her labour for which she has taken birth. The return of Savitri and Satyavan to earth's life will transplant the life divine on earth.

Death in his strong pronouncement tries to justify that the vague ideal after which Savitri is pursuing is really a mirage. Earth ever lies unchanged in spite of the repeated efforts made by the *Avatars*. The thought of the sages, the prophet's voice have proved in vain. The Earth has not changed.

Savitri replies firmly to Death that her love is not a craving of the flesh. She has inherited her love from the great Gods, and to God her love will return when it is purely consummated. Death's inexorable voice peels forth shattering all her hopes. He says that her longing to build heaven on earth is a delusion.

Prolonging her argument with Death, Savitri says that the former has looked on an unfinished world, the world that is not yet sure of its path of progress. Man is yet an infant and clearly bears the stamp to grow in future. The Divine lies hidden in man's imperfect state. It is true that perfect wisdom and joy beyond the earth is waiting for release.

In an informative tone Savitri describes to Death the sacred mission of her and Satyavan's life. Revealing their symbolic role, Savitri says - "For I, the Woman, am the force of God" and Satyavan is "the Eternal's delegate soul in man." She assures Death that her love is the heavenly seal of the Supreme.

Then the three figures journey onwards. Like Dante, Savitri passes through a realm where the figures and motions represent past human toil. Pointing at these figures and motions, Death indicates how hope in those men was an incurable malady of the mind. These conditions point to one thing: "where Nature changes not, man cannot change." The human race is chained to a vicious cycle. Death ridicules Savitri's idealistic stand and her conception in which human race is born and dies to push the world a step further in the path of ignorance. The poet skilfully weaves into the fabric of the theme, the human ideals through the dialogue between Savitri and Death in order to express the futility of these ideals as viewed by a sophist. There is no success without failure. So also the poet could not have established the optimistic view of 'life divine' on earth unless he would have answered all the doubts and misconceptions of human beings.

Death acts like a sophist in this poem because he views everything through His dark eyes having the vanity of a dark god. Veiling the Reality of all idealism, he succeeds distorting the proper meaning. He is an adept in misrepresenting facts.

Further, to test her courage, Death asks Savitri to show her freedom from the inscrutable laws of fate. As in the legend of the *Mahabharata,* we come across here in Sri Aurobindo's poem the same benevolent attitude of Death towards Savitri. He is prepared to grant all earthly pleasures to her except the life of Satyavan. Then the dialogue between Savitri and Death follows the same course as we find in the original *Mahābhārata* story. Her consistent reply to the Lord of Death is that earth can never flower if she returns lonely.

Death categorically replies to Savitri that the limits of man are set by his mind. Man cannot soar beyond the limit of thoughts, the limits imposed by the reasoning mind. Death further informs her that Truth cannot descend to the transient earth. He assures Savitri that if she can show Him the body of living Truth and the outline of her face, He too will obey and worship the Truth; and would give back the life of Satyavan. This is an impossible demand lodged before Savitri by the Lord of Death.

Accepting Death's challenge, Savitri humbly opens her lips. While she speaks this time, her mortality disappears, and the indwelling divinity grows visible. Her answer demolishes the very gloomy existence of the Lord of Death. In her brief speech she points out the play of the opposites that underlies all movements in the universe. She says that all contraries are aspects of God's face. She avers, "The many are the innumerable one." She then challenges the Lord of Death and warns Him:

> Who can show to thee Truth's glorious face?
> Our human words can only shadow her.
> To thought she is an unthinkable rapture of light,
> To speech a marvel inexpressible. [45]

At this stage there lurks a question in Death's mind - if the Manifest and the Unmanifest are not linked, how can earth receive the blessings of heaven? Who is to bring down the light of heaven on earth? To resolve this issue, he puts a direct question to Savitri. It comes to Savitri in the form of a challenge. For a moment she keeps silent while a mighty transformation comes on her:

> A halo of the indwelling Deity, ...
> The Incarnation thurst aside its veil.
> A little figure in infinity
> Yet stood and seemed the Eternal's very house...[46]

After being transformed Savitri through her sparkling eyes looks into the eyes of Death. Then a Voice is heard which is the calm utterance of Infinity. This incident is absent in the original legend. The poet has introduced these typical dialogues into the theme of the poem to give it a symbolic overtone. The voice of Infinity makes it clear that Savitri is not an ordinary woman.

Death is still unconvinced and protracts the same resistance and stubborn attitude. But the situation changes. He shows this attitude no more now. His self is poised with a conflict. His spirit and will obey the law. But His being towers in the darkness calling for help to all His acolytes. In a desperate bid to defy heaven he calls out all his accessories, but none come to His rescue. He disappears taking refuge in the retreating Night. With the disappearance of Death into the Void, Savitri and Satyavan are left alone. But none stirs due to the presence of a mute invisible and translucent wall.

Death being totally defeated by Savitri disappears leaving behind an invisible presence, becomes a disguised foe. It is necessary to transform Death so that He no longer behaves as a disguised foe, but becomes a generous friend. Then the fear of death can be extirpated from earth and the secret of life and death can be revealed.

Savitri steps into the bright light of the "Eternal Day". In the region of that brilliant light she sees the transformed figure of Death emanating "A sum of all sweetness gathered into his limbs." It is a marvellous form. Gazing at the transformed figure of Death, she realises the struggle of Nature, the Universe and its agony. In this transformation the mystery of the nameless one is revealed to her. This episode is totally absent in the *Mahābhārata* legend. Probably with the help of this episode the poet wants to strike a symbolic note. Savitri sees in this form the "fourfold Being" of Death. The dreadful shadowy physical form of Death is now no more.

Savitri sees Death in this new form as *"Hiranyagarbha"*, the Golden Egg symbolising the creative activity of the mind. Then she comes across the second aspect of Death as the Mental Being, who rules over the realm of the imagination like a magician with a sceptre - the omnipotent wand of thought.

The third aspect of Death is a "mass of superconsience closed in light", the "creator of things in his all-knowing sleep." He symbolises wisdom that does not come by thought. When he is awakened, he is the Eternal and the supreme because His slumber is Almightiness in things.

The Fourth aspect is bliss that has made the world. All forms of Love, Delight and Beauty are there. Savitri sees all these Beings working harmoniously in that embodied Light. The two mighty powers look at each other — "Soul saw soul." Being full of bliss Death, is transformed. So there is no fear of death. Savitri's love thus transforms Death into such a blissful and lovable form.

Savitri is offered a choice by Death that she and Satyavan could remain united together in an ecstatic communion to serve the dual law of ecstasy. They will remain one, but willingly be separated for work. This polarity will be suffused with their mutual love and attraction. The other alternative offered to Savitri by Death is to renounce all care and anxiety for the world, leave aside her sympathy for the mortal beings and ascend into the realm of bliss to live eternally with Satyavan. But for this she has to ignore the ambiguous myth of earth's desire. To Savitri, both these offers are unsuitable. She can neither become contented with her lover in the world of bliss renouncing all responsibility for earth's desire, nor accept the law of polarity to function in two different realms with Satyavan. She rejects both these offers on the ground that she has come down to earth with a particular mission to carry out. The acceptance of these offers by her will be contrary to her nature and her mission on this earth.

Death expresses his own limitations by saying that he is to look after the requirements of Fate. If Savitri is not prepared to wait for Time and God, then she should endeavour to change Fate; and for this she has to rise to a higher level. It is the realm of Timelessness where fate ceases to exist. As Savitri ascends to the Timeless state, Death ends. She comes across a Voice here, which assures her the descent of the Superman on earth. Not only this but also the spirits' force shall merge into the Nature's force. All things shall manifest the latent divinity. In "Matter shall be lit the spirit's glow" is the prophecy given by the Voice to her. This is the pith and kernel of Sri Aurobindo's philosophy. With such nectarean assurance Savitri returns to the earth. Then what happens afterwards follows the original legend.

Thus, we find the character of Savitri is raised to that of the "saviour" of man. The range of *Savitri* comprises the cosmos and takes into its sweep the worlds of beings, which are connected with humanity but are not perceived by them due to our ignorance. It also includes the unmanifested higher planes of consciousness, which are waiting for manifestation on earth. These higher planes contain beings and powers not known to us. Savitri, herself being the power of Truth-consciousness prepares the ground on earth for the manifestation of Light Supreme. The epic presents through its panoramic view the problems of man's imperfection, his thirst for spiritual light, his groping in the Darkness of ignorance, the problems of his mortality and his search for immortality.

The epic, *Savitri* accomplishes two difficult tasks, it creates a personality, Savitri, a human-divine character, and secondly it succeeds in making all the spiritual experiences of man real and ineffable. Even though it is well known that the highest spiritual experiences defy expression in language.

Savitri enunciates a new world of transcending consciousness and makes it a natural part of the vision of man; so that man can attain it. In *Savitri* the seer poet presents the evolutionary spiral at its highest rung and Savitri, the Divine Grace incarnate establishes victory over the cosmic Ignorance, the Inconscient represented by its extreme form of death. She presents a solution to the basic problem of man, the cause of his imperfection, suffering, death and evil. So *Savitri* is symbolically more inward in its solution of the basic human problems. What man is and what he shall be? The epic lifts the veil existing between man and the Divine, and establishes a direct relationship between them. Raymond Frank Piper has made a pertinent comment: "*Savitri* is perhaps the most powerful artistic work in the world for expanding man's mind towards the Absolute."[47]

The reading of *Savitri* lifts us from our mundane level to see from above the play of life and the working of cosmic forces; and the working of the Divine veiled behind the play. *Savitri* gives the vision of the relation between Eternity and Time in its varied ways.

Sri Aurobindo's prophetic words in his *Future Poetry* regarding the form and possibilities of an epic poem in modern days hold true in the case of *Savitri*. He writes: "The epics of the soul most inwardly seen as they will be by an intuitive poetry, are his greatest possible subject, and it is this supreme kind that we shall expect from some profound and mighty voice of the future. His indeed may be the song of the greatest flight that will reveal from the highest pinnacle and with the largest field of vision the destiny of the human spirit and the presence and ways and purpose of the Divinity in man and the universe."[48]

Savitri is the sublime poetic utterance of the integral and cosmic truth-vision of one of the great seers of the modern age that moves with aspiration of man for an ultimate divine fulfilment on earth. In a letter Sri Aurobindo has explicitly laid down the grand design of *Savitri*: "*Savitri* is the record of a seeing, of an experience which is not of the common kind and is often very far from what the general mind sees and experiences."[49] The wide vision of the author sees the all-pervading delight even in the terrestrial existence of death, incapacity and doom. It is a "song of the life divine".

Sri Aurobindo has revived the spiritual glories of the past in *Savitri*, the active present and the future possibility of the establishment of an earthly paradise. The poetic genius has blended the visible and the occult, the material and the spiritual, the terrestrial and the cosmic in the epic action. The symbol has changed the legend to an ambrosial sweetness; the symbol and the legend commingle and are not separated from each other.

Both the streams of the Eastern and the Western thought find expression in the epic. Starting from the evolutionary theory advocated by the Western scientists, Sri Aurobindo visualises a positive advancement in the process, giving rise to the descent of a new consciousness called Supramental-consciousness that transcends the human mind.

The journey of Savitri, Satyavan and Death in the symbolic worlds of Eternal Night, the Double Twilight, and the Everlasting Day, are the realms beyond our Time and Space. Sri Krishna Prem's remark on *Savitri* is of eternal value and bears the truth of *Savitri*'s symbolic interpretation. As he indicates:

> Savitri is neither subjective fantasy nor yet philosophical thought, but vision and revelation of the inner structure of the cosmos and of the pilgrim of the life within its sphere—Bhu, Bhuvar, Swar, the Stairway of the Worlds reveals itself to our gaze - worlds of Light above, worlds of Darkness beneath - and we see also ever circling life ("Kindled in measure and quenched in measure") ascending and descending that stair under the calm unwinking gaze of the Cosmic Gods who shine forth now as old... Poetry is indeed the full manifestation of the Logos...[50]

Indeed, *Savitri* is a song of the divine. In the *Mahābhārata* and the *Rāmayana* human egoism in its sublime aspect is fought and destroyed. But in *Savitri*, the original evil, the Inconsient, the cause of man's subjection to imperfection is defeated and eliminated.

The epic deals with the original evil power and not with any of its manifestation. Viewed in its different perspective, it is the study of Man, what he is? What is within him? What he is likely to be? It envisions the Golden Age in the history of mankind that is to come. It can be said that *Savitri* synthesizes all the spiritual gains of humanity acquired down the ages. It lifts man from his mundane sphere to an apocalyptic vision of his highest cherished ideals. And it is such a vision that will impel man to unfold the indwelling Divine and enact the heaven on earth.

In the following chapters a detailed discussion of the different symbols in *Savitri* beginning with the symbolic journey of Aswapathy will be made.

References

1. *Modern Man in Search of a Soul,* trans. from German by W.S. Dell and Cary F. Baynes, New York, 1934, p.188.
2. Lillian Feder, *Ancient Myth in Modern Poetry,* New Jersey: Princeton University Press, 1971, rpt.1973, p.27.
3. Ibid., p. 32.
4. *Standard Dictionary of Folklore Mythology and Legends,* ed. Maria Leach, London, 1975, p.518.
5. J.M. Macfie, *Myths and Legends of India,* Edinburgh, 1924, p. XXII-IV.
6. Sri Aurobindo, *Vyasa and Valmiki,* 1964, p.21.
7. K.R. Srinivasa Iyengar, *Dawn to Greater Dawn,* 1975, pp.13-4.
8. Letters on Savitri, p.727.
9. Ibid., pp. 731-32.
10. Sri Aurobindo, *Savitri,* p.817.
11. Sri Aurobindo, "The National Value of Art" in *The Complete Works of Sri Aurobindo,* Pondicherry: Sri Aurobindo Ashram Press, 2003, Vol.I, p. 450
12. Ibid., 451.
13. Nolini Kanta Gupta, *Poets and mystics,* 1951, pp.20-21.
14. K.R. Srinivasa Iyengar, "The First Canto of Sri Aurobindo's Savitri", *Mother India,* Vol.XX, No.7, 1967, pp.451-24.
15. A.B. Purani, *Savitri: A Study and an Approach,* p.133.

16. Sri Aurobindo, *Collected Poems*, p.99.
17. Sri Aurobindo, *Savitri*, op.cit., 1977, p.341.
18. Ibid., p. 341.
19. Ibid., p.345.
20. Ibid.
21. Ibid.
22. Ibid.
23. Ibid., p.17.
24. Nolini Kanta Gupta, "Editorial Comment", *The Advent*, February 1947, p.63.
25. Sri Aurobindo, *Savitri*, op.cit., p.15.
26. Ibid., p.416.
27. Ibid.
28. Ibid., p.418,
29. K.R. Srinivasa Iyenger, *Dawn to Greater Dawn*, 1975, p.66.
30. Sri Aurobindo, *Savitri*, op.cit., p. 418.
31. Ibid., p.419.
32. Ibid., p.424.
33. Ibid.
34. Ibid., p.425.
35. Ibid., p.426.
36. Ibid.
37. Ibid., p.428.
38. Ibid., p.431.
39. Ibid., p.432.
40. Ibid.
41. Ibid., p.441.
42. Ibid., p.445.
43. Ibid., p.460
44. Ibid. p 461.
45. Ibid., p.583.
46. Ibid., p.663.
47. Ibid., p.664.

48. Raymond Frank Piper, "Sri Aurobindo's Savitri - A Note", *Mother India,* December 5, 1958, p.38.
49. Sri Aurobindo, *The Future Poetry,* pp. 3777.
50. Sri Aurobindo, *Savitri,* op.cit., p.794.

5

Aswapathy's Psycho-Spiritual Odyssey

Sri Aurobindo takes the idea of the soul's journey through different worlds beyond our physical world from the *Vedas* and the *Upanishads.* In the *Life Divine* he quotes with approval from *Shwetaswatara Upanishad:*

> The Soul of man, a traveller, wanders in this cycle of Brahman, huge, a totality of lives, a totality of states, thinking itself different from the Impeller of the journey. Accepted by Him, it attains its goal of Immortality.[1]

Yoga is the art of finding one's own *self.* This finding of the self entails all knowledge and the secret knowledge, which Aswapathy in the course of his journey achieves. A.B. Purani's scholarly discussion of Aswapathy's journey is worth noting. He points out:

> It is the epic of man's ascent from level to level of consciousness rising from world to world, from peaks of mind to the peaks of the spirit till he reaches the supreme Divine and by his unfailing aspiration invokes the Divine to descend into himself so as to create divine life on earth. But this cannot be so long as the human soul is tied like an animal with the triple cord of mental, vital and physical ignorance to the sacrificial post in the vast cosmic sacrifice to be offered as a victim. As long as human consciousness lives in the ego, lives subject to desire, conflict, dualities, suffering and pain, so long he cannot fulfill the deepest longing and the highest aspiration of his being. He must liberate himself from the bondage of ignorance.[2]

Savitri traces the spiritual odyssey of the soul. In a sense Aswapathy is like Ulysses who is not satisfied with his present-day living and yearns to break the barrier of the mortal world through his ordeal and quest; he is a Moses who led the Israelites out of the wilderness. Aswapathy represents the mortal's need, the world's desire for higher life. D.V.K. Raghavacharyulu observes:

> It is not surprising, therefore, that a major part of *Savitri* is devoted to Aswapathy's Sadhana symbolises the *Pravritti Marga* (Evolution) and the *Nivritti Marga* (Involution) into a single dynamic of spiritual and cosmic action. Aswapathy is the artist of the divine reality modulating its transcendent energy in accents of significant utterance, while Savitri is the divine aesthesis (*Rasa*), the liberating vision invoked by imagination, rescuing man from ignorance, falsehood and limitation.[3]

Aswapathy's task is to bring down Divine Grace and to prepare the Earth-consciousness to receive it. He is the modern man in search of the Soul. His *sadhana* can be identified with the yogic climb of the *Kundalini* through the various *Chakras* and *Mandalas* as described by Patanjali.

In tune with the Puranic tenet Aswapathy like the gods and *Rishis* invokes an *Avatar* when the earth is rife with falsehood, ignorance and suffering, to redeem humanity at large. His journey is an immense experience of seeing and expanding the limit of the soul- force. Identifying Aswapathy's yoga with that of the traditional yoga mentioned in the *Gita*, D.V.K. Raghavacharyulu further observes:

> Aswapathy's forerunning spiritual pilgrimage progresses from *Karma-Yoga* (self-realisation through spiritual action) to *Jnana-Yoga* (self-illumination through the attainment of the supramental consciousness) and finally *Bhakti-Yoga* (communication with the supreme Being through total self-surrender and the attainment of Bliss). The pattern of triplicity also traces Aswapathy's spiritual sojourn through the successive realms of *Tamas* (Darkness-Ego), *Rajas* (Nescience-Power) and *Satva* (Being-Truth) until there is nothing but It (*Tattva*)[4]

The world is a great riddle in which we live in. What is the purpose of this Universe? Such and other questions are of eternal significance. Aswapathy's journey is directed to find out the answers to these questions. He ascends to the highest level of consciousness and learns the function of each level; each helps in the growth of his consciousness. He starts his journey from the lowest rung of ignorance and reaches the peak of the highest knowledge.

In the original story of the *Mahābhārata,* Aswapathy is assigned a simple role. Being an old childless king, he performs eighteen years of arduous *tapasya.* In the present poem the master poet devotes nearly one-half of the poem to Aswapathy's yoga. He becomes a symbolic character in the poem. A.B. Purani analyses the character of Aswapathy:

> The life of the childless king Aswapathy performing *tapasya* in order to have a child has been entirely changed by the poet into a symbol of human soul descended on earth from divine heights trying to acquire knowledge of the self and the world. The entire Second Book, in fact, is Aswapathy's travel over worlds heaped upon worlds in a complex cosmogony mounting from the plinth of the plane of Matter right up to levels of Higher Mind and the plane of the Cosmic Being Tending to worlds of greater knowledge. Aswapathy represents the aspiring human soul down the millenniums of evolution in his search for the truth of himself, of the world and of God.[5]

In the earlier draft of the poem, the legend was no more a symbol. So Sri Aurobindo made revisions of these drafts at Pondicherry, and enlarged Aswapathy's role. Speaking about the significance of these revisions, K.R.S. Iyengar remarks:

Sri Aurobindo fused in his Aswapathy the two ideas - a childless man desiring issue and mankind seeking redress against current discontents and ills - and metamorphosed him into a Seer-King, a representative leader of the human race and also the Forerunner of the *avatar* or redeemer to come. The basic situation - Aswapathy seeking out or invoking the World-Mother and asking for a child - is retained still, but the whole context and the psychological and spiritual backgrounds have now undergone so great a change, so marvellous a transformation, that we can at once see that we are in a symbol-world of portentous cosmic import, that the theme is not Savitri's personal history alone, but rather the future of the race itself upon the earth.[6]

While explaining to a disciple in 1946 about the structural organisation of the yoga of Aswapathy, Sri Aurobindo explain:

Aswapathy's spiritual development consisted of two yogic movements, one a psycho-spiritual transformation and the other a greater spiritual transformation with an ascent to a supreme power... Aswapathy's yoga falls into three parts. First, he is achieving his own spiritual self-fulfilment as the individual and this is described as the yoga of the king. Next, he makes the ascent as a typical representative of the race to win the possibility of discovery and possession of all the planes of consciousness and this is described in the Second Book: but this too is as yet only an individual victory. Finally, he aspires no longer for himself but for all, for a universal realisation and new creation. That is described in the Book of the Divine Mother.[7]

King Aswapathy has come to this earth from "larger spheres" with a special mission – "His birth held up a symbol and a sign." His prophetic mission is to prepare the conditions for a divine descent. The first ray of spiritual light enkindles his heart when he realises that the bodily appearance – is not all; behind the appearance lies the hidden reality. The 'flame of God' abides in man, which is the centre of Godward in man. When the universal transcendental realisation comes to Aswapathy; he grows into his larger self. Something superhuman, divine comes into his mortal frame. His human person gets erased and his self-centred ego personality gets dissolved and becomes one with the Divine Being. His "intellect's hard and lustrous lid" gets broken up. The outward form deceives him no more. He attains a new status of consciousness; which extends wider and deeper, and embraces the consciousness of all. His systems keep magical accord with the rhythm of subtler kinds that start vibrating in his inner being. As a result of this, his bodily self becomes an instrument of the soul. His inner sight opens up. He comes to a threshold watched by a serpent where he hears a secret voice. He comes across beings possessing subtler bodies, objects too fine for his material grasp. When his mind leans out to meet the hidden world, his nostrils quiver with celestial fragrance, the tongue tastes the honey of paradise. Such marvellous things are revealed to him which none can express. He crosses the border of Matter and the zone where thought replaces life:

> Out of this world of signs suddenly he came
> Into a silent self where world was not
> And looked beyond into a nameless vast.[8]

From the world of signs and symbols he comes into the world of the formless, where the objects are not perceived by touch or by the senses. All things in this region can be known through light of identity:

> Love is a yearning of the One for the One,
> And beauty is a sweet difference of the Same
> And oneness is the soul of multitude.[9]

In this sphere different types of truth coalesce into a single truth and a power of silence pervades his whole self. He comes to the plane of "still consciousness" which sustains all. His soul stands free, no more absorbed in the "moment ridden flux". He understands the world-design and knows the original Divine desire behind the working of this brute material force. He realises:

> All here must learn to obey a higher law,
> Our body's cells must hold the Immortal's flame.
> Else would the spirit reach alone its source
> Leaving a half-saved world to its dubious fate.[10]

He sees the origin and source of all things in this state. He sees in the "illusion and mystery of the Inconscient" the presence of a consciousness, which is in a condition of self-involution. He sees God and Nature in their mutual fulfilment in this manifested universe. His soul, mind and heart become a single sun, although the lower nature remains reluctant to receive the transforming light. Inspiration comes as a sudden messenger from the 'all seeing top' to the corridors of his mind.

Aswapathy's consciousness wandering through space enters the regions that are covered by ignorance and Inconscience. He sees the unused powers and faculties of man hidden deep in the subconscient region whose priceless value can save the world. Thus, his mind and body undergo the first spiritual change, which the poet describes as the "soul's release from ignorance." A wide

God-knowledge descends from the viewless region to his mind, and within his mind a new world-knowledge broadens. All his actions spring up from the inner light. The human in him paces with the divine, and his strength gets linked with the universal strength. To help mankind and earth in her progressive evolution, he draws "the energies that transmute an age".

Before Aswapathy can take up any further spiritual adventure, he needs "Secret knowledge" for his guidance. The Canto IV of Book I points that for any spiritual explorer this world is the "beginning base." K.S. Srinivasa Iyengar integrates the theme of this canto to the poet's metaphysical speculations that has immense spiritual significance:

> It would not be very wide of the mark to say that the canto entitled "The Secret knowledge" is almost a poetic summary of The Life Divine, a cataract of Aurobindonian metaphysics; and as the eager mind tries to catch the shower in the sunshine, Truths flash upon the inward eye draped often in rainbow colours. It is the impassioned Song of the Spirit, reiterating the spiritual basis of all existence, but the improvisations cast a spell while they reinforce the meaning.[11]

Life and Mind are the two aspects of our earthly existence, which can create ideals for individual as well as for collective perfection. Even if we lie embedded in the earthly consciousness, some parts of our being grow towards the Divine Light. Sometimes when we turn within, earth's 'ignorant veil' is lifted from our eyes. A greater personality sometimes possesses us, as a result of which our bodily ego falls down leaving us one with Nature and with God. A wider consciousness opens its pathways before us. A secret Voice calls within our soul, which our mortal ears have never heard. But it perishes with our mortal body. This happens when instead of human consciousness ascending the higher planes; Grace descends here from those higher planes into the human consciousness. But all this is "screened, subliminal, mystical." To realise the Divine presence we need an intuitive heart, the inward turn, and the power of a spiritual gaze. Otherwise we human beings are here on this earth by some chance factor and our "goalless voyage seems our dubious course." Our life is a vague experiment, and the earth we live in, is a "brute mechanic accident." In the opinion of the poet- "Out of the unknown we move to the unknown." He further points out:

> Along a path of aeons serpentine
> In the coiled blackness of her nescient course
> The Earth-Goddess toils across the sands of Time.[12]

Mind keeps the soul of man a prisoner in this earth. Man does not know the meaning of his life. He does not know what he shall achieve and when. But this state of inertia, ignorance and incapacity will not prevail upon earth forever. A truth-light will surprisingly capture Nature. The prophetic voice of the poet sings of the coming golden age in these words:

> A stealth of God compel the heart to bliss
> And earth grow unexpectedly divine,
> In Matter shall be lit the spirit's glow,
> In body and body kindled the sacred birth;
> Night shall awake to the anthem of the stars,
> The days become a happy pilgrim march.[13]

The Transcendent Divine is not in a hurry to untie the cosmic knot. An outstretched hand is felt upon our lives. He is very near to us through "unnumbered bodies and births," but we are not always aware of his presence. Nature goes through a process of slow evolution with the help of the intervention of the Divine from high above. Aswapathy realises that his world is not only a "brute mechanic world", which has its trap of death and suffering set for human beings. Even though we make errors, these are the steps in the path of our success. The Divine is not mute and inactive. He is ever busy watching everything.

All that we see in this universe is the play of the Transcendent Divine. There are "Two who are one and play in many worlds." These two are *Purusha* and *Prakriti,* Soul and Nature. His unseen presence regulates every movement of this universe. He was there before the cosmos came into existence. He is the creator and He is the World that he has made. In every work of apparent opposition, we find his dual appearance like knowledge and ignorance, light and darkness, pleasure and pain. The *Purusha,* the Soul has assumed a diminished Godhead here, relinquishing all his omnipotence. He has become subservient to *Prakriti,* Nature. As the poet points out, "He knows her only, he has forgotten himself." He has left everything to her to make her great. Here the poet echoes the philosophy of the Sankhya. The ideas contained in these poetic lines have been fully elaborated by Sri Aurobindo in *The Essays on the Gita*. The roles of these primal principles have been explained as:

> For it explains existence not by one, but by two original principles whose inter-relation is the cause of this universe – *Purusha*, the inactive, *Prakriti*, the active. *Purusha* is the Soul, not in the ordinary and popular sense of the word, but of pure Conscious Being immobile, immutable and self-luminous. *Prakriti* is Energy and its process. *Purusha* does nothing, but it reflects the action of Energy and its process; *Prakriti* is mechanical, but being reflected in *Purusha* it assumes the appearance of consciousness in its activities.[14]

The Soul follows Nature in her every movement and draws the experience of life. With this relationship between Soul and Nature, creation goes on. All is their play; the whole world is only "he and she." This is the Truth-Law of the One Divine who governs the manifestation.

When the evolutionary development reaches certain maturity, the divinity embedded in man finds articulate expression. When *Purusha* awakens from within, Nature unmasks her significance, till then the Soul is a plaything in Nature's game. Nature moves him at her sweet will. The Absolute, the Perfect, the Alone has taken the tenement of human flesh, so that man may rise to the divine nature. The Divine has shown us that with His help transformation of human nature is possible.

Man does not stay confined to his narrow physical limits. His soul needs growth and expansion. He awakes to the larger worlds of feelings, emotions, and spiritual thoughts. The physical grows into vital, mental and aesthetic consciousness in his way of getting spiritual experience. Once he takes such a turn, Life changes for him its time constructed scenes. He crosses the limits of "mortal thought and hope," his mind is poised for a leap into Immortality. The realms beyond summon him - "the fire speaks and the unknown grows near."

Armed with this Secret knowledge, Aswapathy crosses the limit of mortal nature and enters the bright realms of the spirit, where all knowledge is spontaneous and the laws of material life hold their sway no more. He finds the mystic door of the occult cave near to the well of vision in the soul. The direct light of the soul in this region lights all. He finds the Truth-knowledge in this realm. On this subtler level of consciousness, he finds the "record graphs of the cosmic scribed." Here he discovers the clues to all the mysteries of material universe. After witnessing these supra-physical realities, a greater will seizes Aswapathy's heart. He directs his inward gaze into the unknown spiritual heights. He lives in the great realm of Silence; his being now exceeds "thinkable space" and he gets universal vision. His being passes through the "Immobile's ocean-silence." He feels his progress arrested by the dragon tail of the black Inconscient' but he mounts "burning like a cone of fire" because a flaming aspiration for the Divine is there in his whole being.

It is true that only upon a chosen few such gods like vision is bestowed. Aswapathy is one among such a group of 'fated few'. He is the hero of the struggling human soul, who has grown fit to receive this Grace. He is a man of knowledge. He has lived and guided himself by the "Shastra", the scriptures, the moral and social code.

Whem Aswapathys being towers into 'pathless heights' casting away behind him his human trappings, visibly leaps down a "strong Descent". The Descent is "A Might, a Flame, a Luminous Beauty." He can no more bear the thrill of this epiphany and faints. Then a "power more ruthless than Love, happier than Heaven" hails him with unalloyed bliss. His spirit shines out wide, blank and pure; and his mind becomes an empty state. A mystic fire consumes his past self so that he is purged in the divine fire. He experiences greater force and strange energy - "his spirit breaths super human air." His sight is no more confined to the physical plane.

Nature reveals herself to his eyes as the mediating agency between the Supreme Creator and the created universe. She opens to his sight all the mystic fields of her working and power. As he transcends the physical range of the universe, he faces new worlds of beauty, calm, knowledge. These worlds surprise his vision. These are the worlds of "Sunbelts of knowledge, moon belts of delight." Venturing across enormous realms, he breaks into another space and time. For him each plane of existence has its own space and time. An ascending and a descending order of worlds from Time to Eternity and vice versa are thus revealed to his vision. He sees the divine unity and the reconciliation of all diversity.

Aswapathy enters the realm of the unknown, which is an existence beyond earth. This is a region, "Where space is a vast experiment of the soul." One experiences the unity of consciousness in everything. His subtler senses awake to new objects of experience. He finds there everything the Infinite has manifested itself but 'only is missing the sole timeless word" that makes the world of perfection. Looking still inward, he sees worlds pile on worlds. It rises from the Conscience towards a Superconscient Light. He perceives it as a ladder of delivering ascent for the evolution in Nature by which Matter can discover itself in the Spirit. It makes possible man's journey from Inconscience to the level of light of Superconscience. These steps are originally formed for the descent of the godhead to save and redeem the spirit from nescience. These grades of consciousness are the powerful steps in the evolutionary progression of the earth.

Beyond our world of Gross Matter, Aswapathy enters the world of Subtle Matter. He finds life in this World has no flesh and light that makes visible all immaterial things. Here the eyes are the "doors to a celestial sense"; all shapes are beautiful and all things true. All things of the earth have their origin here. Aswapathy has entered the world of subtle material existence. It acts like a shield protecting the gross world from subtle forces, which is very strong. The union of mind and form takes place on this plane. There is a sense of purity in everything in this world, which we never feel on earth. This pure sense is linked with perfect beauty and shape of things. It is a world where matter and soul meet in conscious union. The spirit is not enclosed in mortal form of the physical world. This subtle body has its subtle senses; it is more enduring. After death, the physical body of man perishes and the subtle body enters this realm.

There are dangerous nether planes with demonic forces in the lower levels of this subtle material world. Our material world is a fall from this subtle material world. It is this fall that has created a possibility of evolution from the Inconscient to the Superconscient. Earth is a fragment of "heaven's design"; else we could never have hoped for a greater life. There is a continual attempt to create perfection from imperfection, completeness from incompleteness. The nescience has kinship with the Divine. So there is this progressive evolutionary movement of Earth. Beyond this physical world of matter, there is a subtle physical world, which has perfect symmetry in form and a marvellous design. This world gives Aswapathy a moment's fine release. His being leaves that "fine material paradise" and turns to realms of still greater light, larger vistas of Infinity.

While he is on the lower planes of life, he sees the image of a happier life. He comes to the kingdom of griefless life, a gleaming sphere of strange felicity. The life in this domain is impervious to suffering, struggle, and grief, untarnished by anger, gloom and hate, absorbed in its own beauty and bliss. Thus, to the vast vision of Aswapathy is revealed the higher vital life full of joy and laughter and the lower life full of sorrow, pain and suffering. There is an intermediate region of Life, amidst these antipodal lives. It is a region that is on the path halfway to heaven, and can receive the direct Divine light. The beings that inhabit this world are the embodiments of joy and delight. An atmosphere of divine inspiration pervades this region. Beauty lives here without any deformation, spreads without any physical obstruction. Falsehood has no place and none is weak. Contraries of life here are complementariness. Ignorance is a protecting light and "imagination the free-will of Truth." Worship, obedience and faith come spontaneously. Here "work" is "play and play the only work." Aswapathy feels attracted towards this world of bliss but he finds an impediment - a darker air encircles still his soul. His mind bears still things of earthly sorrow.

In the beginning of the mortal world "Life was not mind's play nor heart's desire." Before life could establish itself fully, a dark power of Nescience imposed an ordeal on spirit. Life's growth got arrested; her immortality became veiled. Life was subjected to joy, sorrow, struggle, suffering, desire, etc. It is because of man's craving, the formless yearning passion in him has added care and discontent to life, so man has become an insatiate seeker. Matter first awoke in man from its long, obscure trance. Thus, was life turned away from Matter and went on to form Mind.

The next world Aswapathy sees is a vast animal world, a world of "great puissant creatures with a dwarfish brain." Human beings here live like animals. They are not troubled by any thought. Life here is driven by some needs. For them body is all that matters. The mind at this stage is only preoccupied with sensational joy.

Next, Aswapathy sees a third order of life, which has the capacity for pure thinking. The world becomes organised out of such obscure beginning. He sees the growth of mind. Still the life of man does not participate in the soul's experience.

Aswapathy sees the kingdom of the little Life, with its rigid forms. He wants to know the secret of this world, so he plunges his gaze into the "mask", and all lurking creatures are revealed to his gaze, such as:

> Imps with wry limbs and carved beast visages,
> Sprite prompters goblin-wizened or faery-small,
> And genii fairer but unsouled and poor
> And fallen beings, their heavenly portion lost,
> And errant divinities trapped in Time's dust.[15]

These creatures can play havoc in the world. They exert their influence on everything on earth. These beings take pleasure in opposing good with evil, and bring failure and disappointment to man. They make "knowledge a poison, virtue a pattern dull." Wherever there is absence of love, and light, these "crooked fashioners take up their task." The region of our unconsciousness is their lurking place. They speak to us with the "voices of the Night." This state lasts so long as man's soul is not free. When man awakes to his inner self, "Then only ends this dream of nether life." In the beginning, the world seems to be a brute machine, but when we observe more closely, there is a gradual unveiling of an indwelling spirit, a consciousness. Life is subjected to the law of Matter. The World vibrates with the Light of God. Behind the struggling nature, the whirling of the brute mechanical world, a power watches from above and leads everything.

Aswapathy advances through chaotic expanses; darkness surrounds him. He feels as if he is inside a cave. From the region of the lower vital plane he comes to the region of higher vital where he finds a streak of dubious hope. He comes to an ineffectual world where the birth of things is arrested. It is a strange and uncertain world. Beauty and Power from higher regions try to enter this world, but they are unable to do so. All is vague here; life drifts towards an uncertain goal. Everything is unsafe, strange and half-true.

He sees from this region a wider zone of greater promise, where the self-conscious spirit seeks its own self. The beings and forces of this symbolic vital-world influence human activities on this earth. All that we seek on earth is prefigured here. The greater Life is in pursuit of the unseen, to express the Eternal in Time. He sees the creative Life Force. This Life Force is the same on earth, in heaven and in hell. This Life Force creates "god-like marvels out of mud", she keeps her search day and night. She is a power of the Divine Being to fulfil His will and to manifest His glory. She has been working so hard for her great Lover, the *Purusha*.

Aswapathy finds that the beings of the higher vital world are not incomplete, and not subjected to the control of the outside forces. They are self-assured and act according to their inner urge. The soul within them is not passive, participates in the destiny. They are the beings that are the "Kinsmen of our earthly race." Nature is not here a mechanical energy but a conscious force. They have their own ideals, which they seek to realise. They aspire for truth; their action confirms to Truth and they grow in the spirit. Not all the beings of this world seek Truth; some of them also choose the ideal of falsehood, of darkness. Both good and evil exist here with equal force. All beings have the complete freedom to develop. There sin, too, is a divinity. Those who worship a crooked god, the evil power, admit, "the black Idea twists the brain" and slays the soul. The vital beings of this plane of Life seek either a "mighty victory or a mighty fall", a "Throne in heaven or a pit in hell." Matter is the soul's result in the world, and the gross weighs less there, "the subtle counts for more." The vital beings of this world need no speech to communicate their thoughts. Mind meets directly with mind; two hearts come together. With all these interchanges there exists a barrier between the souls. All in this world is imperfect, still, half-known, and half-done.

Aswapathy further follows the trails of the vital world of life and tries to scan the tangled design spread before him. He sees all as a play of life and spirit. The spirit tries to possess life, but loses itself in the pursuit. He watches closely the activity of the Life Force. He sees also the negative aspect of life. He hears the divine call from afar.

Aswapathy tries to find out the causes of the failure of this vital world with a calm and detached mind. His gaze rends the veil that covers Nature's face, sees the fount of the world's misery and pain, and discovers the mouth of the black pit of Ignorance. He sees the haunting shape of Death, the agent of error, grief and pain. He sees a hostile and perverted mind at work, which defiles Light and Love, and the other divine things. No visible form is seen, yet the agents of evil wreak havoc. These agents of evil lay the foundation of an order of crookedness, sin, and adverse fate. Aswapathy sees such ominous beings, which pass him on the road, whose very gaze forebodes a calamity. Their beauty is like a snare. He follows the dark path and enters a "no-man's-land of evil air." It is a place where nothing is true. Deception is the very law of this world. Here joy becomes tears, and good becomes evil and love ends in hate. All these seem to be the work of an evil power, which is masked by light. Truth has no place here. Then the scene changes; he sees a city of Ignorance having the same main features. It is a country which neither has a ruler nor a capital and injustice and error reign high. Light has no access to it. Ego and falsehood dominate this realm.

Aswapathy passes through this region with the name of God on his lips. He is constantly aware of treachery at his back. He descends into the abyss where he faces a greater darkness. He fails to see, so his soul becomes the guide. Cruelty, lust, and ugliness reign in this zone. The undivine is worshipped, and evil is cherished. It is hell in its naked form. Demoniac forces impel the inhabitants of this region. Pity and love have no place.

When Aswapathy sees the core of that dark Night, he finds there a sheer unconsciousness at work revealing a horrid infinity. There is no Light, no divine soul. The atmosphere is rife with evil and pain. A time was there when a vast Non-Being, a Nescience came to live and occupied the earth. Death, pain, and falsehood emerged out of it and denied light to man. In spite of this, the divine spirit grows in man. Under the cover of Ignorance these powers fight against Light, Peace and Truth. They interfere with the working of God.

Aswapathy goes deep into this black Night and finds formidable powers hindering happiness, inflicting pain and misery. He suffers all sorrows of this hell and gathers nauseating experience. Though his thought ceases and senses do not function, his soul still sees and knows. At last he arrives at the entrance of the subconscient and sees the divine hand guiding the sphere. He perceives the wisdom and the will that work behind the veil of nature. When he realises this truth, the whole aspect of Night changes, divisions cease, sorrows end.

From the region of the dark Night, Aswapathy comes to a region of felicitous daylight. Life in this zone is under divine command without fear or grief. The course of life is smooth. Pain is transformed into joy. Peace, Love and Strength reach the acme. Aswapathy hears a divine music, creative thought comes to his mind. His senses acquire a new range. He sees before him a road stretching toward timelessness. These are the realms of lucent mind. He first meets a "silver grey expanse, where Day and Night meet. Nothing here is certain and definite. It is the meeting ground of knowledge and Ignorance. At the lower end of this region there is the physical mind akin to our earthly nature. This mind is the base of our evolving soul's ascent. This material mind serves the need of the body.

Aswapathy steps above this region into the realm where intelligence is at work mediating between the Supermind above and the Nescience below. It enables Matter to think. Powers from the higher realms of consciousness bring certain faculties like intuition and inspiration.

There are three gradations of the Mind power: the physical mind, the mind of desire and the reasoning mind. The reasoning power of the mind is the greatest power. Aswapathy reaches now the bright kingdoms of the rising Sun where "all is a birth into a power of light." He marks two more powers overshadowing the three powers of mind. These two are the "huge high-winged Life-Thought" and a "power Thought Mind" which hold the key to the higher Gnosis. These two enable man to arrive at the supernal Light.

After crossing the limits of the human mind Aswapathy enters the regions of a vaster transcending Thought. This world of Ideal Mind intervenes between the divine and the human and strengthens the link between man and God. This Ideal Mind lies beyond the reaches of imagination and thought. Over it is the sky of eternity. In this region power and beauty go together. These regions are far away from earthly toils and tribulations. Thought comes down from the ideal worlds to this region and "moves us to new-model." Living gods dwell in this region whose knowledge is permanent, joy is ineffable and powers spontaneous. In fact, human beings are not alien to this region. In our present state of divisive consciousness and ignorance we are exiled from that home of ours.

Our thought is a ray from that region but in course of its career it has become the "servant of Ignorance." In this region all things are real which to our earthly minds appear only as dreams. Our soul can ascend that luminous region. This thought-world is a triple realm. The first is akin to human mind. Aswapathy ascends the triple realms and comes to the great-ruling consciousness, where Mind unwittingly serves a higher power. This is such a plane of consciousness from which wisdom guides this world. Chance, necessity and fate come under its control; the forces of knowledge and power arrange the movement of upward evolution here, "When naked of ego and mind" man hears the Voice from this plane. When mind thus transcends the barriers of thought, the Truth that is unmanifest can reflect its form on our mind. Here itself a timeless Ray descends to our hearts. But man must always remember, "Truth is wider, greater than her forms."

Aswapathy finds that the Ideal is beckoning from afar. He finds the stairs to heaven for the ascent of the human soul. He finds on one side the blue heavens of the ideal mind and on the other, a lovely "Kingdom of the deathless Rose". This world of the deathless Rose, exists "unseen, unguessed by the suffering world." It blooms forever at the feet of God. When the bud of this deathless Rose blooms in the human heart:

> Then by a touch, a presence or a voice
> The world is turned into a temple ground
> And all discloses the unknown Beloved.[16]

At its summit this realm verges on the regions of the Immortals. When man opens to the "house of flames", he touches the "immortal kind." Even in rare moments the soaring aspiration of Earth can touch the "imperishable beatitudes", and can see:

> A million lotuses swaying on one stem,
> World after coloured and ecstatic world -
> Climbs towards some far unseen epiphany.[17]

The world of deathless Rose has similarity with the poet's early poem "Rose of God". The visions in the "Rose of God" come to fruition in Book Two Canto Twelve. The powers and the forces that he invokes to manifest in the poem on earth are really seen manifested in this Canto. If the earlier poem of Sri Aurobindo is an aspiration, this canto is the consummation of that aspiration. The "Rose of God" exists in a state of vision and that vision is made concrete a reality in this Canto.

Aswapathy sees on the other side of the eternal staircase, the "sorrow and darkness of the world" where a deathless Flame burns upwards to heaven and humanity is at the base of its sacrifice. The efforts to support this upward Flame in man are difficult to maintain. Only the strength of the Eternal in us can dare to sustain this Flame and fulfill what we cherish here.

Aswapathy moves beyond the Heavens of the Ideal, because "All there was an intense but partial light." He comes to a region where silence listens to the cosmic Voice. He finds himself on a wide summit where he is alone with the "enormous self of Mind" which is omnipotent but immobile, taking no part in the world's movement from which it has originated. It is unperturbed in its observation of good and evil. This silence is the real base of the Thinker in man; from here takes birth all his expression. Aswapathy becomes one with this self. Thus, being with it he grows powerful and free. It appears as though he knows everything. He has no more any desire or will. Then all of a sudden he feels a revealing touch in everything and realises that he has not known everything. Still he is far away from the source of knowledge. This "Sceptic Ray" strikes at the very root of thought and sense and disrupts all that is known. He realises that the ignorant mind seeking knowledge is like a labourer in the "dark dazzled by half-light." In this condition what we know is an image in a broken glass. This self of mind is like a veil and not the living God.

Aswapathy realises that for the greater satisfaction of the spiritual need of a man, a greater spirit than this self of mind is needed because here is no firm clue and no sure road. He looks above but "all is blank and still;" he looks down, "all is dark and mute." The soul moves in between these two firmaments of Darkness and Light. It seems as if "to be was a prison, extinction the escape."

He moves on led by a mysterious Voice. Arriving at the heart of the space and heart of the Time - he comes to a "bodiless realm". Here is the silent soul of the entire world. It is at the same time a Being, a Presence and a Power. This Soul loves spontaneously without caring for a return of Love; it extirpates the bitter cruelties of earth and nourishes the growth of the Divine manifestation in the cosmos. It leads evil things towards their secret good; turns falsehood to happy truth. It has the power to reveal divinity. Here is a feeling of divine intimacy.

It is the origin of finite creation in the bosom of infinite. The whole region is a vast soul. All is seen here in a spiritual light. Life is experienced here as a spiritual power. All beings take here rest after death and before they are born on earth. This is the centre of creation. Aswapathy finds beyond this world the domain of peace, delight, hope and love. He becomes conscious of the presence of Eternity. He travels along a road "of pure interior light" under the guidance of a nameless God and arrives in the region which is the "source of all things, human and divine." There he beholds "The figure of the death-less Two-in-One" seated in deep creative joy, whose rapture sustains the whole creation.

Behind this biune Divinity stands the Great One, the Divine Mother who "guards the austere approach to the Alone." She pervades all planes of existence; she reigns over the whole cosmos. This is the posture of the Divine Mother as seen by Aswapathy:

> Above them all she stands supporting all,
> The sole omnipotent Goddess over-veiled
> Of who, the world is the inscrutable mask;
> The ages are the footfalls of her tread,
> Their happenings the figure of her thoughts,
> And all creation is her endless act.[18]

Aswapathy's spirit is made a vessel of Her force. In passionate cry he stretches out his hands and prays. In a supreme gesture, the Divine Mother half uncovers her face. He sees the unending light and bliss in Her face and eyes. He falls down at her feet losing all awareness and drunk with" a deep golden spiritual wine."

Spending an eternal moment in this state of the soul, Aswapathy returns to the surface fields where he hears once more "the slow tread of the hours." He now stands in a realm of "boundless silences." Around him is a white and pure light. Leaving behind him Nature's hues, he comes out of the sphere of Mind - it is "a plane of undetermined spirit." It is the place where all cease and all begin. Here is the knowledge by which the knower is known; here is the still voice which human ear cannot hear. Herein the birth of spiritual things takes place. From here a thousand roads lead towards Eternity. Here he sees the flaming miracle of transcendent life. All here are a glorious "multiple of one radiant self;" everything here is the embodiment of Divine Bliss. He moves through regions of transcendent Truth. He is completely freed here from the limitations of mind and Time. To him, is revealed a universal beauty. He then, traverses in the regions of the cosmic Mind, and reaches the region of unchanging Truth. Above him he sees "The sun-eyed Guardians and the golden Sphinx."

Aswapathy thus reaches the "top of all that can be known," his vision extends beyond the summit of creation. He sees the triple heaven of light and the obscure Abyss of darkness. The ultimate mystery is only left to him to be known. The self's infinity begins to unveil. There is here no division in consciousness. Each moment of time contains in itself the Eternity. He is reborn in his knowledge. Even Gods begin to converse with him behind Life's veil. His being reaches the peak of Nature. He is now able to scan the secrets of the Overmind as he bears the rapture of the Oversoul. He has reached the border of the empire of the Sun – the Kingdom of the Supramental Truth. He is in tune with celestial harmony. At the end of his journey he finds that all his knowledge ends in an Unknownable. A silence overcomes his striving heart. He turns to the "Ineffable's timeless call", whose presence makes the smallest thing divine. He comes to the edge of the peak where the mind has to surrender to the Light of Truth or dissolve in the 'naked blaze of It like a moth.' At last a stark companionless Reality answers his soul's passionate search. This Reality has no kinship with the universe. It is a formless, featureless and silent Being, self-existent, and immobile. The presence he has yearned for draws close to him. He stands face to face with the Divine Mother.

Observing the inward journey of Aswapathy, one can also explore the occult worlds, meet the denizens and study their behaviour. It is a cosmic tour (exploration) starting from the occult regions of Gross Matter to the Supernal region, the region in which the Gods have their peaceful abode. Dante's three worlds, Hell, Purgatory and Paradise, are not only geographical regions; his journey through them describes psychological states of man's mind. Sri Aurobindo's exploration of these worlds and the states of consciousness is occult and spiritual. What the poet has done here is to trace the lines of descent of consciousness from spirit to Matter and the ascent of the consciousness from Matter to spirit. It is the poet's original contribution to literature.

The whole journey described in the poem may be considered as a self-contained epic within the larger framework of the poem. In K.R. Srinivasa Iyengar's scholarly assessment, it is "a poetic encyclopedia of occult knowledge and experience."[19] He brings out its symbolic significance by saying; "... it is more properly the matrix of the phenomenal world, the blue print on the divine plan, the key to the drama that is being enacted in the theatre of possibilities."[20]

Aswapathy not only points out the causes of man's suffering and ignorance but also indicates the possible ways and means for liberation of the human soul from its earthly nature and obscurity. Although the journey starts on a personal level, Aswapathy soon becomes the forerunner of human race and his journey assumes cosmic significance. Not only does he present an individual solution to the problem of earthly ignorance but also a universal, a cosmic solution for the liberation of consciousness which is enmeshed in Matter. During his journey he finds out the cosmic design, the forces working behind the veil, working of the universe, the action of the Divine, and the unknown supernal region not yet known to the earthly mind of man. He interprets the working of the universe, the forces behind the working of this world; and indicates how these occult forces influence our life on earth. He interprets the mysterious slow working of the evolutionary process in this universe - its past, present and its future course. His journey is not a discovery of the life on earth, but it is a discovery of the cosmos, a discovery of the life of subtle bodies, invisible beings, their nature and activities. It is a cosmic book on life, Nature and God.

Voyaging through the world-stairs, he passes through the "Kingdoms of Subtle Matter", "The World of the Vital", and "The Kingdoms of Godheads of the Little Life" - the "Powers of the Ignorance", "The Kingdoms and Godheads of the Greater Life." He then makes a descent into the abyss of the Night, finds the reigns of Falsehood, Evil and Darkness, the worse perversions of Life. Like Dante, he goes to the deep core of Hell. In his Ascent he journeys through "The Paradise of the Life of Gods"; "The Kingdoms and Godheads of the Little Mind", "The Kingdoms and Godheads of the Greater Mind"; "The Heavens of the Ideal", "In the self of Mind", "The World-Soul", "The Kingdoms of the Greater Knowledge" and at last he gets the "Beatific Vision and the Boon".

Thus, exploring those many regions Aswapathy records the various levels and gradations of consciousness. He scans the boundaries of human "thought" and analyses the working of the mind of man, its different grades and the characteristics of each type of mind. His journey comprises the psycho-spiritual analysis of human mind. His spiritual ascent presents a concrete proof that the possession of all the planes of consciousness by the human race is not at all alien and unattainable. Through the Integral Yoga of Sri Aurobindo man can ascend the higher planes with steady efforts and self-surrender. He also gives an assurance that a day will come when man will be in possession of these various levels of consciousness and life-divine will be established on earth. His journey is not a romantic escape into other worlds rather it is the subjective effort to reach the higher levels of consciousness. Sri Aurobindo's concrete vision of the occult worlds is the stuff of Aswapathy's journey. His journey appears symbolic to the readers because the earthly mind of man with its terrestrial limitations cannot comprehend these visions as realities. Hence, we attach symbolic significance to the findings of Aswapathy during his journey.

The journey of Aswapathy has no physical reality; it being a journey in spiritual field we confront in it certain psychological states or psycho-spiritual experiences. He descends into the pit of Inconscience and then step-by-step ascends the higher planes of consciousness. He descends to the rungs of Gross Matter, Subtle Matter, insect life, animal, primitive human life, life in the Heroic Age, Kingdom of Falsehood where the Mother of evil is the ruler. He then emerges into light and takes his ascent. Speaking about the ascending series of experiences, Sri Aurobindo records the following lines:

> The principle which underlies this continually ascending experience and vision uplifted beyond the material formulation of things is that all cosmic existence is a complex harmony and does not finish with the limited range of consciousness in which ordinary human mind and life are content to be imprisoned. Being, consciousness, force, substance, descend and ascend a many-runged ladder on each step of which being has a vaster self-extension, consciousness a wider sense of its own range and largeness and joy ..."[21]

How does this ascending series affect the possibilities of our earthly existence? Sri Aurobindo has explained this from a scholarly point of view:

> Our material world is the result of all others, for the other principles have all descended into Matter to create the physical universe, and every particle of what we call Matter contains all of them implicit in itself... And as Matter is the last word of the descent, so it is also the first word of the ascent; as the powers of all these planes, worlds, grades, degrees are involved in the material existence, so are they all capable of evolution out of it... Evolution comes by the unceasing pressure of the supramaterial planes on the material compelling it to deliver out of itself their principles and powers that might conceivably otherwise have slept imprisoned in the rigidity of the material formula.[22]

Viewed from this angle, Aswapathy's symbolic journey opens up the secret wealth of spiritual possibilities for man. We learn from this that man must rise above his title every day self through 'Integral Yoga' as envisioned by Sri Aurobindo. This symbolic journey is a microscopic observation of the structure and functions of different subtler worlds. Pointing out the symbolic significance of Aswapathy's journey, R.K. Singh shows various dimensions of it in his excellent study *Savitri: A Spiritual Epic*:

Aswapathy's yogic movement relates to the philosophical content of the epic which in thematic terms is cosmic salvation through evolution, the characteristic rhythm of which is spiritual transformation: man strives to reach upward from below and brings about a change of his consciousness as also transforms the consciousness of others by an 'inner oneness.' In terms of the main course of action, it concerns the purpose of man is to go beyond his present state of human aspiration for a kingdom of heaven on earth: the consciousness.[23]

Notes

1. Sri Aurobindo, *The Life Divine*, Sri Aurobindo Library, New York, 1951, p. 42.
2. A.B. Purani, *Savitri: An Approach and a Study*, 1970, p.151.
3. D.V.K. Raghavacharyulu, "The Immense Journey Awapathy's Sadhana: An Outline", *Aspects of Indian Writing in English*, ed. M.K. Naik. Macmillan, 1979. p.65.
4. Ibid., p.67.
5. A.B. Purani, op.cit., p.5.
6. K.R.S. Iyengar, *Dawn to Greater Dawn*, Simla: Indian Institute of Advanced Study, p.39.
7. Sri Aurobindo, *Savitri*, op.cit., pp.773-4.
8. Ibid., p.31.
9. Ibid., p.32.
10. Ibid., p.40.
11. K.R.S. Iyengar, op.cit., p.41.
12. Sri Aurobindo, *Savitri*, op.cit., p.50.
13. Ibid., op.cit., p.55,
14. Sri Aurobindo, *Essays on the Gita*, p.65.
15. Sri Aurobindo, *Savitri*, op.cit., p.152.
16. Ibid., p.315.
17. Ibid., p.317.
18. Ibid., p.295.
19. K.R. Srinivasa Iyengar, op.cit., p.45.

20. Ibid., p.45.
21. Sri Aurobindo, *The Life Divine,* Part I, 1977, p .257.
22. Ibid., p.258.
23. R.K. Singh, "The Structure of Savitri" in, *Savitri: A Spiritual Epic,* Bareilly, Prakash Book Depot, 1984, p.76.

6

Major Symbols

Fire Symbol

In ancient times the *Vedas* were regarded as a sacred book of wisdom. It is a great bulk of inspired poetry. Down the ages the *Vedas* have been revered as the "Book of Knowledge." Pointing out the significance of the *Vedas,* Ralph T.H. Griffith, the brilliant commentator and translator of the *Vedas* records:

> These four Vedas are considered to be of divine orgin and to have existed from all eternity, the Rsis or sacred poets to whom the hymns are ascribed being merely inspired seers who saw or received them by sight directly from the Supreme Creator. In accordance with this belief these sacred books have been preserved and handed down with the most reverential care from generation to generation and have accompanied the great army of Aryan immigrants in their onward march from the Land of the Seven Rivers to the Indian Ocean and the Bay of Bengal.[1]

The Vedic *Ṛishi*'s poetic utterances as revealed in the *Vedas* were inspired from higher hidden planes of consciousness. The name given to these Vedic seers 'Kavi' afterwards came to mean any poet. But in those days the word meant a seer of truths. Under the pressure of necessity the Vedic seer poets masked their meaning in symbols and symbolic words. Hence we come across many a symbol and the dominant use of symbolism. The central theme around which all the thoughts move in the *Vedas* is the search for Truth, Light and Immortality. The same is the theme of Sri Aurobindo's *Savitri.*

In the *Vedas,* Fire *(Agni)* is hymned as the supreme and universal God, symbolised as the Divine Will-Force. This Divine Flame, *Agni,* destroys all the powers of falsehood and evil that distracts us from heavenly bliss. According to Sri Aurobindo:

> All puissance of action, strength in the being, beauty of form, splendour of light and knowledge, glory and greatness are the manifestation of *Agni.* And when he is entirely delivered and fulfilled out of the envelope of the world's crookedness this deity of flame and force is revealed as the solar godhead of love and harmony and light.[2]

Such is the symbolic significance of *Agni* as perceived by the ancient Vedic seers. While expounding the Madhuchandas Vaiswāmitra's "Hymn to Agni", written in the *Gāyatri* metre, Sri Aurobindo brings out the symbolic as well as the spiritual significance of fire, *Agni,* in the *Hymns to the Mystic Fire.* The poet explains it in the following lines:

> Because it is he that stands before Yajna, the Divine Master of things; because he is the god whose burning eyes can gaze straight at Truth, at the *Satyam,* the *Vijnānam,* which is the Seer's own aim and desire and on which all Veda is based; because he is the warrior who wars down and removes all the crooked attractions of ignorance and limitation *(asmajjuhuranam enāh)* that stand persistently in the way of the Yogin; because as the vehicle of Tapas, the pure divine superconscious energy which flows from the concealed higher hemisphere of existence, *(avyakta parardha),* he more than any develops and arranges Ānanda, the divine delight.[3]

Fire (*Agni*) is revered as a God in the Hindu Tradition. Fire, as recorded by J.C. Cooper in *An Illustrated Encyclopedia of Traditional Symbols* as per Buddhism symbolises wisdom, which burns all ignorance. Cooper has further catalogued the symbolic significance of fire in different countries and nations. To the Chinese, flame signifies the presence of divinity.[4] In the Christian tradition "Tongues of fire" is the advent of the Holy Spirit; the voice of God; divine revelation.[5] The Hebrew tradition also regards fire as divine revelation.[6] J.C. Cooper mentions: "The Parsee temple has the fire as the Sacred Centre, the place of divinity and the divine light in the soul of man...It is also associated with law and order. In Zoroastrianism the seeds of men and bulls have their origin in fire, not in water."[7] Sri Aurobindo says, "Strength, heat, brilliance, purity, mastery of knowledge and impartiality are his (Fire's) attributes."[8] Fire also destroys in order to create. In its spiritual meaning it is the psychic Godward flame, force, and will of the inner being. Taken symbolically it is a mental power. Fire symbolises the awakening of man's knowledge. In other words, in the esoteric symbolism *Agni* is the manifestation of the flame of divine will and knowledge, divine wisdom and delight in the physical life of man, turning his material life into a spiritual existence. *Agni* is the immortal in mortals, the divine power in man. *Agni* in the *Vedas* is always presented in the double aspect of force and light. "He is the divine power that builds up the worlds, a power which acts always with a perfect knowledge..."[9] Fire also symbolises the inward force of Light and Power. "Fire," according to Sri Aurobindo in the *Veda*, stands as a symbol of "the guardian of Truth, of the ṛtam in man and defends it from the powers of darkness; ..."[10]

The sacrifice made by the Hindus also bears symbolic meaning. The sacrificial fire is the energy of fulfilment through which gods do their work in man. Our passions and baser emotions are the curls of the smoke of *Agni*. Fire destroys, devours, purifies, perfects and then rises upwards. In the *Vedas*, it is said that *Agni* carries our offering to higher powers and brings back in return their force, light and joy into our lives. *Agni* is worshipped first among all the gods because he removes our crookedness, ignorance and limitations and brings to us divine delight. Rightly Sri Aurobindo remarks, "It is a continual self-offering of the human to the divine and a continual descent of the divine into the human which seems to be symbolised in the sacrifice."[11] Sri Aurobindo further draws our attention to the spiritual meaning: "Fire is also the upholder of the Bliss and the Truth by which men attain to the supreme–seated godheads."[12]

The First *Rik* of the *Rig-Veda* begins with an invocation to Agni, adoring the pure, mighty and brilliant God:

> *Agnimile purohitam yajnasya devamrtvijam, hotaram ratnadhatamam.*

The English version of these runs as:

> Agni I adore, who stand before the Lord, the god who seeth Truth, the warrior, strong disposer of delight.[13]

It is very important that in the beginning of the *Rig-Veda,* before all other gods *Agni* alone is invoked. It is *Agni* who stands before *Yajna* the Divine Master of things. *Agni* is also a God – the Master of light. *Agni,* observes Sri Aurobindo, "is a Devata, one of the most brilliant and powerful of the masters of the intelligent mind."[14]

Buddha and Gavishthira invoke *Agni* in Sukta-l of Mandala Fire of the *Rig-Veda.* These are called the 'Hymn of the Morning Sacrifice'.

Dwelling on the symbolic meaning of these hymns, Sri Aurobindo would like the spiritual seekers to take a significant note of it:

> Agni rises towards the luminous paradise, his goal, feeding on the works of the Discernment which distributes the gifts and activities of the sacrifice, becomes a pure energy leading our days and ascends to the Vastness and the Truth. By the Truth he fashions anew our two firmaments, the physical and mental consciousness. This is the golden Affirmation of him in our heavens.[15]

One of the shlokas moulds the symbolic meaning of *Agni* in an affirmative tone. The English version of this shloka rendered by Sri Aurobindo runs as:

> The minds of men who grow in the godhead move entirely towards the flame of Will even as all their seeings converge in the Sun that illumines. When two Dawns of opposite forms are delivered of him, he is born as the White Steed in front of the days.[16]

Sri Aurobindo adds explanatory notes to this *shloka*:

> ..instead of the groping thoughts of other men, their mentality tends to convert itself into a luminous flame of Will that is knowledge and all their thoughts become a blaze of direct vision, the rays of the Sun of Truth.[17]

Explaining the significance of two Dawns, he further writes:

> Day and Night the latter the state of Ignorance that belongs to our material Nature, the former the state of illumined Knowledge that belongs to the divine Mind of which our mentality is a pale and dulled reflection.[18]

M.P. Pandit, a Vedic scholar brings out the symbolic meaning of Fire in the *Vedas* as:

> He is equally the Will in Prana, the dynamic Life-energy... Devouring and enjoying, purifying, preparing, assimilating, forming, he rises upwards always and transfigures his powers into the Maruts, the energies of Mind. Our passions and obscure emotions are the smoke of Agni's burning. All our forces are assured of their action only by his support.

If he is the Will in our nervous being and purifies it by action, he is also the Will in the mind and clarifies it by aspiration..He leads the thoughts towards effective power; he leads the active energies towards light... is the Truth, the Infinity, the vast cosmic Intelligence in which Knowledge and Force are unified. For there all Will is in harmony with the truth of things and therefore effective; all thought part of Wisdom, which is the divine Law, and therefore perfectly regulative of a divine action. *Agni* fulfilled becomes mighty in his own home – in the Truth, the Right, the Vast. It is thither that he is leading upward the aspiration in humanity, the soul of the Aryan, the head of the cosmic sacrifice.[19]

Taking the clue from the Vedic context, Sri Aurobindo seems to have employed 'fire' in *Savitri* as a poetic symbol implying various connotations. In Book One Canto One it appears as follows:

> A fire has come and touched men's hearts and gone;
> A few have caught flame and risen to greater life.[20]

'Fire' symbolises divine energy and power, transcendental light and knowledge. Divine grace and Light has many a time come to earth through the sages and prophets to raise mankind from their murky and mundane existence. Only a few have been inspired by spiritual teachings of those seers, the rest grovel under the same wretched conditions.

There are moments of inspiration, which pour knowledge into us. The activities of the mind come to silence in the presence of a vast luminous knowledge. In the depth of one's being in such a state, lit by the flame of aspiration, one is overwhelmed with the bliss of the Godhead's touch. This is brought out in the following few lines with the help of a fire symbol:

> Our minds hush to a bright Omniscient;
> A voice calls from the chambers of the soul;
> We meet the ecstasy of the Godhead's touch
> In golden privacies of immortal fire.[21]

The "immortal fire" referred to in the lines above is the flame of aspiration in the depth of man's being.

It is not only from above that a change comes; sometimes it comes from within too:

> Or through the earthly coverings something breaks,
> A grace and beauty of spiritual light,
> The murmuring tongue of a celestial fire.[22]

The "celestial fire" symbolises the divine Will and energy in man, his inner inspiration.

'Fire' in the following passage symbolises Power and Light of the Divine Conscious-Force. While Aswapathy's being towers into pathless height his spirit gets a novel experience, divine knowledge drives away his old mentality, his ignorance.

> All that represses our fallen consciousness
> Was taken from him like a forgotten load:
> A fire that seemed the body of a god
> Consumed the limiting figures of the past
> And made large room for a new self to live.[23]

"All that represses our fallen consciousness" are eliminated in a trice by the action of the descending power and Light of the Divine-Conscious Force.

'Spirit's Climbing Fire' symbolises the flame of God-ward aspiration in the heart of every human being in the following lines:

> Always a nameless goal beckons beyond,
> Always ascends the zigzag of the gods
> And upward points the spirit's climbing Fire.[24]

Divine light illuminates the god-ward path and beckons the spirit of man to cross beyond his limitations.

'Enlightening Fire' is the symbol of divine Will and power, God-ward knowledge in the following passage:

> Even while her fingers fumble at the knots
> Which bind them to their strange companionship,
> Into the moments of their married strife
> Sometimes break flashes of the enlightening Fire.[25]

The secret spiritual knowledge that man endeavours to acquire is not in the outside world, it is concealed within his own self "hid behind our minds."

There persists in man's heart an aspiration that one day the highest truth will be known and the face of the divine Reality will be revealed to him through intuitive knowledge. Prophesying the future, the poet-anchorite envisions:

> A fire shall come out of the infinitudes,
> A greater Gnosis shall regard the world
> Crossing out of some far omniscience on
> Lustrous seas from the still rapt alone to
> Illumine the deep heart of self and things.[26]

The 'Fire' referred to in the above passage is the symbol of aspiration, Will of the Supreme.

Aswapathy in his yogic search comes to know that beyond the world of knowledge there is a longing for a Truth, infinite and absolute. His inner self supports this flame of aspiration, which burns upward slowly, mounts to the invisible throne-ascending plane after plane. This flame is a guiding angel on the way to the Infinite. 'Fire' as the symbol of Power, Knowledge, the flame of aspiration occurs again in the following lines:

> A fire along the mystic paths of earth,
> It rises through the mortal's hemisphere,
> Till borne by runners of the Day and Dusk.
> It enters the occult eternal Light
> And clambers whitening to the invisible Throne.[27]

The poet emphatically says that once the flame of aspiration is enkindled, it cannot be extinguished. The above passage contains another symbol, the symbol of Light.

> Armed with the immune occult unsinking
> Fire, the guardians of Eternity keep its law.[28]

'Fire' is the symbol of Divine Will and Force. Aswapathy finds powers equipped with Divine Force guarding the Law of the Eternal entrenched in Truth.

At the end of his journey in consciousness, Aswapathy comes face to face with the Mother of All, the mediatrix between the earth and the supreme. He finds the secret of existence veiled by Nescience in her keeping. She is the 'golden bridge' between earth and heaven, Matter and Spirit and darkness and light. She is described in the epic as the 'wonderful fire'. The 'Fire' symbol has been used to indicate that the Divine Mother through her divine power builds up the worlds, a power which acts with perfect knowledge, a marvellous Flame that leads the creation to its goal. The lines that glow with this symbolic meaning run as follows:

> Hers is the mystery the Night conceals;
> The spirit's alchemist energy is here:
> She is the golden bridge, the wonderful fire.[29]

'Fire' is also referred to as the indwelling invisible Divine, waiting to be realised by man:

> But dim in human hearts the ascending fire,
> The invisible Grandeur sits unworshipped there.[30]

'Fire' symbolises the psychic God-ward flame, the fire of aspiration that burns dim in the human heart, but the Divinity within remains unadorned.

Analysing man's present state, the poet speaks emphatically that man is in love with Ignorance. It is the root of all his pain and suffering. Man has lost contact with the truth that is within his own self. The following passage elucidates the present spiritual state of man:

> The great Illusion wraps him in its veils,
> The soul's deep intimations come in vain,
> In vain is the unending line of seers,
> The sages ponder in unsubstantial light,
> The poets lend their voice to outward dreams,
> A homeless fire inspire the prophet tongues.[31]

'A homeless fire' refers to an errant inspiration which is momentary yet revelatory. Such is the paradox of our life that we fail to understand properly its nature: the life we lead hides spiritual light in us. The ascending flame of spiritual aspiration burns dim in our heart. The invisible grandeur of God sits unadored within us. But intimations from the depth of one's being come in vain intermittently to him. The wise words of the seer, poets and prophets fall flat on our ears.

Human life in this earth follows a scheduled course and no more attempts can scale the difficult paths. As the poet affirms:

> Life was consigned to a safe level path,
> It dare not tempt the great and difficult heights...
> Or leave the world's bounds and, where no limits are,
> Meet with the heart's passion the Adorable
> Or set the world ablaze with the inner Fire.[32]

The 'inner Fire' refers to inner inspiration, the psychic God-ward flame in man. Savitri enters deep into her consciousness in her yogic *sādhanā;* she does not take her "surface person for the soul." She encounters the reasoning mind which governs life within fixed rules and systems. Even religion is narrowed down to conventional worship by this reasoning mind of man. Life is made to move on "a safe and level path." There is no freedom of the spirit. Life does not dare to see the face of the unknown, the Infinite. No one inspires other to accept spiritual life by overcoming mundane existence here.

One of the luminous gods that thronged near her in the course of Savitri's yoga reveals to her "inner divinity". He advises her to follow the path of Truth, the winding highway of the world to its source. There in the silence she would find:

> There in the silence few have ever reached,
> Thou shalt see the Fire burning on the bare stone
> And the deep cavern of thy secret soul.[33]

The 'Fire' refers to the Godward flame, the Tapas. Savitri continues her search of the "birth -place of the occult Fire." She realises that she must search her soul first if she has to save others. One of the Powers admonishes her to follow "the world's winding highway" which leads to the door of man's hidden soul. There in silence she can see the fire burning in the cavern of her secret soul.

Aswapathy comes to know that when a man rises higher and higher in his consciousness and scales the heights of his being, he can realise and perceive a tremendous change in him:

> Ignorance was a thin shade protecting light,
> Imagination the free will of Truth,
> Pleasure a candidate for heaven's fire.[34]

'Heaven's Fire' symbolises in the above lines higher Truth, divine Power and Energy. Aswapathy enters the world of the higher levels of life leaving behind the limits of his physical mind. He sees the blue expanse of life mounting up the Infinite where there is no grief, sorrow, struggle, anger, gloom or hate. The beings of this world experience immortal happiness.

Then Aswapathy comes to know that in the very beginning of the cosmos Spirit was completely immersed in Matter. This indwelling Spirit urged Matter to reveal life, mind and consciousness. 'Immortal fire' symbolises Life in the following passage:

> As comes a goddess to a mortal's breast
> And fills his days with her celestial clasp,
> She stooped to make her home in transcient shapes;
> In Matter's womb she cast the Immortal's fire ..[35]

Fire or flame is thus variously used to symbolise human aspiration for the Divine, Divine Will, Force, and Light, Consciousness, and Truth.

Solar Symbol

The Sun is a Vedic symbol. The Vedic hymns are undoubtedly among the greatest poetic utterances of humanity. The seers of the Vedic hymns depended for knowledge on intuitive mind. Illumination of ideas rather than logical argumentation was their main intention. In the minds of the ancient mystics, everything, the names and sacrifices were turned into potent symbols to cover a secret meaning. Thus, Sun, Cow, Dawn, Wind, Horse, Gold, Light, Night, Fire etc., are used as symbols in the *Vedas* as these have spiritual significance in human life.

Surya, the Sun is conceived in the *Vedas* as the master of Truth, the Illuminator. The solar energy is the physical form of *Surya,*

Lord of Light and Truth on the material plane. It is through Truth that man can arrive at Immortality – such is the final aim of the Vedic seers. Under the images of Sun and its rays, of Dawn and Day and Night, the life of man, his progressive illumination of soul, passes.

Surya enlightens the mind and the thoughts of man with the illumination of Truth and widens its limited movement. *Surya* is conceived by the Aryan seers as the seer and revealer of Truth, the Truth that lies in us, in the phenomenal world. Sri Aurobindo has explained the role of the Sun as the creator in these cogent words:

> Surya, as the creator, as the supreme good, manifests in our human consciousness its concealed heavenly summit on the levels of the pure mind, and we are able to look up above from the earth of our physical existence and are delivered from the obscurities of the night of Ignorance...
>
> All the other gods follow in this march of Surya and they attain to his vastness by the force of his illumination. That is to say, all the other divine faculties or potentialities in man expand with the expansion of the Truth and light in him; in the strength of the ideal supermind they attain to the same infinite amplitude of right becoming, right action and right knowledge.[36]

As the creator, *Surya* creates everything from the burning light and the truth of the infinite Being. Human beings after liberation from Ignorance can attain the first aspect of *Surya* that is the Supreme Light of Truth. He is the impeller of illuminating thought in man. He is the father, fosterer and enlightener of our souls. Thus, in the images of physical Nature, the Vedic seers contemplated our spiritual ascension. Sri Aurobindo wisely points out the struggle of the various forces to possess man's soul:

> The soul of man is a world full of beings, a kingdom in which armies clash to help or hinder a supreme conquest, a house where the gods are our guests and which the demons strive to possess; the fullness of its energies and wideness of its being make a seat of sacrifice spread, arranged and purified for a celestial session.[37]

Savitri herself is the Divine Flame and the Divine Illumination who descends to earth as the Divine Grace. The other name of the Sun is Savitri. The Sun as Savitri is the Creator.

The solar symbolism is very powerful in the *Vedas*. It is interesting to find that Sri Aurobindo has largely drawn the solar symbolism from its Vedic context and has profusely employed it in *Savitri*. The sun represents that Higher Light which leads man to the knowledge of God. K.D. Sethna points out the importance of the Sun symbolism worked out in the fabric of the poem:

> At the back of this tale of conjugal devotion armed with an extreme Will to Life, Sri Aurobindo intuited a wealth of symbol; for the name "Savitri" the *Rig Veda* had given to the supreme creative consciousness emblemed forth as the Sun. It means the Truth-force of the divine Light and by analogy "Satyavan" would mean that Light's Truth-being. So the carrying away of Satyavan by Yama, the God of Death and the combat of Savitri's heart and mind with that inscrutable darkness were felt by Sri Aurobindo to be hinting vaguely the effort celebrated in the Vedic hymns to reclaim by means of Yoga what they call the lost Sun, the divine Light that has got submerged in a material Nature..[38]

The 'Sun' symbolises an inner truth. It is the symbol of the concentrated light of Truth. The "Sun" is also the divine illumining power. Truth is Light, the body of *Surya*. There are four powers of *Surya* as presented in the *Vedas*. These four powers are: Varun, Mitra, Aryaman, and Bhaga. Varuna, points out M.P. Pandit, is the symbol of "a vast purity and clear wideness destructive of all sin and crooked falsehood."[39] Mitra represents "a luminous power of love and comprehension leading and forming into harmony all our thoughts, acts and impulses."[40] Aryaman is the symbol of "an immortal puissance of clear-discerning aspiration and endeavour."[41] Bhaga represents the more puissant aspects of the Sun: "a happy spontaneity of the right enjoyment of all things dispelling the evil dreams of sin and error and suffering".[42]

Discussing the active and passive aspects of the Sun, M.P. Pandit further says: "The name of Surya is seldom used when there is the question of this creation; it is reserved for his passive aspects as the body of the Infinite Light and the revelation. In his active power he is addressed by other names; then he is Savitri, from the same root as Surya, the Creator; or he is Twashtri, the fashioner of things; or he is Pushan, the Increaser—appellations that are sometimes used as if identical with Surya, sometimes as if expressing other forms and even other personalities of this universal Godhead. Savitri, again, manifests himself, especially in the formation of the Truth in man, through four great and active deities, Mitra, Varuns, Bhaga and Aryaman, the Lords of pure Wideness, luminous Harmony, divine Enjoyment, exalted Power."[43]

In the epic Savitri is herself the main symbol etymologically associated with *Surya*, the sun. In the *RigVeda* we come across the word *savitar* which is given to the supreme creative consciousness embodied by the sun that stands for the truth-force of the divine light. The name Satyavan suggests truth. Therefore Savitri and Satyavan conjointly stand for the eternal pair, the primal principles of this great creation that is enshrouded in mystery.

The Sun symbol recurs in the poem, "Heaven's messenger"; it descends to earth to preach their 'sun-thoughts' but the suffering humanity 'bears ill the eternal's touch.' As a result of which the sun-thoughts' of the sons of God get eclipsed. 'Sun-thoughts' are flashes of the higher Truth that have an ethereal origin. In the poem the 'sun' symbol appears in the following lines:

> A glory of lightning traversing the earth-scene,
> Their sun-thoughts fading darkened by ignorant minds.[44]
> The events that shape our lives are born from—
> ...the spirit's sun of hidden powers,
> Digging a tunnel through emergency.[45]

The 'sun' in the above lines is the symbol of the creator.

Speaking of the coming New Age, Sri Aurobindo envisions a transformation of Earth-Nature, when the living breath of the Spirit will animate Matter. New changes will take place:

> Night shall awake to the anthem of the stars;
> The days become a happy pilgrim march,
> Our will a force of the Eternal's power,
> And thought the rays of a spiritual sun.[46]

The 'rays of the spiritual sun' symbolise the outpouring of the Light of knowledge, the Truth-force of the divine light.

As Aswapathy traverses beyond his mortal consciousness, the physical range of the universe, he comes across new worlds quite different from the earth. Realms glowing with higher knowledge and streams of bliss appear before him:

> Sunbelts of knowledge, moonbelts of delight
> Stretched out in an ecstasy of widenesses
> Beyond our indigent corporeal range.[47]

The 'Sun' symbolises higher Truth, Knowledge, and 'Moon' stands for spiritual *Ānanda,* bliss in the lines quoted above.

Aswapathy reaches at the summit of all that can be known. His vision stretches beyond the zenith of creation:

> His sight surpassed creation's head and base;
> Ablaze the triple heavens revealed their suns,
> The obscure Abyss exposed its monstrous rule.[48]

The word 'sun' is the symbol of truth in the above passage. The 'triple heavens' refer to the triple divine worlds of the Supreme *Sat, Chit* and *Ānanda.*

Aswapathy reaches the top of all that can be known. In his new experience in the luminous kingdom of the spirit he feels a new birth of his self:

> He came newborn, infant and limitless
> And grew in the wisdom of the timeless Child;
> He was a vast that soon became a Sun.[49]

His being gathers prophetic knowledge as the "Sun' is the symbol here for seerhood, the revealer of vision. As he is bestowed with seerhood he possesses the ability to know the ultimate truth of all things. In him "A million energies joined and were One."

The Divine Mother is the revealer of our vision, the illuminator and the mistress of truth; thanks to whom we open our path towards the divine and receive truth. These aspects are symbolised by the word 'Sun' in the following lines:

> She is the Force, the inevitable Word,
> The magnet of our difficult ascent,
> The Sun from which we kindle all our suns,[50]

The Divine mother is the light of all things, the origin of all our power and delight. All human efforts for knowledge are directed towards this Divine Power. It is through Her that man will realise unity with all beings.

In a scholarly way Narad explains the importance of pain in human life to the royal couple. He foresees what would have happened if there were no pain in the life of human beings:

If the heart were not forced to want and weep,
His soul would have lain down content, at ease,
And never thought to exceed the human start
And never learned to climb towards the Sun.[51]

The 'Sun' is here the symbol of higher Truth, and supramental knowledge.

A 'superconscient Sun' is the symbol of the supreme Life of Truth–knowledge. In the lines noted below the poet affirms that the Truth-Ray strikes at the very root of thought and sense which are developed in 'a universe of Nescience'. This Truth-Ray aspires towards the supreme Light of Truth-Knowledge:

The sceptic Ray disrupted all that seems
And smote at the very roots of thought and sense.
In a universe of Nescience they have grown,
Aspiring towards a superconscient Sun..[52]

The sun symbolism is invariably couched in supramental and spiritual connotations through out the epic.

Symbol Dawn

The Vedic seers view Dawn as a potent symbol in the *Rig Veda* as the goddess symbolic of new openings, of divine illumination in man's physical consciousness. The light of Dawn is the symbol of an inner illumination. Dawn comes to earth as the bringer of Truth. In the *Rig Veda, Ushā* (dawn) is described as following effectively the path of Truth. The ancient conception of Truth is the path to bliss. *Ushā*, the light of Truth, also brings joy and beatitude. Dawn, too, dispels darkness and evil.

Night in the Vedic writings as a symbol connotes man's obscure consciousness that is full if ignorance. Metaphorically night is unillumined, darkened state of mind. Dawn by the power of its visible dim light dispels this state of ignorance. She is the medium of awakening, the activity and the growth of other gods; and she is indispensable for *Vedic* realisation. As the light of the immortal existence, divine dawn brings out for man the power of Truth and Joy. Dawn is the opening and awakening of the consciousness to truth that comes from above and beyond. It is the opening out of the Supreme illumination on the night of human ignorance. Referring to the symbolic significance of the Divine Dawn, Sri Aurobindo points out:

> This Dawn illumines not only our earth but all the worlds. She brings out into expression the successive planes of our existence so that we may look upon all 'the diverse lives' of which we are capable. She reveals them by the eye of the Sun and fronting the worlds of the becoming she stands aloft over them all as the vision of immortality.[53]

The idea of Truth is associated with *Ushā*. It is from the seat of the Truth that the dawn awakes, say the *Vedas*. In the *Vedas* it is mentioned that she leads man on the divine path. She gives to mortals the impelling force and vast energy to proceed on the path of Truth. The opening line of the poem, "It was an hour before the Gods awake", refers to the time between the last phase of night and the first phase of dawn. The time, though not extraordinary, is yet replete with symbolic significance. A short account of 'mute' stirrings—"something in the inscrutable darkness stirred" and "insensibly some where a breach began" while the night "Lay stretched immobile"—are presented in the poem as the description of dawn. Dawn is not only the beg- inning of a day but also a period of transition called twilight. For Savitri, it heralds the day her husband is destined to die. Thus, dawn is both an optimistic and a pessimistic symbol as Savitri's – the human potential for godhead – heart is filled with "anguish" in her spiritual odyssey. Dawn for Savitri symbolises both mortality and immortality. It is also a day of her conquest over Death.

The "divine event" also symbolically means the Dawn of the Supermind. Night too is used here as a potent symbol. It may refer to Inconscience. The coexistence of 'dawn' and 'night' is fraught with symbolic significance in regard to Sri Aurobindo's philosophical pronouncements. Matter like night is 'opaque', 'impenetrable'. The 'mind of Night' refers to the spark of consciousness involved in Matter. The movement from the stage of night towards dawn through twilight can be viewed as the process of evolution. Evolution took place in the past from Matter to Life and to Mind. The evolution of Matter is possible only because there has been an involution of the Spirit into Matter. Explaining Sri Aurobindo's theoretical treatment of the process of terrestrial evolution, V. Madhusudan Reddy says:

> This inevitable evolution first develops, as it is bound to develop Matter and a Material Universe. In Matter, Life appears and living physical beings. In Life, Mind manifests embodied thinking and living beings; in Mind, ever increasing its power and activities in forms of Matter, the Supermind or Truth-Consciousness must appear invevitably.[54]

The secret burden and intention of evolution is the manifestation of a spiritual being, the divine life of supramental consciousness on earth. Dawn refers to the manifestation of a race of supramental being or superman. Thus, the opening few lines implicitly refer to Sri Aurobindo's philosophy of evolution. In Nature's primal works Matter alone appeared as "the sole, dumb and stark cosmic reality".

Sri Aurobindo makes use of the "symbol dawn" in the poem with its varied undertones. As in the darkness enveloping the earth dawn comes as a bringer of light and illumines the whole of earth, so also in the crucial period of human life Savitri comes down as the dawn, the bringer of light. Nolini Kanta Gupta finds out a new aspect of the use of symbol dawn in the beginning Canto:

> Savitri represents one such divine dawn at a crucial moment of earth-life. She embodies creation's entire past and shows in her life how that past is transformed through the alchemy of Divine Grace to a glorious future – the inevitable destiny that awaits man and earth.[55]

Cantos One and Two of Book One of *Savitri* are the poetic explication of the symbolic role of Savitri. She is to bring the god-light, immortality to earth from the clutches of Death, Yama, who is the godhead of Inconscience by reviving the life of Satyavan. The Dawn also symbolises the descent of Grace from above. This

Dawn illumines the consciousness of man and dispels ignorance, which he is steeped in. The "divine Event" alluded to in the opening Canto of the poem signifies the outbreak of consciousness in man. Dawn also symbolises the outbreak of spirit in Matter, which is the central theme of *Savitri*. The goal of man is to find out the secret light of Truth, which leads to divine existence – the symbol dawn illumines this path. Dawn symbolises the emergence of Knowledge from Ignorance in which man is entrenched and entrapped.

Dawn in the beginning of the poem is the herald of the establishment of the Supramental Age. But this Supramental Age is not going to be established until there is advancement in the growth of the consciousness in man. K.D. Sethna explains the 'Symbol Dawn' in an insightful manner giving a new twist to the symbolic implication:

> ..the 'Symbol Dawn' unfolds the panorama of a gradual rousing of consciousness on its way to the archetypal Superconscience and then the advent of this Superconscience itself in a passing spell of spiritual light - presage of Earth one day receiving and embodying the Divine in a supreme transfiguration of Mind and Life-force and Matter through the Soul's full awakening to the Suprmmental Reality that has to emerge and evolve here. The work that Savitri will do, bringing Satyavan back from the clutch of Death, of Yama who is the godhead of Inconscience, and making possible to earth the immortality of the superconscient Gods of Light, is prophesied by this dawn of the very day on which Satyavan must die.[56]

Dawn in its mystical note symbolises the descending of the light from the Supramental region to the lower Nature in order to transform it. She will open the way to the Truth of divine existence. Like the stages in the coming of the physical dawn, there are also stages in the growth of man's consciousness. So 'Dawn' symbolises the coming of a New Consciousness. Sri Aurobindo calls this new consciousnes—Supermind, or Supramental Truth–Consciousness. As in the *Vedas* so also in Sri Aurobindo's epic, dawn symbolises the coming of Savitri, who will bring joy and truth. As the physical dawn dispels darkness, Ṣavitri as the lady messiah in the vision of the poet in his literary treatment will dispel falsehood, ignorance, and suffering from the bosom of

Mother Earth. Hers is the "labour of the battling gods" to implant the divine life on earth. Like the dawn in the *Vedas,* Savitri will bring the Truth of immortal existence, the truth of life on earth. By this Truth, she will establish bliss, *Āanandā,* and extricate mankind from the evils of suffering and death.

The "greater dawn" mentioned at the end of the poem, reveals to us another existence of life, the divine-life. If sincere efforts are made, mankind is capable of establishing divine-life. The 'dawn' in the end gives us a vision of immortality, truth and harmony of life. Dawn spreads the message that a new race of human being will live on earth leading a life of peace, harmony, beauty and bliss. The "divine Event" referred to in the beginning of the poem portends this sort of achievement for mankind. Dawn brings the message that Supramental Truth allied with Love and Grace will raise man up from his limitations of death, desire and incapacity.

Dawn also symbolises the evolutionary rise of earth and the descent of Savitri from the region of Superconscience into human consciousness. Reading the literal meaning of dawn, K.R. Srinivasa Iyengar points out:

> The movement from darkness to light; the movement from the cosmic drowse of inconscience to the first stirrings of consciousness and then to the full awakening of consciousness; and the movement of Savitri from her superconscient divine calm and felicity towards earth consciousness in response to the stir of human life and human need and her resolute awakening to meet the human need and earth's challenge, - these three movements coalesce in the "Symbol Dawn" to set the stage and start the action of the poem.[57]

Sri Aurobindo reveals the symbolic meaning of dawn as the outpouring of divine light in *The Secret of the Veda*:

> Dawn the daughter of Heaven, the face or power of Aditi, is the constant opening out of the divine light upon the human being; she is the coming of the spiritual riches,a light, a power, a new birth, the pouring out of the golden treasure of heaven into his earthly existence.[58]

Sri Aurobindo has rendered a few hymns of the *Vedas* into English with his own commentary. These verses in English are known as

"Hymns to the Dawn". In this connection he says, "The Rishi hymns the divine Dawn, daughter of Heaven, as the bringer of truth, the bliss, the heavens of light, creator of the Light, giver of vision, maker, follower, leader of the path of Truth, remover of the darkness, the eternal and ever youthful goddess of our godward journeying."[59] He has translated a few hymns, which connote the meaning of the above passage. Some of these hymns in English version run as:

> Dawn of the luminous journey, Dawn queen of truth, large with the Truth, how wide is the gleam from her rosy limbs, - Dawn divine who brings with her the heaven of light! Her seers adore with their thoughts.[60]
>
> This is she who yokes her cows of rosy light; her journey does not fail and such is the treasure she makes that it passes not away. She hews out our paths to happiness; divine is she, far-shining her glory, many the hymns that rise to her, she brings with her every boon.[61]
>
> Lo, how brilliant is her body when she is found and known! How she stands on high as if bathing in light that we may have vision! Driving away all enemies and all darkness, Dawn, the daughter of Heaven, has come with the Light.[62]

Sri Aurobindo is the first poet and scholar to have made an authoritative exposition of the symbolic significance of the *Vedas.* As it has already been indicated earlier, M.P. Pandit enlists the symbolic meaning of a number of words used in the *Vedas.* Indicating the symbolic meaning of dawn, Pandit too, points out:

> Dawn is ..the illumination of the Truth rising upon the mentality to bring the day of full consciousness into the darkness or half-lit night of our being. The goddess is symbolic of new openings of divine illumination on man's physical consciousness. She alternates with her sister Night; but that darkness itself is a mother of light and always Dawn comes to reveal what the black-browed Mother has prepared.[63]

Pandit identifies the divine Dawn as the force or face of Aditi. Dawn, the daughter of Heaven, and Night, her sister are the obverse and reverse sides of the same "Eternal Infinite." If 'Night' symbolises Inconscience (nescience), dawn symbolises the breaking out of a new age, new consciousness. As night conceals the dawn in her, so also Inconscience hides Superconscience. Dawn gradually emerges from the deep darkness of night; so also consciousness is supposed to emerge from Inconscience through the medium of human mind and progress towards Supramental consciousness. Night and dawn in Sri Aurobindo's poetry have been consistently employed as complimentary symbols, which focus his futuristic vision of earth's evolution.

There is a constant rhythm and alternation of night and dawn, illumination of the light and periods of exile from it, openings up of our darkness and it's settling upon us once more till the celestial Birth is accomplished. In a metaphorical way in the Vedic context 'night' and 'dawn' are of different forms but supposed to be of one mind that suckles alternatively the same luminous Child.

The Triple Dawn is the symbol of the three luminous realms of Swar, the Divine Mind, on the human mentality.

Savitri is psychic, mystic and spiritual poetry. The symbols used in *Savitri* are very unfamiliar to the common readers of poetry. In the opening Canto of the epic, the symbol-Dawn is related to the Vedic goddess *Ushā*, dawn. Far from these symbolic meanings A. B. Purani makes a different interpretation of the symbol dawn. To him it symbolises the continuity, the ever-fresh continuity of the process of Time. It is in effect Time-Eternity in contrast to Timelessness-Eternity of the Absolute. In his poem "In Horis Eternum" Sri Aurobindo calls the sun – "A blazing eye of Time watching the motionless day." For, in the sight of the sun the day is eternal. Ordinarily dawn stands for life eternal – life ever fresh, life ever beautiful. But, "In *Savitri* it symbolises the perpetual awakening of the light of consciousness from the Night of Nescience which gives rise to the cosmos and awakens in man the aspiration for the Spirit from the normal state of ignorance."[64]

In the epic 'The Symbol-Dawn' is an intimation of the coming of a new Age of Consciousness to put an end to the reign of ignorance. K.R. Srinivasa Iyengar provides a lucid explanation to the symbol Dawn to the human divine role of the protagonist:

> It means really a sharp ascent of consciousness, from the somnolence or nightmare or inconsciene of sleep to the normal waking consciousness governed by the affections and by the faculty of reason. But this Dawn also means, for

> a realised Yogi like Savitri whose habitual stance of consciousness is the supramental, for Savitri the physical dawn could mean the necessity for a descent from her habitual poise in the spirit to meet the demand of day..[65]

In summing up we can say that the symbolism of dawn as used by the poet in the epic is central and implies the dawning of a new consciousness in human society. It proposes a new age for man on earth, hence the establishment of a new race of human beings.

LIGHT

Truth and Light are synonymous words in the conception of the Vedic Seers. *Surya* is the supreme Light of the Truth attained by human beings only when they are liberated from the clutches of Ignorance. The light of *Surya* is the body or the form of divine vision. Describing the symbolic meaning of Light in the *Vedas*, Pandit explains that Light is, "A symbol of knowledge, of spiritual illumination. *Surya* is the Lord of the Supreme Sight, the vast Light, *bṛhat jyotih*, or as it is sometimes called, the true Light, *ṛtam jyotih.*"[66]

The Sun is the source of all light and life. At the literal, metaphorical and symbolic levels in *Savitri* the symbol of light plays a significant role. Poets have invariably taken recourse to light symbolism to describe their ineffable vision of the Supreme, the Absolute. Prema Nanda Kumar makes an insightful interpretation of light symbolism in *Savitri*:

> *Savitri* is of course a blaze of light. We begin with the symbol dawn and watch all the different shades of light in the course of a single day. Nor is this light-symbolism of the mystics to be wondered at, for that is the purest form of nature that can be used by them for conveying their feelings.[67]

Savitri's charismatic personality reveals to her playmates her inner divinity. The poet indicates her divine qualities through light-symbolism:

> Almost they saw who lived within her light
> Her playmate in the sempiternal spheres
> Descended from its unattainable realms
> In her attracting advent's luminous wake.[68]

'Light symbolises the manifestation of divinity, the action of certain hidden divine forces in Savitri even in her human body.

Aswapathy frees himself from the sight of the world of 'Names and Forms in Ignorance' and enters the realm of Spirit. He is confronted by a tremendous and vast silence:

> A formless stillness called, a nameless Light.
> Above him was the white immobile Ray,
> Around him the eternal Silences.[69]

This 'nameless Light' refers to divine illumination. The "white Ray" symbolises purity and power of divinity. When man transcends his mortal limit:

> A line of the Transcendent meets our road...
> A ripple of Light and glory wraps the brain,
> And traveling down the moment's vanishing route
> The figures of eternity arrive.[70]

Light is the symbol here of illumination of consciousness.

"Earth's doubting future" paradoxically contains a bright future for man. The poet prophetically utters with singular clarity:

> Earth's doubting future hides our heritage:
> The Light now distant shall grow native here,...[71]

'Light' stands here for the opening of subtle vision and the establishment of Truth.

All the movements of the cosmic *Shakti* are governed by the Being of the Eternal. In creating this solid universe of Matter out of the womb of the Infinite, the creative puissance is governed by the Truth–Idea at the origin. Light as the symbol of omniscient knowledge is used in the following lines:

> Out of the Void's unseeing energies
> Inventing the scene of a concrete universe,
> By his thought she has fixed its paces, in its blind acts,
> She sees by flashes by his all-knowing Light.[72]

The Wisdom, *Prajnā* of the Eternal is symbolically suggested as the expression 'all-knowing Light.'

Aswapathy gathers horrible experience in his "Descent into Night". The air in this realm is rife with evil and falsehood. Things are in a state of topsy-turvy and Truth is deliberately perverted in this region. He develops a feeling that to walk in this domain safely, one has to invoke the presence of God. Speaking about the courage of such people the poet indicates:

Only were safe who kept God in their hearts:

> Courage their armour, faith their sword, they must walk,
> The hand ready to smite, the eye to scout,
> Casting a javelin regard in front,
> Heroes and soldiers of the army of Light.[73]

The "army of Light" symbolically suggests the defenders of Truth in the lines above. These defenders of Truth possess unfailing courage and strong faith for they can wield their weapons potently against the enemy who are safe in this realm of falsehood.

In the "Kingdoms of the Greater Knowledge" beings having wider consciousness make friendship with him. He gathers a novel experience like that of:

> The primal Energy took him in its arms;
> His brain was wrapped in overwhelming Light,
> An all-embracing knowledge seized his heart.[74]

'Light' refers to divine illumination, to knowledge.

Aswapathy in his ascent reaches a height where hope and search cease: where all forms fall off and there the poet affirms:

> On a dizzy verge where all disguises fail
> And human mind must abdicate in Light
> Or die like a moth in the naked blaze of Truth,
> He stood compelled to a tremendous choice.[75]

'Light' stands for manifestation of divine qualities, of spiritual illumination in man's heart and mind.

Aswapathy's being grows too wide for his single self in the presence of the Divine Mother. His heart's demand remains unfathomed, measureless:

> His single freedom could not satisfy,
> Her light, her bliss he asked for earth and men.[76]

The Mother's Light symbolises spiritual manifestation of Divine Grace. The same meaning of the light symbol is conveyed in the following lines:

> This Light comes not by struggle or by thought;
> In the mind's silence the Transcendent acts
> And the hushed heart hears the unuttered Word.[77]

Aswapathy's realised Knowledge becomes the seed of a new creation. He now realises a living oneness with the surging multitudes. The cosmos seem to rise out of the secret knowledge of him. This knowledge does not need any sheath of ignorance. He is able to see by the light of this knowledge a new marvellous creation. So the poet points out that light in the following lines symbolises divine knowledge:

> This knowledge was now made a cosmos' seed:
> This seed was cased in the safety of the Light,
> It needed not a sheath of Ignorance.[78]

Savitri in Book IV Canto I is referred to as 'flame' and 'incarnate flame' – the Wisdom and Power of the Supreme. The poet says that her mind has a divine origin:

> A mind of light, a life of rhythmic force,
> A body instinct with hidden divinity
> Prepared an image of the coming God.[79]

'Light' above refers to the divine and intuitive knowledge of Savitri.

Even those who come nearer to Savitri find in her a hidden divinity. 'Ray' and 'Light' refer to Savitri's divine qualities, her wisdom and knowledge in the following lines:

> For even the close partners of her thoughts
> Who could have walked the nearest to her ray,
> Worshipped the power and light they felt in her
> But could not match the measure of her soul.[80]

The poet prophetically utters divine help for Savitri in terms of light symbolism. 'Light' below symbolises the Grace of the Divine:

> One force shall be your mover and your guide,
> One light shall be around you and within..[81]

In terms of light symbolism the poet suggests sage's sacrificial work. 'Light' in the following lines symbolises Truth and Knowledge.

Taught the great Truth to which man's race must rise
Or opened the gates of freedom to a few,
Imparting to our struggling world the Light...[82]

One in the crowd apprises Savitri of their functions:

In evil we light the deathless flame of good
And hold the torch of knowledge on ignorant roads;
We are thy will and all men's will towards Light.[83]

'Light' points to the divine path that leads mankind to the Absolute.

Light in the sense of divine illumination, the Supreme appears in the following passage:

A few I guide who pass me towards the Light;
A few I save, the mass falls back unsaved;
A few I help, the many strive and fail.

But my heart I have hardened and I do my work:
Slowly the Light grows greater in the East,
Slowly the world progresses on God's road.[84]

In terms of light symbolism the Woman reveals to Savitri her divine power.

In the following passage flame is a symbol of spiritual force, the presence of divinity, and the unseen energy in existence; so it is referred to as deathless Flame:

On the other side of the eternal stairs
The mighty kingdoms of the deathless Flame
Aspired to reach the Being's absolutes.
Out of the sorrow and darkness of the world,
Out of the depths where life and thought are tombed,
Lonely mounts up to heaven the deathless Flame.[85]

On one side of the ascending stair of the new realm Aswapathy sees the" Kingdom of the world of Bliss", the deathless Rose. On the other side he sees the great and potent 'Kingdom of Knowledge' aspiring to reach the Supreme Being. This flame of knowledge, the unfolding consciousness breaks out from the depth of the nescience, where there is pain and suffering.

NIGHT

In the *Vedas* darkness or night is the symbol of the ignorant mentality. It is the symbol of our obscure consciousness, of the stumbling will and act that obstruct all progress. It also symbolises evil, sin and suffering. From among the listed Vedic symbols, M.P. Pandit draws our attention to the symbolic meaning of Night in the *Vedas*:

> The great darkness of the Inconscient is the *Vedic Night*, which holds the world and all its unrevealed potentialities in her obscure bosom. Night extends her realm over this triple world of ours and out of her in heaven, in the mental being, Dawn is born who delivers the Sun out of the darkness where it was lying concealed and eclipsed and creates the vision of the supreme day.[86]

'Night' and 'Day' taken from their Vedic context stand as poetic symbols of the alternation of the divine and human consciousness in man.

It is not the physical manifestation of night that is described in the epic. The vivid presentation of night in the beginning of the epic is quite symbolic and calls for deep understanding of the total meaning of the poem. The following passage is quite suggestive in its symbolic interpretation.

> It was the hour before the Gods awake.
> Across the path of the divine Event
> The huge foreboding mind of Night, alone
> In her unlit temple of eternity,
> Lay stretched immobile upon Silence'marge.[87]

The poetic description of Night that prevails before the outbreak of the Dawn does not refer to physical darkness. This darkness is subjective of many layers of meaning. It indicates Nescience, a term typically designed by Sri Aurobindo that reigned before the cosmos was created. A.B. Purani is of the opinion that the condition of the darkness described as Night here has a resemblance to the primordial condition described in the *Rig Veda* in a hymn generally called the Hymn of creation.

Based on his observation of the *Rig-Veda,* A.B. Purani makes pertinent remarks about these beginning lines of *Savitri*:

> The condition described here is pre-existent to Being as well as Non-being. Nor was there 'day and night' i.e. time. In the beginning darkness was hidden by darkness – all this was an ocean of inconscience. That is the Night of Savitri, a condition of Nescience in which nothing had yet emerged – not even matter – and yet everything was there from which the cosmos could emerge.[88]

The premeditated thought to employ night symbolism in the epic is clear the way the poet himself explains the significance of the symbol to meet the query of a reader in a letter:

> The attempt at mystic spiritual poetry of the kind I am at demands above all a spiritual objectivity, an intense psychophysical concreteness... That darkness itself is described as a quietude, which gives it a subjective spiritual character and brings out the thing symbolised, but the double epithet 'inert black' gives it the needed concreteness so that the quietude ceases to be something abstract and becomes something concrete, objective, but still spiritually subjective.[89]

K. D. Sethna interprets the double suggestiveness of the night-symbol as: "..the night-symbol may be considered a double one. It is suggestive or representative not only of a temporary relapse into Inconscience but also of a fundamental fall which constitutes the God-oblivious state on a cosmic scale."[90] The growth of divine potentialities in man is described in the *Vedas* as the growth of a Child. Sri Aurobindo uses the same Vedic symbol in the following lines along with the symbols of 'night' and 'dawn':

> His mind could not rest on a supernal ground
> And look down on the magic and the play
> Where the God-child lies on the lap of Night and Dawn
> And the Everlasting puts on Time's disguise.[91]

The divine potentialities in man grow alternatively through the state of Ignorance, i.e., symbolised by Night and the rise in one's consciousness that is suggested by the word Dawn in the lines above. The coexistence of night and dawn symbols is significant in human life.

Primordially life on the earth has passed through the obscurity of the Inconscience. But in the depth of the Inconscience burns a flame of aspiration that yearns for the supreme consciousness. Life and mind, which embody the ray of Light, the tongue of Fire to grow upward, are the various forms of the cosmic movements. 'Night' in the following passage is the symbol of darkness, Inconscience

> An aspiration in the Night's profound,
> Seed of a perishing body and half-lit mind,
> Uplifts its lonely tongue of conscious fire
> Towards an undying Light for ever lost.[92]

In the above lines 'Light' symbolises the Supreme consciousness, which is the source of all knowledge.

The evolving being on this earth is borne by the Nature-Power from the beginning of his emergence in the Nescience of Matter to the summit of superconscient Existence. The poet employs 'Light' and 'Night' symbols to convey this theoretical assumption:

> His spirit survives amid the death of things,
> He climbs to eternity through being's gaps,
> He is carried by her from Night to deathless Light.[93]

All organisms perish, body dies in this changing world but our soul survives, it has no death. The soul passes through various lives to ascend towards Godhead.

In the transformation of earth-nature Matter will be inducted with Spirit to become in future completely spiritualised which is set goal of earth's evolution otherwise known as God's *līlā*, Illusion. Night that symbolises unconsciousness will be lit with flashes of consciousness. The mind of man being no more couched in Ignorance will become a vessel for steady outpouring of divine knowledge and truth. The seer gives prophetic utterance to the transformation of Earth-Nature:

> In Matter shall be lit the spirit's glow,
> In body and body kindled the sacred birth;
> Night shall awake to the anthem of the stars,
> The days become a happy pilgrim march,
> Our will a force of the Eternal's power,
> And thought the rays of a spiritual sun.[94]

'Night' symbolises the states of unconsciousness. The spiritual sun refers to the supramental Knowledge.

In a world perverted by Inconscience, unconsciousness, the Life Force struggles to manifest higher consciousness. In the midst of death, decay and suffering, life continues to grovel under eath's weight because Nature labours hard to execute the mysterious covenant made by God with the Nescience, which is symbolised by Night in the following lines:

> The will to know in an inconscient world,
> The will to live under a reign of death,
> The thirst for rapture in a heart of flesh,
> And works out through the appearance of a soul
> By a miraculous birth in plasm and gas
> The mystery of God's covenant with the Night.[95]

Aswapathy describes the mysterious changes that have come to Life since the beginning of the cosmos when Spirit was completely immersed in Matter. The imprisoned life in the transformation of earth was compelled to release mind and then mind developed various types of consciousness. But before life could establish its perfect glory upon earth with the fully manifested perfect consciousness "A dark, ambiguous Presence questioned All." Thus, we see that darkness itself is a part of the working of the process of the Divine Will. The poet reveals this metaphysical concept in the following lines:

> The secret Will that robes itself with Night
> And offers to spirit the ordeal of the flesh,
> Imposed a mystic mask of death and pain.[96]

Night being the symbol of darkness, ignorance and nescience covers the secret Will. In another passage 'Night' symbolises the contraries of life – suffering, failure of consciousness. The creation is based on contraries. The creative triune states *Sat, Chit* and *Ānanda* in the distant past was confronted with their opposites in its downward plunge. *Chit,* consciousness turned into Nescience, absence of consciousness. *Ānanda,* Bliss was transformed into pain and suffering. Life was forced to make a compromising existence with Death and nescience which is indicated in the lines below:

> Life here was intimate with Death and Night
> And ate Death's food that she might breathe awhile;
> She was their inmate and adopted waif.[97]

Aswapathy expresses his worry for the precarious state of man, a mid-being who is a compromise between beast and God. Using night symbolism, he reverentially complains his worriness to the Divine Mother. How long man has to suffer the pangs of ignorance? The pity is man suffers defeat and death even though he carries in him the immortal Force, even though he is said to be the architect of divine humanity. Night symbolism recurs again to indicate cosmic Evil:

> How long shall our spirits battle with the Night
> And bear defeat and the brute yoke of Death,
> We who are vessels of a deathless Force
> And builders of the godhead of the race?[98]

When Aswapathy gets the "Vision and the Boon", 'Night' symbolism is used to suggest evil power, the forces of darkness that rule over earth:

> A witness to God's parley with the Night,
> It leaned compassionate from immortal calm
> And housed desire, the troubled seed of things.[99]

References

1. Ralph T.H. Griffith, *The Vedas,* p.1.
2. Sri Aurobindo, *The Secret of the Veda,* Centenary Edition, Vol. X, p.358.
3. Sri Aurobindo, Hymns to the Mystic Fire, *Centenary Edition, 1971, p.439.*
4. *J.C. Cooper,* An Illustrated Encyclopedia of Traditional Symbols, *1978, p.67.*
5. Ibid., p.67.
6. Ibid., p.67.
7. Ibid., p.68.
8. Sri Aurobindo, Hymns to the Mystic Fire, *Centenary Edition,* Vol.II, 1971, p.442.
9. Sri Aurobindo, *The Secret of the Veda,* op.cit., 1871, p.61.
10. Ibid., p.63.
11. Ibid., p.62.
12. Ibid., p.397.
13. Sri Aurobindo, *Hymns to the Mystic Fire,* op.cit., Vol.II, 1971, p.40.

14. Ibid., p.443.
15. Sri Aurobindo, *The Secret of the Veda,* op.cit., p.364.
16. Ibid., pp.364-65.
17. Ibid., p.364.
18. Ibid., pp.364-65.
19. M.P. Pandit, *Key to the Vedic Symbolism,* 1973, pp.7-8.
20. Sri Aurobindo, *Savitri,* p.7.
21. Ibid., p.48.
22. Ibid., p.48.
23. Ibid., p.81.
24. Ibid., p.238.
25. Ibid., p.258.
26. Ibid., p.258.
27. Ibid., pp.279-80.
28. Ibid., p. 321.
29. Ibid., p.314.
30. Ibid., p.371.
31. Ibid.
32. Ibid., pp. 496-97.
33. Ibid., p.502.
34. Ibid., p.124.
35. Ibid., p.130.
36. Sri Aurobindo, *The Secret of the Vedas,* Centenary Edition, 1972, p.278.
37. Sri Aurobindo, *Hymns to the Mystic Fire,* Centenary Edition, vol.xi, p.34.
38. K.D. Sethna, *The Poet Genius of Sri Aurobindo,* 1974, p.106.
39. M.P. Pandit, *Key to Vedic Symbolism,* op.cit., 1971, p.76.
40. Ibid.
41. Ibid.
42. Ibid.
43. Ibid., pp. 76-7.
44. Sri Aurobindo, *Savitri,* op.cit., 1977, p.7.
45. Ibid., p.52.
46. Ibid., p.55.
47. Ibid., p.91
48. Ibid., p.300.
49. Ibid., p.301.

50. Ibid., p.314.
51. Ibid., p.443.
52. Ibid.
53. Sri Aurobindo, *The Secret of the Veda,* op.cit., pp.431-32.
54. V.Madhusudan Reddy, *Sri Aurobindo's Philosophy of Evolution,* Hyderadabad: Institute of Human Study, 1966, p.233.
55. *Collected Works of Nolimi Kant Gupta* IV (Pondicherry: Sri Aurobindo International Centre of Education, 1971), p.307.
56. K.D. Sethna, *Sri Aurobindo: The Poet,* (1970), p.183.
57. K.R. Srinivasa Iyengar, "The First Canto of Sri Aurobindo's Savitri," *Critical Essays on Indian Writing in English,* 1968, pp.142-3.
58. Sri Aurobindo, *The Secret of the Vedas,* op.cit., p.527.
59. Ibid., p.527.
60. Ibid.
61. Ibid., p.527.
62. Ibid., p.528.
63. M.P. Pandit, op.cit., p.24.
64. A.B.Purani, *Savitri: An Approach and a Study,* 1970.pp.126-7.
65. K.R.Srinivasa Iyengar, *Dawn to Greater Dawn,* 1975.p.100.
66. M.P. Pandit, *Key to Vedic Symbolism,* p.39.
67. Prema Nanda Kumar, *Dante and Sri Aurobindo,* p.132.
68. Sri Aurobindo, *Savitri,* p. 16.
69. Ibid., p.102.
70. Ibid., p.110.
71 Ibid.
72. Ibid., p.121.
73. Ibid., p.211.
74. Ibid., pp. 301-02.
75. Ibid., .306
76. Ibid., p.315.
77. Ibid.
78. Ibid., p.323.
79. Ibid., p.357.
80. Ibid., p.363.
81. Ibid., p.374.
82. Ibid., p.383.
83. Ibid., p.501.
84. Ibid., p.510.

85. Ibid., p.279.
86. M.P. Pandit, op.cit., pp.52-3.
87. Sri Aurobindo, *Savitri*, p.1.
88. A.B. Purani, op.cit., pp.127-8.
89. *Savitri*, pp.750-52.
90. K.D. Sethna, *Sri Aurobindo - The Poet*, p.183.
91. Sri Aurobindo, *Savitri*, p.36.
92. Ibid., p.50.
93. Ibid., p.64.
94. Ibid., p.55.
95. Ibid., p.75.
96. Ibid., p.130.
97. Ibid., p.135.
98. Ibid., p.341.
99. Ibid.,p.340.

7

Other Symbols

Let us analyse other *Vedic* and *Upanishadic* minor symbols that Sri Aurobindo was so fond of, and artistically employed them in the poem to lend a mystical meaning. In the psycho-spiritual journey that expanded his consciousness, Aswapathy passes beyond the workings of earthly Nature to reach the height of Godhood. The downward pull of the laws of the Inconscient no more holds back his winging spirit. In "The Yoga of the King" there occur the following lines:

> The python coils of the restricting Law
> Could not restrain the swift arisen God: ...[1]

A.B. Purani makes a pertinent comment on this passage by bringing out the symbolic meaning of 'python-coils', with the support of some lines from the *Rig Veda.*

> The 'python-coils' reminds us of *Ahi-Vritra* of the *Rig Veda* where it is symbolic of the coils of Ignorance enveloping the human being restricting his freedom and knowledge.[2]

Savitri in the Canto entitled "The Entry into the Inner Countries" comes across a Voice who advises her that God has to accept human limitations as he did as a Dwarf to measure the cosmos with triple strides:

> For man thou seekest, not for thyself alone.
> Only if God assumes the human mind
> And puts on mortal ignorance for his cloak
> And makes himself the Dwarf with triple stride,
> Can he help man to grow into the God.[3]

The 'Dwarf' refers to a story of Indian mythology and instantly brings to the Hindu mind the Incarnation of Vishnu as Vamana, who is believed to have measured the three worlds (in 'triple stride') – the material, the vital and the mental. In the *Rig Veda* there is a symbolic reference to this story, which was later on enlarged in the *Puranas.*

One of the *Vedic* hymns reverberates in the following passage with its symbol of 'red-Wolf', which indicates Aswapathy's journey:

> In menacing tracts, in tortured solitudes
> Companionless he roamed through desolate ways
> Where the red Wolf waits by the fordless stream.[4]

The original hymn as quoted by A.B. Purani in his book reads as:

> *Aruno mā sakrit patha yantam dadarsha hi.*[5]

The English translated version quoted by Purani runs as: "Once the red-Wolf saw me walking on the path."[6]

The Red Wolf is the symbol of evil force that suddenly falls upon, destroys and tears its prey. The beast is the symbol that glows with the meaning of destructive, cruelty and unscrupulous powers of the lower Darkness. Sri Aruobindo in *Savitri* makes the symbol more effective, improving spontaneously upon the original in the alchemy of his poetical process by the image of 'fordless stream'. In the original hymn there is only 'path'. The "fordless stream" brings in the needed element of danger and difficulty on the path of the aspirant when he has to cross this dangerous region."[7]

Aswapathy comes to know how Ignorance yields ground to Knowledge. Out of darkness the light of wisdom emerges slowly. The movement of thought pours down from the realm of Light into the Material world. The *Vedic* herds of the Sun penetrate the hidden obscurity of the earth. This descent of the "gold-horned herds" into the Inconscient in terms of Vedic symbolism appears in the following lines:

> Thus streamed down from the realms of early Light,
> Ethereal thinking into Matter's world;
> Its gold-horned herds trooped into earth's cave-heart.[8]

The symbol of luminous-herds appears in some *Vedic* hymns:

> They drove upwards, the luminous ones-the good milch-cows, in their stone-pen within the hiding cave.[9]

Another similar hymn:

> By a mind seeking the Ray-cows, they rent the firm massed-hill which encircled and repressed shining herds, man desiring, laid open the strong pen, full of Ray-Cows by the Divine Word.[10]

The "gold-horned" cows symbolise richly laden waves of knowledge, which descended into the Inconscience of the earth, its 'cave-heart' in the distant past. The *Vedic* hymn connotes the following meaning, as observed by Purani: "Generally, in the *Vedas* the action is that of breaking open the Cave of the inconscient and releasing the pen of cows, the imprisoned Rays of Light for the conscious possessions by the seeker."[11]

Sri Aurobindo's skill in adopting this *Vedic* symbol lies in reversing the process – the descent of the Ray of Knowledge into the Inconscient. His vision makes clear the act of involution of the Light into the darkness of the Inconscient.

As has already been discussed earlier, the development of the 'divine potentialities' of man is symbolically indicated in the *Vedas* as the growth of a child. In *Savitri* the poet poetically employs the symbol of 'God-child' to focus on the divine potentialities in man without twisting the symbolic meaning. The 'God-child' in man is fostered alike alternately by Ignorance and a state of awakening. Ignorance is not something anti-divine. It contributes to the growth of spiritual possibilities of man that is indicated in the following lines:

> His mind could rest on a supernal ground
> And look down on the magic and the play
> Where the Godchild lies on the lap of Night and Dawn
> And the Everlasting puts on Time's disguise.[12]

The *Vedic* symbol of the 'God-child' certainly reminds the reader one of the following *Vedic*-hymns of course in different context but having the same implication:

> Two are joined together, powers of truth, powers of Maya
> They have built the Child and given him birth and they nourish his growth.[13]

It should not be presumed that the poet has taken recourse to Vedic symbols only to enrich the symbolic dimension of the epic. Sri Aurobindo uses symbols from other areas with appositeness and artistry. Prominent among these are the colour symbols. We have already discussed the various ways he employs colour symbolism in his shorter poems. The poem, "Thought the Paraclete" is replete with this. In his use of colour symbolism the poet maintains a pattern. In short poems such as "The Blue Bird", "The Bird of Fire", "Thought the Paraclete", "Rose of God" and "Silver Foam" the colour symbolism that appears is consummated and intensified in *Savitri,* where it reappears as blue skies of Infinity, white foamed oceans of Eternity, flame-red passions of Divine desire suggesting Infinity, Peace, Love and Compassion.

Colour symbolism is used in Aswapathy's psycho-spiritual odyssey. His interest lies in unearthly matters. He gazes upwards the higher spheres of supramental regions. His mind is illumined by wisdom and knowledge. "White rays" indicate in the poet's scheme of mystic colour symbolism divine consciousness in the following lines:

> A skyward being nourishing its roots
> On sustenance from occult spiritual founts
> Climbed through white rays to meet an unseen Sun.[14]

In the mystic colour symbolism of Sri Aurobindo, 'white' is the symbol of purity, a ray of timeless glory. This symbol with these implied meanings appears again in the following lines:

> A ray of the timeless Glory stoops awhile
> To commune with our seized illumined clay
> And leaves its huge white stamp upon our lives.[15]

Rose is another potent symbol Sri Aurobindo uses both in his short poems and *Savitri.* Great poets are fond of the rose symbol. This, however, has already been discussed in the chapter on shorter-poems. But Sri Aurobindo disapproves to imitate any poet in the use of rose symbolism.

Savitri, the daughter of infinity, is compelled to receive both life and doom on earth.

> Her passion-flower of love and doom she gave.[16]

'Passion-flower' in Savitri's life refers to symbol rose implies immaculate bliss and her heart's ardent love.

Aswapathy continues his journey in consciousness through the region of "The Heavens of the Ideal" and presents a picture of heavenly peace, beauty and bliss. The poet employs an apposite symbol 'rose' to symbolically present such a picture:

On one side glimmered hue on floating hue,
In a glory and surprise of the seized soul
And a tremulous rapture of the heart's insight
And the spontaneous bliss that beauty gives,
The heavenly kingdoms of the deathless Rose.[17]

The 'deathless Rose' refers to a kingdom, which is filled with immaculate bliss and untainted love.

Sri Aurobindo glorifies the flower in "Rose of God" – as bliss, light, power, life and love. Savitri is like a rose. After her rendezvous with Satyavan in forest when she returns home and graciously approaches the throne of her father as he is with the divine sage, Narad, the latter casts at her his immortal look and finds:

She stood before her mighty father's throne
And, eager for beauty on discovered earth
Transformed and new in her heart's miracle-light,
Saw like a rose of marvel, worshipping,
The fiery sweetness of the son of Heaven.[18]

'Rose' can refer to Savitri who is the agent of divine love on earth. Again the same symbol appears with immense significance:

She burned in the passion and splendour of the rose
She was the red heart of the passion-flower,
The dream-white of the lotus in its pool.[19]

Another flower used in the epic as a symbol is lotus. Savitri's secret soul is revealed to her as an image of a lotus:

In its deep lotus home her being sat
As if on concentration's marble seat,
Calling the mighty Mother of the worlds
To make this earthly tenement her house.[20]

Lotus is the symbol of divine wisdom. The 'red-lotus' is supposed to be a favourite flower of Sri Aurobindo for its spiritual significance. In Hindu religion lotus has a symbolic and scriptural significance and it is offered to Goddess Lakshmi.

Aswapathy's thought crosses the horizon of the knowable sphere to scale the peak of the Unknown. At each stage of his ascent he sees new world of wonders and bliss. He sees God's multiple creations that emerge from one caul, linked to one placenta. This supporting base is an integral organ of the Infinite Being. The Supreme Power is manifested in world after the world of bliss. While presenting a mystic vision, the poet employs lotus symbol with apposite artistry:

> A million lotuses swaying on one stem,
> World after coloured and ecstatic world
> Climbs towards some far unseen epiphany.[21]

In the Hindu tradition the lotus is the symbol of the heart of being, the seat of Brahman, the visible manifestation of his occult activity.

Human beings possess the sparks of the Divine Being in them. Man's inner being is nourished by the pure Power of the Spirit. Bathed in the sweetness of the higher Grace, rocked by divine Ecstasy, it will become fully conscious. 'Rose-fire' refers to Divine Grace. Sometimes we come across a compound symbol linked together as in the following passage:

> It shall be caught to the breast of a white Force
> And, flaming with the paradisal touch
> In a rose-fire of sweet spiritual grace,
> In the red passion of its infinite change,
> Quiver, awake, and shudder with ecstasy.[22]

In the following lines 'shadow' is the symbol of the state of gloom and despondency, an accessory power of the Lord of Death. It is Savitri's mission on earth to defeat the absolute power, Death on the governance of the earth:

> To wrestle with the Shadow she had come.[23]

The 'gold-Hawk' in Hindu mythology is the symbol for Garuda, the king of the birds. The king of birds as per myth is supposed to be Garuda , the vehicle of Lord Vishnu.

> And the gold Hawk can cross the skies no more.[24]

Every thing is in transition in this world. There seems to no certainty in any thing in this world. All appears to be a play of chance of a "fortuitous fate." No one has complete knowledge about the actual world-movement; we have no inkling of where all things lead to. Human life itself is an enigma; no philosophical school of thought has a complete grasp over life. The obscurity of the Inconscient casts its ominous shadow over all that exists. 'Grey' is the colour that symbolises infertility, and grief; whereas 'shadow' stands as the symbol of gloom, obscurity in the following lines:

> Out of the unknown we move to the unknown.
> Ever surround our brief existence here
> Grey shadows of unanswered questionings.
> The dark Inconscient's signless mysteries
> Stand up unsolved behind Fate's starting line.[25]

Behind the terrestrial existence Aswapathy comes across a cosmos of graded planes of beings, each plane of existence with its own world. The Spirit manifests in Time and gets enriched with various experiences in the field of its deployment. When this Spirit climbs back from Time to the Eternal Self, it forms a ladder of ascent through evolutionary labour. The Inconscient is linked with the Absolute, Existence-Consciousness-Bliss by an increasing order of consciousness. The 'golden-ladder' stands for the connecting link from one supramental plane to another, from mind to the higher ranges of consciousness as in the following lines:

> Up a golden ladder carrying the Soul,
> Tying with diamond threads the Spirit's extreme.[26]

Aswapathy comes to know that the domain of the deathless Light is a graceful region of peace well fed by perennial streams of joy. 'Violet' is the colour of Divine compassion and God's grace in the lines below:

> Illumined continents of violet peace,
> Oceans and rivers of the mirth of God
> And griefless countries under purple suns.[27]

'Purple' according to Sri Aurobindo is the colour of vital force. The 'sun' stands for the supramental region in the above lines.

The spirit of man is guided by a higher Power that can aid him to scale superman's height. Being himself a mortal being, man draws upon the riches of supernature and hews his path towards immortality. With the help of the symbol 'Gold' which indicates purity and richness the poet shows aspiration of human beings for immortality.

A borrower of Supernature's gold,
He paves his road to immortality.[28]

Sri Aurobindo aptly presents the pangs and sufferings of the world redeemer in his short poem "The God's Labour". The reader is advised to go through this poem to get a first-hand knowledge of the insurmountable problems and difficulties the redeemer of the world has to face to save the world from doom and peril. Thematically, "The God's Labour" has strong link with the suffering of Savitri. The world redeemer has to make an eternal quest so as to find out the enigma of life and death:

He too must grapple with the riddling Sphinx
And plunge into her long obscurity.[29]

Sphinx is a piece of stone in the Egyptian desert which is conceived as an image of the sun god, Ida, but in Greek myth the sphinx is conceived as a monster that takes away the life of travellers who fail to answer the riddles it puts to them. In his poem, "The Second Coming" W. B. Yeats symbolically imagines it coming alive in the form of a universal destructive force. The Christian myth of prophetic hope as projected by the Christian monks and apostotles from time to time has been artistically displaced by Yeatsean vision of despair, anarchy and doom manifested in the contemporary events of the world – "the growing murderousness of the world." The ancient mythical image is used by Sri Aurobindo to stand as the symbol of destructive force in the lines quoted above.

In her march towards man's liberation by reclaiming the life of Satyavan from the deadly clutch of the God of Inconscient, Death, Savitri encounters several primordial figures in the form of abstract universal forces before she musters up her inner courage, arouses the *Brahma* within. Pitying on one such figure, the Madonna of suffering, Savitri assures her of a 'transformation in power and being':

•Thy love shall be the bond of human kind,
Compassion the bright king of Nature's acts:
Misery shall pass abolished from the earth;
The world shall be freed from the anger of the Beast,
From the cruelty of the Titan and his pain.[30]

The 'Beast' in the above line is the symbol of the evil force, pestilence and destruction.

After encountering the Madonna of suffering in her inward journey, Savitri comes across a beatific vision. The poet renders this vision into a memorable frame by employing the image of the Eternal Female:

> Here on a boulder carved like a huge throne
> A Woman sat in gold and purple sheen,
> Armed with the trident and the thunderbolt,
> Her feet upon a couchant lion's back.[31]

The description is obviously that of Durga, one of the Emanations of the Divine Mother in her fearsome personality, but her beneficent aspect is known as Bhavani.

A serpent is one of those reptiles that can cause man a great harm, put an abrupt end to his life. The poet uses the expression "flaming serpent" as a symbol in the epic with the implication of carrying evil force:

> As if a world were shaken and found its soul:
> Out of the Inconscient's soulless mindless Night
> A flaming serpent rose released from sleep.[32]

'Wood' and 'stone' symbolically stand for obstacle, firmness with an obvious indication of the rigidity of human nature which after God-touch can become the abode of the Divine.

> Out of the wood and stone of our nature's stuff
> A temple is shaped where the high gods could live.[33]

The "three-bodied trinity" refers to the physical mind, the vital or desire-mind, and the thought or reasoning mind, in the line:

> A dwarf three-bodied trinity was her serf.[34]

Bird is a popular poetic symbol in Sri Aurobindo's poetry so also in the *Vedas*. In the poem 'Bird of Fire' it appears with "gold-white wings" which symbolises the *agni*-bird, the psychic *tapas*. In one of the short poems the symbol- bird appears in the form of Hippogriff with "face, lustred, pale blue-lined" which stands for divinised thought. In *Savitri* the symbol bird occurs in the following lines where the poet describes the divine nature of Savitri:

In her attracting advent's luminous wake,
The white-fire dragon bird of endless bliss
Drifting with burning wings above her days:[35]

The 'white-fire dragon bird' as perceived by Sri Aurobindo symbolises eternal *Ānanda* in the mystical region.

The river of human consciousness that seeks to merge with the oceans of Eternal and Infinite Existence in Sri Aurobindo's one of the short poems "To Sea", "To R", "In Infinite Adventure" and "Ocean Oneness" finally does achieve merger in *Savitri*, where the Divine and the human unite inextricably in a spiritual bond. The following lines glow with this meaning with regard to the union of Savitri and Satyavan:

As when a soul is merging into God
To live in Him for ever and know His joy,
Her consciousness was a wave of him alone
And all her separate self was lost in his.[36]

The poet projects Narada's departure from earth-atmosphere toward his heavenly abode steeping the poetic expression in colour symbolism:

A brilliant arrow pointing straight to heaven
The luminous body of the eternal seer
Assailed the purple glory of the noon...[37]

"Griffin" as popularly known is an imaginary animal that has a lion's body and the wings and hand of an eagle. Such a creature possesses the potency to be used in poetry as symbol. Sri Aurbindo has taken full advantage of this image in his epic by employing it as a symbol to present the description of the yogic development. The context runs as:

A Seer was born, a shining Guest of Time.
For him mind's limiting firmament ceased above,
In the griffin forefront of the Night and Day
A gap was rent in the all-concealing vault.[38]

Nolini Kanta Gupta had once explained the 'Griffin' symbol to Sethna, which the latter has quoted in an article. "Griffin" as the "Golden Hawk-Winged Lion", explains Nolini Kanta Gupta, the symbol stands for "The piercing eye of soaring aspiration + Upsurging energy of the pure vital and asked us to remember 'Vishnu's Garuda + Durga's Lion." Finally, he points out: "With these twin powers you cross safely the borderline between the lower and the upper hemispheres – the twilight world (Night and Day) – Griffin is the guardian God of the passage – *dvāra-pālaka*."[39] In a long discourse, Sethna opines that 'griffin' fused in itself holds some of the powers and functions and forms the *Rig Veda* ascribes to the Fire-god, *Agni*.

Thus, from the foregoing discussion we find that without toeing in any English or French poet's use of symbolism in poetry but taking the support of the *Vedas* as the storehouse of knowledge Sri Aurobindo has built up a scheme of symbolism piling on powerful images from diverse fields with consummate artistry. The poet in Pondicherry has established a tradition of his own with regard to symbolic expression of one's devotion to God in poetry. The Aurbindonean influence on the budding poets of Pondicherry has been discussed in detail by the present writer in the book *A Critical Response to Indian English Literature*. No doubt, it can be universally acclaimed that Sri Aurobindo established a mystical trend in poetry in which myths and symbols form an integral organ. As a modern *Rishi* and well-read sage of great repute, he tenaciously believes that a new age in mystical and spiritual poetry is dawning upon human civilisation the glimmering of which can be gleaned in the poetry of Whitman, A.E., Carpenter, Tagore, etc. Use of poetic symbol is considered no more an ornamental decoration but a part of poetic language indispensable to the technique and thematic framework of a poem. Symbolism is the medium through which an accredited poet delves into psycho-spiritual regions and occult world more efficaciously. This is not what the poet anchorite believes but has amply demonstrated in the great bulk of Sri Aurobindo's poetic out. Posterity has to toe the line set by him and make profitable use of the vast wealth bequeathed by the modern Vyasa. He has sagaciously showed that the typical Indian mythical figures, the characters of the *Puranas* and the great epics can be symbolically used in Indian English poetry with deep implication and strong spiritual import. In a way the days of the Indian Classics are never over for artistic reuse. As far as the technique of symbolism in Indian English poetry is concerned *The Vedas* continue to remain the original source material inexhaustible for the posterity particularly in spiritual poetry.

References

1. Sri Aurobindo, *Savitri,* p.83.
2. A.B. Purani, *Savitri: An Approach and A Study,* p.19.
3. Sri Aurobindo, *Savitri,* p.488.
4. Ibid., p.230.
5. A.B. Purani, *Savitri: An Approach and A Study,* p.50 (Quoted from Rig Veda, V.105-18).
6. Ibid., p.50.
7. Ibid., p.51.
8. Sri Aurobindo, *Savitri,* p.243.
9. A.B. Purani, op.cit, p.51.
10. Ibid., p.51. (Rig-Veda IV, 1-13).
11. Ibid.
12. Sri Aurobindo, *Savitri,* p.36.
13. A.B. Purani, op.cit., (Quoted from the Rig Veda X - 5.3.), p.52.
14. Sri Aurobindo, *Savitri,* pp.22-3.
15. Ibid., p.48.
16. Ibid., p.7.
17. Ibid., p.277.
18. Ibid., p.418.
19. Ibid., p.557.
20. Ibid., p.528.
21. Ibid., p.279.
22. Ibid., p.171.
23. Ibid., p.17.
24. Ibid., p.18.
25. Ibid., p.50.
26. Ibid., p.89.
27. Ibid., p.120.
28. Ibid., p.339.
29. Ibid., p.449.
30. Ibid., p.507.
31. Ibid., p.508.
32. Ibid., p.528.
33. Ibid., p.531.
34. Ibid., p.245.
35. Ibid., p.16.
36. Ibid., p.410.
37. Ibid., p.462.
38. Ibid., p.25.
39. K.D. Sethna, "Agni in the Rig-Veda and Aswapathy in Savitri", *Mother India,* Pondicherry, 15 Aug.1982, p. 524.

8

Symbolism in *Savitri* and Dante's *Divine Comedy*

J.B. Fletcher's remark about the poet of mankind made in the 'Introduction' to his book *Symbolism of Divine Comedy* is highly significant and true when we consider the poetic output of Dante and Sri Aurobindo:

> Of the millions of human voices a few score are heard for a generation, perhaps as many as a dozen for a century, and but very, very few for all time.... The poet of mankind must speak a particular language, but he may speak it in a way that will confound the Tower of Babel and make the whole world understand. This has been done by Homer in Greek, by Dante in Italian, by Shakespeare in English, and by Goethe in German. Each of the four was in and for his time not only poet but philosopher; and it is the philosophy which has made the poetry live and which has given it a universal appeal.[1]

This statement is singularly true of Sri Aurobindo. It is rewarding to find out how both Dante and Sri Aurobindo have used some common symbols. Dante calls his poem a multiple allegory that uses so many medieval symbols. Sri Aurobindo has proclaimed that Savitri is mystic poetry cast into a symbolic mould. In both these epics allegorical elements prevail.

Both Dante and Sri Aurobindo have taught men to think and feel about the noblest experiences, the spiritual way of progressing, which is the loftiest aspiration of human life. Both are prophets who herald man's progress on the path of spirituality.

They have dealt with the common interest of mankind. Like a 'cameo-worker', Dante arranges symbols after symbols in his poetic pattern. In their poetic treatment Dante and Sri Aurobindo have poured centuries of Christian and Hindu meditation to determine what the outline or the path of journey to God 'in the soul and in this life' would be. Both of them do not formulate any conception, the path is shown through the unfolding of the action in the poems. The Hinduistic incarnational art of Sri Aurobindo envisions the earthly life of man as embodying the potentialities of establishing a 'life divine' on earth. The observation made by scholars like George Santayana about Dante is most appropriate and can indeed be regarded as the century's salutation to Dante:

> Here, as in some great symphony, everything is cumulative: the movements conspire, the tension grows, the volume redoubles, the keen melody soars higher and higher; and it all ends, not with a bang, not with some casual incident, but in sustained reflection, in the sense that it has not ended, but remains by us in its totality, a revelation and a source for ever. It has taught us to love and to renounce, to judge and to worship. What more could a poet do? Dante poetised all life and nature as he found them. His imagination dominated and projected the whole world. He thereby touched the ultimate goal to which a poet can aspire; he set the standard for all possible performance, and became the type of supreme poet... Dante gives a successful example of the highest species of poetry. His poetry covers the whole field from which poetry may be fetched, and to which poetry may be applied, from the inmost recesses of the heart to the uttermost bounds of nature and of destiny.[2]

What is said here of Dante can equally be applied to Sri Aurobindo. Both exemplify the concept of a consummate poet.

Sri Aurobindo's epic *Savitri* in some ways is an extension of Dante Alighieri's *Divine Comedy*. *Savitri* transcends the Dantean model of the universe, which is based on theology. Sri Aurobindo reconstructs a universe based on a spiritual and mystic foundation. Both are spiritual and mystic poets to whom vision and revelation count much. For both these epics record visions in concrete forms. Sri Aurobindo's visions are from occult planes. Visions and revelations from plane after plane pile upon one another. As mystics both have used some common symbols. But neither imitates the other in the use of symbolism. For Sri Aurobindo the symbols were concrete realities and no more abstractions that he found on different planes of inspiration. *Savitri* and *Divine Comedy* encompass cosmic comprehension. The mystic visions of both the poets are recorded in concrete terms. The symbolism used in both these epics is not far-fetched. It is not through mere allegorical treatment that the themes acquire symbolic significance in both these epics. Ideas are finely chiseled into symbolic form but do not degenerate into vagueness.

As Charles Williams remarks, "The record of Dantean way begins with three things - an experience, the environment of that experience, and the means of understanding and expressing that experience; say — a woman, a city and intellect or poetry; say again, Beatrice, Florence and Virgil. These images are never quite separated, even in the beginning; towards the end they mingle and become a great complex image.[3] In *Savitri* also the three dominating figures are Savitri, Yama and Satyavan representing Love, Death and Truth. Savitri represents Grace; the Lord of Death stands for pain, death, fate and incapacity of man; and Satyavan is the representative of the suffering humanity entangled in death and incapacity. In both the epics a woman is the central figure and symbol; in *Savitri* it is Savitri, and in *Divine Comedy* it is Beatrice.

Beatrice in the epic is represented as an image of nobility, of virtue, of the Redeemed Life, and in some sense of Almighty God himself. Dante brought the figure of Beatrice as closely as possible to that of the Almighty God. To speak of Savitri's divinity, it is worthwhile to quote Nolini Kanta Gupta, a close disciple of Sri Aurobindo who wrote in his editorial comment:

> The Divine Mother is upon earth as a human creature. She is to change the mortal earth into immortal paradise. Earth at present is a bundle of material inconscience. The Supreme Consciousness has manifested itself as supreme unconsciousness. The Divine has lost itself in pulverising itself, scattering itself abroad. Immortality is thus entombed here below in death. The task of the incarnate supreme consciousness is to revive the death-bound divinity to free the human consciousness in its earthly-life from the obscurity of the material unconsciousness, reinstall in its original radiant status of the Divine Consciousness.[4]

Beatrice is a glorious lady of mind. As quoted by Charles Williams from Dante's "Vita Nuova", she is "the destroyer of all vices and the queen of virtues."[5] As Savitri stands for divine Love, so also Beatrice is the Mother of Love. Beatrice arouses Dante's 'valore' or nobility; similarly Savitri also restores the life of Satyavan from the grip of the Lord of Death. Beatrice is a compensation, Savitri is also a compensation, in the sense that she restores the life of Satyavan; even more that that, she is a saviour, whose mission is to release man from death, desire and incapacity and make earth divine, "to hew the ways of immortality" on earth. Both the epics deal with the release and progress of the soul. If Dante's spiritual movement is the pattern of Beatrice, *Savitri* is an expression of Sri Aurobindo's spiritual movement, experience and realisation.

It is a fact that "her beauty has power to renovate nature in those who behold it,"[6] similarly all those who came under the influence of Savitri, felt her inner divinity. Both Savitri and Beatrice have descended from heaven. Dante and Sri Aurobindo, the masterminds of two different ages, devoted their supreme energy to one of the great problems that concerns us all, the great problem of the spiritual world and human life.

Beatrice is a symbol, not for Dante's rescue, but for the rescue of mankind. Savitri's role is also the same on earth. If Beatrice is an instrument of Grace, Savitri, herself is the Divine Grace on earth. The three blessed Ladies in the *Divine Comedy* are symbolic characters. The Mary of the *Divine Comedy* is often portrayed as the "symbol of God's mercy." The Virgin in Christian tradition is thought to be the medium of "divine Mercy," so Beatrice stands for Revelation. Lucia is the emblem of Grace - the Illuminating Grace, as Jefferson B. Fletcher[7] has suggested in his illuminating study of the *Symbolism of Divine Comedy*. The three ladies merely symbolise the three aspects of God's executive acts.

In *Savitri* also we come across three feminine characters having symbolic functions. The Divine Mother herself is a character who is the source of Mercy. Savitri is the Grace of the Divine Mother upon earth, the divine incarnate human being. The Queen, mother of Savitri, is an ordinary human being who has nothing to do with the Grace except that she is the human channel through which the divine Grace is upon the earth. The queen represents earthly wisdom. Her knowledge does not go beyond what she sees. Both Beatrice and Savitri symbolise Love.

Dante and Christian theologians generally built up an elaborate system of symbolic imagery from the obvious analogy between beneficent God and the Sun, the two prime vitalising forces. The later radiates light and heat, Fletcher points out the use of solar symbolism in *Divine Comedy*:

> Not only is God therefore called the Sun, but also by extension any active agency transmitting the divine influence may be so called and be accredited with powers figuratively paralleling those of the physical Sun. Thus Beatrice, infusing into Dante the light of wisdom and the ardour of love, is acclaimed as *his* Sun.[8]

Dante uses the Sun symbolism in the following lines :

> The glory of Him who moves all things soe'er
> Impenetrates the universe, and bright
> The splendour burns, more here and lesser there.[9]

And again,

> The sun that warmed my bosom first with love
> Had brought the beauteous face of truth to light,
> Unveiling it by proof and counter-proof.[10]

On the other hand, Sri Aurobindo takes the concept of solar symbolism from the *Vedas* and employs it in *Savitri* with new dimensions. The solar symbolism is a potent one in his epic. Savitri herself is directly associated with Savitru, the Sun. A detailed discussion of this symbol has been attempted in the chapter - Major Symbols. The Sun as a *Vedic* symbol stands for Higher Truth, knowledge, creator and so on.

The Sun is the mystic source of all light. Light symbolism is found both in *Savitri* and *Divine Comedy*. Mary is compared to light. From her comes the light to Dante in the dark wood. For he constantly invokes her name:

> And hence ascend to have my sight made clear;
> There is on high a Lady wins me grace
> This mortal burden through your world to bear.[11]

Dante insists on the purification of his physical and spiritual vision as he ascends nearer to the divine sun. Figuratively light signifies truth. Beatrice is referred to as the 'light of grace', 'light of faith', and 'light of revelation'. As Fletcher points out further: "Figuratively light signifies truth - St.Thomas. In one aspect, therefore the whole process of Dante's spiritual ascent consists in the accommodation of his eyes, physical and spiritual, to brighter and brighter light."[12] Speaking further about Mary's association with solar symbolism, Mother further draws our attention: "Mary, the Divine Mother, assumes the role of the divine father and represents in the solar symbolism the Sun itself, or generating - power of Light."[13] St. Lucia's' name signifies 'light' which has the magic power of healing weak eyes. Elaborating the light symbolism more lucidly, Fletcher says:

> It is the 'three blessed ladies' who so restore to Dante his native eagle-sight by removing from his eyes the veiling double cataract of sin and sense, and with loving care gradually expose them to more and more light, until at last he, who had groped blindly in the dark forest, can endure the direct and undiminished effulgence of the divine Sun... The medicament is light. Mary is the source of the healing light; Lucia, the healing light itself; and Beatrice, dispenser of the healing light. As it is said, light is given according to the capacity of the recipient. This capacity is measured by charity. Beatrice having the perfect charity of the heaven receives the light - or word - of Mary, transmitted by Lucia, in its fullness and directly. Her intellect is therefore altogether intuitive or angelic.[14]

In *Savitri* light symbolism is found in all the aspects. Savitri is referred to as 'flame' and 'incarnate flame'. She is 'flame born'. Referring to the influence of Savitri on others, the poet makes use of light symbolism:

> Almost they saw who lived within her light
> Her playmate in the sempiternal spheres
> Descended from its unattainable realms
> In her attracting advent's luminous wake...[15]

In her "Journey in Eternal Light" Savitri is armed with the power of light. Her flame bright spirit remains unperturbed as the poet says:

> But still in its lone niche of templed strength
> Motionless, her flame-bright spirit, mute, erect,
> Burned like a torch-fire from a windowed room
> Pointing against the darkness' somber breast.[16]

Light in *Savitri* is the symbol of truth, divine Illumination, inspiration and Grace of the divine. The play of light displays the artistic skill of Dante:

So did those sempiternal roses wreathe
Twofold about us and, antiphonal
In song, the outer to the inner breathe.
Then, when the dance and the high festival
Made up of singing and of leaping flame,
Light upon light serene and joyous, all...[17]

In her illuminating comparative study of Sri Aurobindo's and Dante's epics, Prema Nanda Kumar has made an elaborate discourse on light symbolism. As she points out:

> Light symbolism in *The Divine Comedy* is mostly used to suggest the atmosphere, the sharp differences between the several states of being... The light symbolism in Dante suggests a presence: the presence of sin, the presence of contrite souls that struggle against the shadow of temptation and reach towards the light of celestial happiness. In *Paradise* light symbolises the presence of Grace everywhere, even in the Moon though it is farthest from the source of Grace-Light, the heart of the White Rose. The presence of the blessed ones is also indicated by different colours or formations of light. Virgin Mary appears as a light of sapphire colour encircled by the white lights of saints in the twenty-third canto. Dante almost exhausts all the possibilities of light as an image-carrier.[18]

Not only light but its different colours have been symbolically used by Sri Aurobindo. Describing Aswapathy's life on earth the poet says:

A skyward being nourishing its roots
On sustenance from occult spiritual founts
Climbed through white rays to meet an unseen Sun.[19]

'White rays' symbolise purity and power of divinity. 'Light' symbol is employed by Sri Aurobindo to suggest illumination of consciousness, as in the following lines:

A ripple of light and glory wraps the brain,
And traveling down the moment's vanishing route
The figures of eternity arrive.[20]

'Light' also refers to the opening of subtle vision and the establishment of Truth:

Earth's doubting future hides our heritage:
The Light now distant shall grow native, here...[21]

Both Aswapathy and Dante represent the progressive human soul. Both are representative of human beings who have been granted divine Vision. In his poem "Vita Nuova" Dante presents his personal spiritual growth under the direction of Love. Similarly, it is the love of humanity that urges Aswapathy to proceed along the spiritual path to meet the Divine Mother and to convey to her humanity's inmost aspiration. Both the poets have made Divine Love the protagonist of drama of their epic's action. Both symbolically experience the ways open for man's spiritual advancement and the paths for perfect life. To Sri Aurobindo, yoga is the art of perfection in life.

In his journey through *Inferno,* Dante meets three beasts. The first one is the Leopard:

> And see! not far from where the mountain-side
> First rose, a Leopard, nimble and light and fleet,
> Clothed in a fine furred pelt all dapple-dyed.[22]

Then a lion:

> Of the bright beast so speckled and so gay;
> Yet not so much but that I fell to quaking
>
> At a fresh sight - a Lion in the way.[23]
> Then about the third beast,
> Dante like the other two attaches symbolic significance:
> And the third one is the Wolf:
> And next, a Wolf, gaunt with the famished craving
> Lodged ever in her horrible lean flank,
> The ancient cause of many men's enslaving.[24]

These three beasts are usually interpreted as Lust, Pride, and Avarice. They also signify something more. They are the sins of Youth, Manhood, and Age. The gay Leopard is the image of the self-indulgent sins - Incontinence; the fierce Lion, of the violent sins-Bestiality; the She-Wolf of the malicious sins, which involve Fraud. In Dante beasts signifying human evil in human mind.

The Beast is the symbol of evil force, pestilence, and the destructive force in *Savitri*:

> Thy love shall be the bond of human kind,
> Compassion the bright king of Nature's acts:
> Misery shall pass abolished from the earth;
> The world shall be freed from the anger of the Beast,
> From the cruelty of the Titan and his pain.[25]

The 'Rose' in the Divine Comedy is the symbol of Christ or Mary or the Church or the faithful soul. But the 'White Rose' is the symbol of divine love. Dante contemplates the snow-white rose filled with different ranks of redeemed souls, and angels:

> So now, displayed before me as a rose
> Of snow-white purity, the sacred might
> I saw, whom with His blood Christ made His spouse.
> But the other, winging ever in His sight,
> Chants praises to the glory it adores,
> It's Maker's good extolling in delight.
> As bees ply back and forth...
> So did the host of Angles now descend
> Amid the Flower of the countless leaves,
> Now rise to where their love dwells without end.
> Their glowing faces were as fire that gives
> Forth flame, golden their wings; that purest snow
> The whiteness of their raiment ne'er achieves.[26]

Savitri standing by the side of her father's throne is referred to as a "rose of marvel". She gives her love to Satyavan which is referred to by the poet as, 'Her passion-flower of love and doom she gave."[27] Aswapathy gets the visions of the kingdoms of "deathless Rose" which symbolises kingdoms where untarnished bliss and untainted love prevail.

Dante sees in his final vision the symbolic colours of the Trinity in the mystic triune circle:

> That light supreme, within its fathomless
> Clear substance, showed to me three spheres, which bare
> Three hues distinct, and occupied one space...[28]

These three distinct colours are, according to the medieval symbolism, white, green and red. "White is symbol of faith, the light of the Father; green is hope, the ray of the sun; red is love, the splendour of the holy spirit."[29]

In the colour symbolism of Sri Aurobindo different colours are symbols of certain ideas and forces. In fact, the whole of *Savitri* is a colourful presentation of the vision of the poet.

The *Divine Comedy* ends when Dante is purged of his sins and his life becomes luminous with the light of God. *Savitri*, too, ends with an apocalyptic vision of divinising the entire humankind:

> Drawn by white manes upon a high-roofed car
> In flare of the unsteady torches went

With linked hands Satyavan and Savitri,
Hearing a marriage march and nuptial hymn,
Where waited them the many-voiced human world...
She brooded through her stillness on a thought
Deep-guarded by her mystic folds of light,
And in her bosom nursed a greater dawn.[30]

References

1. Jefferson B. Fletcher, *Symbolism of Divine Comedy,* 1921, p.VII.
2. George Santayana, *Three Philosophical Poets,* 1910, p.133.
3. Charles William, *The Figure of Beatrice,* 1943, p.11.
4. Nolini Kanta Gupta, "Savitri - Editorial comment", *The Advent* (August, 1967), p.10 .
5. Charles William, *The Figure of Beatrice,* p.21.
6. Ibid., p.213.
7. Jefferson B. Flecther, op.cit., p.124.
8. Ibid., pp.169-70.
9. Dante, *The Divine Comedy-3;* " Paradise", Canto I (Tr.) Dorothy L. Sayers and Barbara Reynolds, Penguin Books, 1976, p.53.
10. Ibid., p.73.
11. Ibid., Purgatory, Canto XXVI, p.273.
12. Jefferson B. Fletcher, op.cit., p. 174.
13. Ibid., pp. 174-75.
14. Ibid., pp.182-83.
15. Sri Aurobindo, *Savitri,* Imprt., 1977. p.16.
16. Ibid., p.582.
17. Dante, *Divine Comedy-* 3, *Paradise,* trans. Dorothy L. Sayers, C -VII, p.157.
18. Prema Nanda Kumar, *Dante and Sri Aurobindo,* 1981, p.133.
19. Sri Aurobindo, *Savitri,* pp. 22-3.
20. Ibid., p.110.
21. Ibid.
22. Dante, *Divine Comedy, Inferno,* Tr. Dorothy L. Sayers, p.72.
23. Ibid., Line 43-45., p.72.
24. Ibid., Line 49-51., p.72.
25. Sri Aurobindo, *Savitri,* p. 507.
26. Dante, *Divine Comedy-3:* op.cit, Canto XXXI, p.327.
27. Sri Aurobindo, *Savitri,* p.7.
28. Dante, *Divine Comedy,* op.cit., Canto XXXIII, p.346.
29. Jefferson B. Fletcher, op.cit., p.84.
30. Sri Aurobindo, *Savitri,* p.724.

9

Myth: A Creative Instrument of Knowledge and Vision

The twentieth-century faced the greatest ever crisis from the dawn of human civilisation as it was pushed to two successive World Wars and is precariously poised on the brink of a third one. The superpowers, jealous and scared of one another, run into an arms race and used up the world's precious natural resources and no country has as yet become capable to offer real peace and security to mankind. Most of the developing and the underdeveloped countries have been caught in the suicidal net of poverty and over population. Instead of food, arms production gets top priority in many of these countries. The gap between the affluent and the poor, the privileged and the unprivileged proves far too wide to be bridged.

Civil war, strike, lockouts, suicide and genocide present a horrible spectacle of anarchy. Political, economic, racial, linguistic and religious conflicts have torn human society up into fragments, resulting in hatred, violence and death. Selfish motives have blinded man; nuclear proliferation, maddening conflict, ideological wrangles have made a nation suspicious of another. In such a state of uneasiness man's sense of peace, security and happiness seem to be jeopardised. The literature of the twentieth-century reflects the social, economic and political uncertainty in various forms.

Two basic themes of modern literature indicate the alienation of man, his sense of loneliness and his precarious relation with the morally diseased society. A new ethic of competition has driven society into a system of cash-nexus and has aroused greed and selfishness. The modern writer's depiction of moral confusion and perplexity springs from his deep concern for moral order and anguish over the decay of humanity. Serious artists cannot remain aloof from the pains and suffering of humanity. Instead they hang on to a faith in moral order and continue to cherish a vision of a hopeful future, one of harmony and peace.

An empirical and sceptical spirit of science to a large extent has hastened the degenerations and beliefs. These have been replaced by a new system of empiricism and positivism that never sustains us. Freud's view of the developing psyche rooted in the biological instincts puts great emphasis on the power of the unconscious to affect human behaviour and calls into question human capacity to create civilisation on the basis of rationality and a sense of order.

In the social sphere too, scientific and empirical knowledge strengthened a sense of moral unease and destroyed faith in the efficacy of some customary beliefs and social practices. Advances in anthropology helped to undermine the absoluteness of religious and ethical systems. Behind all these confusion, the fundamental problem remained unresolved – the inability to arrive at a commonly accepted metaphysical picture of man. To the Marxists man became the product of economic, social and political forces. Charles Darwin reduced man simply to a product the impersonal mechanism of evolution and the survival of the fittest. A pessimistic scientific view of man's hopes and aspirations is analysed by Bertrand Russell as "the outcome of chance collocations of atoms." The Christian notion of man as inherently a child of sin whose essence is free self-determination and wrong use of his freedom, yet he embodies the possibilities of salvation by the grace of God is widely accepted in the world. The emotional despair depicted by Kierkegaard as *Angst* gained currency and popularity. In the political and practical sphere imperial expansions aroused moral dilemmas, doubts, despair and uncertainties. Political harmony of the imperial nations created disgust in the heart of the conscious writers. Life in the colonised countries was subjected to inhuman torture, awful harassment, acute sense of deprivation and injustice. Writers such as George Orwell, Joseph Conrad and many others raised their voices against the social and political injustice meted out those poor nations which had lost their sovereignty and freedom.

The aftermath of the two great World Wars gave rise to social despair economic chaos and a break with the past. Various movements fostered in an apocalyptic climate such as Dadaism, Futurism, Surrealism and Existentialism. Disease, want, ignorance, crime, delinquency, squalor, idleness became the general features of the undeveloped countries. In addition to all these, rapid industrialisation helped to destroy the old social fabric and traditional culture of the people. The impersonal machine has generated a state of sterile passivity. In the context of art as well the dehumanising influence of machine on it was manifest in an excessive insistence on form to the exclusion of context, articulating a sense of crisis in humanism. This is what Ortega y Gasset explains in his book *The Dehumanisation of Art.*

Journalistic endeavours, print and visual mass media now cater to popular taste, focused on vulgarity, triviality, sensational and sentimental themes. The prevailing ethics of business enterprise is to boost up material consumption and earn more profit. Advertising agencies in this direction have stimulated the baser aspect of human nature. Various forms of popular literature depicting crime or love stories, which glorify violence, rape, murder, blood bath, arson, plunder, etc. progressively debase popular aesthetic taste, and social conscience. Thus, the deleterious effect of bad art and pop literature on modern society has of incalculable implications in our times.

A major problem in the twentieth century literature is the sense of "moral rootlessness". The facility for mobility of man has forced him for superficialisation of human relationship. The revolt against the discipline necessary for civilisation clearly perceptible in our strife-torn society is a blatant repudiation of human values and moral degeneration which has manifested in the forms of 'hippies', promiscuity, flight into alcohol and drugs, search for momentary sensation, interest in anti-rational and a mindless 'dream image of life' with its stultifying effects. These features of our civilisation have been further accentuated by a fusion of the *avantgarde* and popular culture fermented by the liberal intellectuals, many of whom show rebelliousness, a disregard for authority and frantic search for thrills for a powerful attraction in life.

In the writings of the twentieth century writers, who are vested with a high degree of social and experiential awareness these symptoms manifest in different ways. Bergson asserts the superior claims of intuition over intelligence in the apprehension of reality. The artist, in his opinion "becomes the flag-bearer of intuition in its interminable struggle against logic and reason." Freud, whose psychological theory has revolutionised modern literature, refers to the unconscious as the "true psychic reality." Dreams display a curious blending and intermingling of inner experience that delve below the normal level of logic and rationality in our waking life. It is expressed in a form of symbolism that brings into operation continuity between the individual consciousness and the life of the race. He links this symbolism with sufficient explicitness to fairy tales, myths and legends.

Literature is sustained by social process and it nurtures the society. By focusing its attention on a restricted social aspect of the social situation, literature offends its nature and breaches the norm of civility. Moreover, science and technology have never reduced the significance of literature, although it is a truism that science and technology have altered the face of the earth in the last century. Surely, a scientific and technological age has already set in, dawning upon a central truth of our terrestrial existence. Some primal force is definitely the source of all the "complex interacting rhythms of energy and matter" of which we find our physical universe consists. Beyond science and technology as also beyond myth and religion, lies the realm of spirituality that includes everything. In the diverse realm of ethics, religion and science – in the pattern of individual as well as collective behaviour and objective enquiry – man is overwhelmed by a sense of crisis. This crisis in civilisation could be read as a pre-condition of a new dawn, the resurrection of a new life.

W.B. Yeats, T.S. Eliot, Ezra Pound and W.H. Auden, the major poets of twentieth century grew to artistic maturity by opening up unexplored approaches to myth in their literary productions with the help of the new fields of Anthropology and Psychology. For Yeats and Eliot, myth offers the promise of a light beyond the enlightenment of the self. Yeats's effort to build a mythical system and the creation of his own mythology constitutes an attempt to reach the unconscious and control it. His search for the immortal in the human psyche leads him to face the most painful limitations of everyday reality, to express old age, decay and death so as to depict man's absurd struggle with these factors of life. He further uses myth as a heroic ideal, as a guide to "insight and knowledge", as an interpretation of his dreams and longings. Lilian Fedder provides us an insightful reading of the use of myth both in prose and poetry of W. B. Yeats:

> All of Yeats's adaptations of myth indicate a need to impose order and unity on an apparent anarchy in his own mind and in the universe; he does so by equating individual with universal experience, seeking some eternal element in the human soul. Ultimately his purpose is to use myth as a guide to reality both unconscious or personal, and historical or general.[1]

Yeast's use of certain mythical themes in his poetry, especially in *A Vision,* reveals the construct of super human powers created out of human weakness, despair, frustration, and chaos.

Eliot uses ancient myth in his early poetry as one of the most important means of conveying unconscious feelings and drives. He considers myth as a means of reaching "beneath the level of present and conscious experience." Prufrock's interior monologue, his pathetic efforts to unite his timorousness and desire, his apathy and yearning in "a fantasy of love" imply the need for "a world of spiritual significance." Mr Apollinax is Eliot's most elegant and attractive mythical creation of natural man. The Grail legend provides the dominant symbolism of *The Wasteland,* Eliot's emphasis on the insight reading of the blind prophet, Tiresias, who has power to see, comprehend and predict what is dark to other men. He contains the secret knowledge of male and female, gods and mortals, past and future. It is Tiresias who perceives the structure of the Grail legend beneath the surface of modern society. In adapting this legend, Eliot employs symbols to depict modern man's sense of dissatisfaction and inner struggle. The quest in *The Wasteland* comes to an end with the maimed protagonist having turned away from man and as the society waits for spiritual regeneration. In "Prufrock" and *The*

Wasteland, myth discloses personal fear, despondency, feelings of impotence, which the poet objectifies in relation to society and history. The mythical experience depicted in these poems is similar to Jungian plunge into archetypal unconsciousness because it leads to a transformation of uncertainty into faith and a belief that the self can "emerge with a divine principle."

Eliot makes the figure of Belladona a symbol of enchanting beauty possessing strong sexual appeal that represents the portrait of a modern upper-class woman. This lady is nervous, frightened, vainly seeking some motivating force in her superficial life. Thus, the central myth of sterility and rebirth takes place within the consciousness of the protagonist, who merges with all the characters. The mythical structure of the poem reveals man's inability to resolve his central conflict. In a poetic framework it symbolically indicates that man's only possibility of salvation lies in the enactment of a symbolic search.

Ezra Pound, like W.B. Yeats, makes use of myth as a basic mode of poetic expression. His repeated reference to mythical themes and identification with mythical figures expose "unacknowledged and chaotic feelings beneath the mask of authority." Pound adapts a mythical voice from Hades to expose chaos within the speaker. While discussing the potentiality of myth, Pound acknowledges it as a means of "explicating and disguising psychic experience." His needs to communicate as well as his compulsion "to screen himself" are projected as a series of personae in their expression of feelings through mythical descent to the underworld. His persona releases a curious combination of feelings – rage, contempt, despair, longing for power and immortality – expressed often in a chaotic and exaggerated form.

Ezra Pound's use of persona of Propertius in *Homage to Sextus Propertius* illustrates his adaptation of the myth of Hades. Emerging from the realm of the dead, his voice turns with contempt towards contemporary political and military affairs. It is in Hades that the poet sees his immortality. The persona of Propertius serves him as a means to alienate himself as an artist from the values of the society. It purifies the poet's feelings so as to make an impersonal expression of "his elaborate mask". In *Hugh Selwyn Mauberley* Pound employs a less congenial mask and allows himself to speak through a dedicated form of Mauberley, a disillusioned minor artist defeated by the insensitivity of his age. In the first section of *Hugh Selwyn Mauberley,* the death of the spirit or the emotion is attributed to a cold and unresponsive society. The persona of Mauberley reveals deadness within the soul and the rage and despair which this hell projects on the living. The persona who speaks for a dead poet being destroyed by a hostile society himself dies at the end.

Again in another poem *The Cantos,* Pound resorts to the myth of Hades that is basic to the structure of the poem. His persona Odysseus makes a journey to Hades to obtain the counsel of the dead. This poem establishes a rapport between the dead and the living; the hidden past and the demanding present. Both the mythical themes of descent and metamorphosis have been used for various purposes. The theme of descent is used for establishment of the persona's claim to superhuman authority. Through Odysseus the essential education of Pound takes place in Hades and he comes back from the land of the dead as a different man. An analysis of Pound's mythical persona discloses the poet's approach to history, ethics, and the problems of contemporary man, which constitutes the poet's conscious search for knowledge and experience. Thus, the mythical theme of *The Cantos* can be read as "the diary of a poet's mind." In the first Canto the poet like Odysseus seeks from the shades of the dead, knowledge unattainable to most living men.

Another mythical figure that functions repeatedly as a symbol of beauty, influence and destructive force is Helen. In Canto II Pound's exalted and cursed Helen is Homer's Godlike and Aeschylus's "baneful Helen, man destroying and city destroying." Thus, Helen or some form of the beautiful and destructive female, part goddess and part demonic, a demanding and chaotic biological principle, dominates the external and the inner world of *The Cantos.* Involved in perpetual conflict with the contemporary world, Pound asserts control over time and events through invocation of super human mythical figures.

W. H. Auden emphasizes the inherent need of Eros in opposition to death in his early poems. The secular myth of Eros conveys man's continuous and painful contest for survival. Auden underlines the inevitable unity of individual and social life, "the graceful god" and the creative principle of the universe through the mythical figure of Eros. Both are continually threatened by violence as Eros and Thanatas wage eternal struggle. In "Kairos and Logs" which first appeared in 1941, he develops the theme of man's limitations of accepting a Christian god whose love removes the ever-present fear of death through "a meditation on the significance of the incarnation." Throughout the poem, the poet more effectively than ever before, portrays man's sense of aloofness in a world of his own limitations, "For the Time being" creates an atmosphere of awful decay and despair amidst which the poet envisions the Incarnation as the one possibility of "transcending the limitations of material existence." He believes that man's psychological limits determined by his biological forces, Eros and the death instinct could be transcended only by a superhuman power. It is divine love, which can alone check the destructive power of Eros by making love faithful and honest. The mythical entity of Eros, which dominated Auden's poetry, becomes later on a symbol of cynicism and despair bred by instinctual drives.

In the works of the poets already discussed in this chapter myth reveals experience, which is too deep, personal and complex adapting to the inner voice of the poet. The character of myth, overt or implicit in its narrative discloses deliberately or intuitively the conflict between human frailty and superhuman longings, and the continual recurrence of struggle and at least partial resolution, the drive towards conquest, destruction, metamorphosis or renewal. The early part of the twentieth century was a period of intellectual curiosity, technological revolution that produced religious scepticism. Poets employed myths in their poetry to express profound and even unconscious level of thoughts, feelings and visions to extend the boundaries of readers' as well as their own inner experience. The incantations, prayers, prophecies and adaptation to ritual elements indicate the extension of the boundary of poetry. A greater inwardness seems to be the drive of the creative spirit of the modern poets. Among the precursors of modern poetry great names such as Walt Whitman, Carpenter, W.B. Yeats, T.S. Eliot, Stephen Philips, R.N. Tagore, etc., may be recalled. In the poetry of these poets one can trace the new spirit, an experiment with new forms and technique of poetic expression. The typical characteristics of these poets are the deepening and heightening of thought, a profound and intimate way of seeing life and nature, a high degree of desire to probe deep the powers of language, rhythm and form.

Discontentment with the past seems to be yet another dominant feature of modern poetry. There is a profound psychological and spiritual strain unmistakably found in the field of poetic expression. Modern poetry is more inclined towards subliminal and lower vital regions of human consciousness by a kind of pseudo-subjectivism. True subjectivism will come into force when the limits of intellect enlarge and open themselves into higher ranges of consciousness. There are many modern poets who under the stress of life display a capacity for intuitive perception and psychic insight, a tendency to concretise and objectify inner status or spiritual experience. The modern poets do not employ myth only as a mode of symbolic expression, they make all sorts of efforts to elucidate its rich and complex nature and thereby create a new trend and species. The ultimate end of myth is to envisage its fundamental truth and moral orientation. It is never a distortion of the world or a means of escape from it. The poet's consciousness of the "ultimate end of myth" is an important subject in modern poetry, in which myth functions as a symbolic system of expression to interpretation, and mediates between the inner experience of the unconscious mind and the conscious awareness of everyday reality of a mechanised and dehumanised society already discussed in the beginning of this present chapter.

Yeats, Pound, Eliot and Auden use myth to explore history and amplify its meanings. Eliot and Auden interpret Christian myth, as a particular era of man's existence, filling his psychological and spiritual needs. Some of the writings of Gerard Manley Hopkins, James Joyce, T.S. Eliot and Hart Crane clearly depict a spiritual frame of reference. At the heart of the poems of Eliot and Hopkins is reflected the suffering and trials for spiritual life. Whereas Hopkins emphasizes spiritual growth, Eliot asserts the necessity of – the spiritual redemption of earthly life. The theme of Hopkins's poems — trial and purgation, hope in the Incarnation and redemption of man—become progressively interpreted and united in Eliot's Four *Quartets and* his plays. Hart Crane's *The Bridges* focuses on the need for a reaffirmation of man's spiritual potentialities to discover God's grace. Similarly,

Grace is given prominence in Eliot's "Little Gidding" in *The Four Quartets*. While Hopkins puts much stress on spiritual growth, Eliot underscores spiritual awakening. For the latter modern man has become so self-centred and so involved in pursuit of sensual pleasures that he cannot love properly; he finds himself "revolving on the wheel of defeating experiences." Although the incarnation redeems the society time and again, man has in rare moments the "hints half-guessed, the gift half-understood." So, for Eliot the way to break out of the 'sterility of contemporary life's endless cycle' of suffering is the spiritual life.

In tune with the way of expression of the modern poets, Sri Aurobindo's mythic perception has its origin in myths and legends of the world that deal with love, death and immortality. As a mythical poet, he draws his materials from the great Indian epics, and the *Puranas,* which have acquired social acceptance down the ages. The legendary tales culled from the tradition project the vision of reality in terms of human aspiration, anxiety, heroism, hopes and expectation for a better and glorious life. Western and Indian mythological stories agreeably mingle in Sri Aurobindo's literary works. The mythopoeic vision of the poet during the Baroda period has been embodied in the epyllions, *Urvasie* and *Love and Death* where indomitable love is put under grievous strains of mortality. Victory of love over death in these poems is achieved by paying a high price. Pururavas and Urvasie, Ruru, and Priyumvada are the legendary amorous couples.

The ancient myths, legends, folk tales and history form the source materials of not only Sri Aurobindo's poetry but also of his plays. Once he chooses a legend or a myth, he rearranges the theme and the plot in such a way that it acquires various dimensions. It is a technique already adopted by Shakespeare and other great writers of the world. Sri Aurobindo's plays *Perseus the Deliverer* and *Vasavadutta* are based on the Perseus-Andromeda and Udayana-Vasavadutta myths respectively which have been given dramatic renderings by many playwrights. But Sri Aurobindo's mythopoeic perception projects in these plays a new vision of life. *Perseus the Deliverer,* a serious play celebrates the victory of a new religion of love and knowledge over an old religion of hatred, violence and blind belief. Polydaon, the priest of Poseidon, a religious fanatic irrationally demands

Andromeda's innocent blood. The latter incurs the wrath of Polydaon and Poseidon owing to her compassionate act of releasing the prisoners. She is chained to a rock and exposed to the sea-monsters, but providentially rescued by the heroic valour of Perseus, a figure cast in the play as "divine-human". The play is peopled with gods who are benevolent but evil. It is a play that symbolically presents the dramatist's vision of the triumph of scientific rationalism over the untamed forces of Nature, and the angelic quality of man over the satanic forces.

Like the romantic comedies of Shakespeare, the dramatic romance of Sri Aurobindo, *The Vizier of Bassora, Eric, Vasavadutta,* and *Prince of Edur* are based on the love stories of Nureddene and Anice-al-Jalice, Eric and Aslaug, Vuthsa Udayana and Vasavadutta, Bappa and Comol Cumary respectively. The heroines' love in these plays faces external impediments temporarily, even pushed to the brink of defeat and frustration, yet ultimately it gets over all obstacles and is consummated in a happy union at the end. *The Vizier of Bassora,* the first dramatic romance of the playwright, was written in his Baroda period some time between 1893 to 1906.The plot is based on the various hints and characters taken from the stories of *The Book of Thousand and One Nights* by Sir Richard Burton. However, the play is presented in a new form by the dramatic imagination of Sri Aurobindo.

Eric is based on the Scandinavian mythological stories woven around the sons and daughters of Odin, Thor and Freya. The play is about the struggle for power between Eric, the legendary king of Sweden and his antagonist Swegn, the earl of Frondhjem. Swegn's sister Aslaug and his wife Hertha come disguised to the court of Eric and wait for an opportunity to take revenge on Eric. Love in this play transcends the feelings of hatred and revenge existing between the two families. Aslaug falls in love with Eric and marries him. On the other hand, her presence changes the personality of Eric who turns himself into a lover from that of a conqueror. Swegn and Hertha are given royal pardon. The dramatist calls the play the apotheosis of love.

Prince of Edur is an incomplete dramatic work, the part of which has been drawn by Sri Aurobindo from the various legends, myths and folklores of Rajasthan built around the glorious character of Bappa. Written in 1907 when the playwright was seriously involved in hectic political activities, his deep sense of patriotism and the nobility of the Rajput blood, a race of warriors, find here its full play. *Vasavadutta,* another play of Sri Aurobindo, is based on the Udayan-Vasavdutta legend as mentioned in Gunadhya's *Brihatkatha,* but like Vasa, the great ancient playwright, Sri Aurobindo gives a new dimension to the legend. The world of romance here is pervaded with the descriptions of natural beauty. In the opinion of A.K. Sinha, the play is a celebration of love: "The story of Vuthsa Udayan and Vasavadutta is transformed into a legend of Purusha and Prakriti, of Cupid and Psyche."[2]

Rodogune, the only tragic play of Sri Aurobindo written at Pondicherry, has its source in the many stories about the mysterious legendary character of Cleopatra, the Egyptian queen. Some notable plays written about the love of Cleopatra can be found in Shakespeare's *Antony and Cleopatra,* John Dryden's *All for Love,* Bernard Shaw's *Caesar and Cleopatra* and Corneille's *Rodogun.* But Sri Aurobindo's play makes a significant departure from these plays. For a detailed analysis the reader is advised to study the author's *A Critical Response to Indian English Literature.* Rodogune's selfless love and her sacrifice in this play are pitted against the egoistic filial love of Cleopatra.

With his mythopoeic vision Sri Aurobindo projects the symbolic meanings of the myths, legends, history, and popular stories of various countries and climes of the world to show the catholicity of his mind, global comprehension and taste. *Perseus the Deliverer* is based on a myth of ancient Greece; Rodogune is a Syrian romance; *Vasavadutta* is of Indian origin. *The Viziers of Bassora* refers to the days of Haroun al Rashid of Islamic countries; and *Eric* is a Scandinavian romance. All these plays embody Sri Aurobindo's global vision and understanding which is filled with a humanitarian outlook on the people in various parts of the world. The central female characters of these plays – Andromeda, Vasavadutta, Eric, Rodogune, Anice-al-Jalice, Aslaug, Comol Cumary, etc., are the embodiments of love, compassion and valour. Love for them in its various forms is the supreme reality in life. The playwright stresses the redeeming and alchemic power of love which triumphs over all adverse circumstances, discord, enmity and hatred, brings the plays to happy endings.

Love and war – the ever-tried traditional themes of epic and romance – continued to fascinate the poetic imagination of Sri Aurobindo. He has composed two incomplete epics, *Ahana,* in rhymed hexameter, and the other, *Ilion,* unrhymed hexameter, a rare feat in English poetry. The poet's prefatory note to the poem indicates that Ahana, the God of Dawn descends on the world of mortality and is greeted by the Hunters of Joy, seekers after Knowledge, Climbers in the quest for powers. Love greets the goddess first. She is a link between God and man. She typifies the eternal feminine principle. K.R. Srinivasa Iyengar compares the theme of the poem with the central theme of *The Bhagavad Gita* bringing out their symbolic implications thus:

> Just as in the *Gita* the real Kurukshetra is the battleground of the human soul, just as Arjuna the puzzled devotee and Krishna the divine teacher are *here* within, the former with his perplexities, his trembling hands, his cast-down Gandiva, the latter with his logic, his illuminating gospel, his magic of ineffable transcendence, they are both here within ourselves, however veiled and obscured, even so, the Hunter of Joy, the Seeker after Knowledge, the Climber in the quest for Power – the bhakti-yogin, the jnana-yogin and the karma-yogin – are all here, they are within ourselves and are ourselves, however their identities may be hidden behind our tempestuous passions, cloud-capped ambitions and befogged prejudices; and when Ahana appears at last, in answer to our strivings and prayers and adorations, she too is seen only on the Himalayas of our soul and is greeted with music...[3]

Ilion is a more ambitious poetic adventure than *Ahana.* The Penthesilea-Achilles story goes back to the myths of ancient Greece or still perhaps to earlier myths. The poem is cast in a new mould with a Homeric theme eulogising the valour, belligerent spirit, and the strength of resolution of an Asiatic Queen, Penthesilea. She is pitted against the great warrior Achilles in the battlefield. She glorifies herself in battle, in spilling blood, in martial art. She is unlike the poet's other heroines – Urvasie and Anice-al-Jalice meek and mild, submissive to men's whims. Perhaps, Sri Aurobindo portrays the other side of woman through Penthesilea. Her fight is on the terrestrial plane to save the besieged city of Troy. In Sri Aurobindo's scheme of female characterisation she is the forerunner of Savitri, the immaculate woman in her belligerent spirit and indomitable courage. Thus, the heroines in the poems already discussed have been portrayed as more than the average human mould. These "mortal fighters" as pointed out by the poet himself are "half divine and whose names are like stars in remoteness."

We see that like the great European poets Sri Aurobindo too uses myths and legends, giving them new dimensions to project the theme of love, the theme of self-transcendence and man's thirst for immortality. His intuitive knowledge and poetic vision were in search of a new myth to embody these values. The legendary tale of Savitri-Satyavan provided him with a multi-dimensional approach. The basis for accepting this legend has already been elaborated in the earlier chapters. Savitri not only combines in herself the feminine traits of all those heroines but also she is developed in terms of the archetypal themes of love, valour, death, immortality, and divine consciousness. The poet with the power of his yogic consciousness elevates her from the level of a mythic character to that of a human-divine figure who is able to glorify the divinity of her soul and awaken the *Brahman* in herself. The legend fittingly serves to establish the human conquest of the divine through a symbolic twist. Moreover, by giving a symbolic dimension to the legend the poet demonstrates the efficacy of yoga in the transformation of the human beings into divine prototype, which is definitely a spiritual emancipation of humanity from the history of mankind. In the form of a mythicised romance Divine Love in the epic triumphs over the God of death. The poet's literary and philosophical quests fuse together and culminate in a futuristic vision of mankind.

Sri Aurobindo's theological conception of the incarnation of the *Mahashakti* is presented in the mythical character of Savitri. In his prose pamphlet *The Mother* he emphasises the necessity of the Divine Mother to descend on earth to effect a change in consciousness so as to overcome mortal limitations. If the supramental change is "a thing decreed and inevitable in earth nature", then the Divine Mother alone can "free the Godlike elements in man."

Sri Aurobindo's poetic mind is strongly inclined towards rendering his scriptural vision into poetic lines to focus his conception of the redemption of man from eternal suffering. The pivotal point in the poetic mind is the presence of the seeds of death within the experience of love, which is mythicised and raised to a universal level as the opposition between Savitri, the goddess of Love and Yama, the god of Death. The hell consciousness present in the poetic psyche is transformed into the legendary figure, Aswapathy's "Descent into Night", a region more hideous and frightening due to the presence of evil, falsehood, sin, violence and crimes. The experience of the hell-bound world like that of the Dantean "Inferno" is presented through the mythic experience of Aswapathy. Hell in the poet's vision is a foul and noisome region inhabited by the corrupters of the contemporary political, social, ethical and cultural values. Not only have the contemporary life and values been scanned under the search light of Aswapathy's journey but also the images of the evolution of life are revealed to him in its various stages, starting from the smallest organisms to the most sophisticated ones. His quest for knowledge culminates in the rise of the individual soul to unite with the divine soul, the World Mother, which itself is an archetypal theme in yoga. Aswapathy's journey dramatises the various levels of the spiritual transformation necessary for emancipation of human mind from the bondage of Ignorance. Thus, one can say that the archetypal motif of Aswapathy's journey signifies that every man has a divine seed hidden in him, which needs to be activated for perfection of life and spiritual transformation. The psychological change necessary to transcend the barrier of ordinary mind is to first emerge from the opposition of psychic pulls. Aswapathy gathers the knowledge that man's present holds the seeds for the future. To win over Aswapathy's soul "The gods of light and titans of the dark" wage a war. Like that of Ezra Pound's mythical figure, Proportius, Aswapathy in his descent into Night discovers the causes of the failure of the higher worlds due to Ignorance that corrupts everything in life. Evil powers deceive him with the very voice of God. But he realises that no one can reach heaven without passing through hell because "Night is the Eternal's shadowy veil."

Allegorically, Aswapathy's yoga is a *tour de force* of the poet's mental and spiritual development to bring down the supramental power to earth. As Wordsworth's *The Prelude,* a psychological epic, elucidates the growth of the poet's mind; so does Sri Aurobindo's *Savitri* project the rise of human consciousness from the mental to the supramental level. The action of the epic is inward and psycho-spiritual in its probe into the interior region of the human mind. It is a poem of inner action that is directed toward God through the psycho-spiritual process of ascent and descent. In the mythical character of Savitri, the poet creates the opportunities for Nirvanic experience so as to prepare the ground for the descent of the divine into the human soul. Like a mythic protagonist she becomes the founder of a new way of life on the earth leaving behind the age-old one like that of Lord Buddha, Christ or any other prophet. Thus, Sri Aurobindo's seminal doctrine of cosmic salvation through spiritual transformation of individual soul is enacted through the mythic characters of Savitri and Aswapathy. It is a definitive attempt to re-enact the spiritual heritage of India for transcendence of the chaotic situations of the contemporary society, which is probably the only way for liberation out of an age of doubt, anxiety, confusion, anarchy and violence.

The poet focuses on the vast differences between unconscious and the conscious life. His vision of the emergence of a collective consciousness, a divine community can only be possible when the fusion between Matter and Spirit takes place on earth. He believes that the purpose of man's existence should be to rise above his present disturbed form of consciousness to a state of divine consciousness, for man is not only a mental being, but also a spiritual being with inexhaustible spiritual potentialities. Within the mythic contexture of the epic the poet inter-weaves multicultural values, symbolic and allegorical allusions, mystical experience, his hypothesis on evolution, soul's vision and occult knowledge. In such a literary adventure the poet reveals his inward vision, a sort of soul-seeing, to interpret profound spiritual experience inwardly in terms of images, symbols and allusions as the greatest poets possesses "a large and powerful interpretative and intuitive vision of Nature, life and man." The external world stimulates his yogic and poetic vision, which he thinks are highly essential for poetic composition.

Sri Aurobindo extends the canvas of the legend so wide as to include the cosmos, which takes into its purview the extra-cosmic realms that indirectly affect human beings. Due to the limitations of our ignorance we fail to perceive the influence of these unearthly beings on our lives. The epic points out possibilities of the higher levels of consciousness waiting for manifestation on earth. The mythical figures of Savitri and the God of death build up the poetic tension between man's mortality and his ago old aspiration for immortality, and his imperfection and unquenchable thirst for perfection. Indian mythological stories are replete with themes of man's aspiration for immortality. Man alone cannot attain this impossible status of divine life; the Supreme Lord has to descend on earth to facilitate this process. It was necessary for the poet to cast Savitri in a human divine mould. Whenever any crisis arises, man has always sought divine intervention and vice versa in ancient Indian literature. Thus, the archetypal fate of Satyavan is bound up with the destiny of mankind in the epic, which is rescued by divine intervention. Moreover, the greatest battle fought in man's soul for its possession by either god or Titan as in the case of Lord Buddha, Christ and other prophets is enacted in the character of Savitri. The purpose of lending a symbolic dimensions to the characters of Savitri and Aswapathy is to demonstrate that man's life is the field for divine manifestation and possession of higher consciousness.

A.B. Purani draws our attention to an important aspect of *Savitri*. Within the mythic framework of the epic Sri Aurobindo resolves the opposition between Time and Timelessness. Time is poised as contradictory to Timeless, the Eternal. Referring to the Vedic concept of the timeless Eternity flowing into the time-Eternity that rolls the cosmos, Sri Aurobindo points out in *Savitri*: "The Eternal's quiet holds the cosmic Act." It is believed that the Eternal beyond Time alone is the Real. In a supreme vision of the Reality both eternity and time are indivisible. The opposition between time and eternity can alone be resolved in human life by the intervention of the power of the Divine. In Sri Aurobindo's epic it is Savitri who acts as a mediator between eternity and time. She embodies the power of the Divine Love in herself. For the poet's philosophical speculation indicates that death is a shadow of love.

The "Yoga of the King" is laced with Sri Aurobindo's yogic terminologies, with the main thrust invariably being on the ascent to the Divine. Action in the timeless sphere is sought through the rituals of the Yoga for the intervention of the Divine power. Yoga in India from the ancient times has been treated as a field of man's metaphysical quest for union with the Divine. Through the mythical character of Aswapathy the poet conveys to the Divine Mother man's age-long sufferings, trials and tribulations. Hope for a reincarnation and descent of Divine Grace as envisioned variously by Hopkins, Eliot, and Hart Crane, has also been dramatised by Sri Aurobindo in the evolving soul of Aswapathy, who tries to break out of the sterility of man's endless suffering. First he frees himself from his desire ridden self and later from his ego and all human weakness, like George Hebert and Hopkins. At some certain stage of his yogic discipline, *sadhana,* he experiences supreme calm and "the human in him keeps pace with the divine."

The symbolic contexture of *Savitri* is built up in the framework of an ancient legend, which has glorified the life of inner action. Sri Aurobindo as a seer poet presents visions, which he considers are essential for great poetry. Yogic *sādhanā* empowers his poetic genius with "a means of contact with the Divine." He has bequeathed to the posterity a strong tradition of poetic creation from Overmind level. He has left a legacy of allegorical and symbolic techniques, which very few can successfully adapt. He has lucidly explained in various letters how arduously he has evolved a suitable form and technique in the composition of his great epic, *Savitri* that the posterity will not willingly lay aside. It is worthwhile to be familiar with the contents of these letters in order to form a total impression of his symbolic epic. *Savitri* is indeed a literal transcription of the great poet's yogic *sādhanā* and experience that is a treasured gift to humanity.

Since the spiritual epic is a record of the visions of a great *Yogi,* it demands intense study and spiritual reflection on the part of reader. The composition of the spiritual epic was a staggering task stretching over many decades. At the compositional stage of the poem, the poet is believed to have confided to the Mother of the Ashram that he found himself adrift in a rudderless boat in a vast ocean. The poem reveals the poet's meticulous care he took in composing it as a symbolic epic and a precursor to the "future poetry". The composition of *Savitri* was an arduous task, calling for new experimentations. The poem can itself be a test case as to see how far poetry could be written from one's yogic consciousness. A new type of art, he hopes, for the posterity will become "a predestined instrument for the new poetic language of the intuitive spirit."

The world is changing fast and people are becoming more inclined towards spiritual themes and expecting poetry as well as other forms of art to overpower them with values that can sustain human civilisation. In such a context the creator of future poetry has to perform a stupendous task, which Sri Aurobindo has already visualised and recorded as guidelines:

> It is in effect a larger cosmic vision, a revealing of the godhead in the world and in man, of his divine possibilities as well as of the greatness of the power that manifests in what he is, a spiritualised uplifting of his thought and feeling and sense and action, a more developed psychic mind and heart, a truer and deeper insight into his nature and the meaning of the world, a calling of divine possibilities and more spiritual values into the intention and structure of his life that is the call upon humanity the prospect offered to it by the slowly unfolding and now more clearly disclosed Self of the universe.[4]

In the composition of *Savitri* Sri Aurobindo has broken new ground by adopting the English language for *Upanshadic* and Kalidasian verse movement. Given the supremely difficult rhythm and 'structure' that Sri Aurobindo wanted to deploy, he had to wait for the right type of higher inspiration to aid him to accomplish the arduous task. But the poem was originally written from a lower level – "a mixture of the inner mind, psychic, poetic intelligence, sublimised vital, etc." Not being satisfied with this stuff the poet made several successive revisions and recasts of the poem with a view to lifting "the general level higher and higher towards a possible Overmind poetry." The Overmind is essentially a spiritual power. It brings out the essential truth that lies behind falsehood and error. It brings out the truth that lies between the Inconscient and the Superconscient. In this new venture he could give the myth a symbolic dimension.

REFERENCES

1. Lilian Feder, *Ancient myth in Modern Poetry,* New Jersey: Princeton University Press, 1971, rpt. 1973, p.63.
2. A.K. Sinha, *The Dramatic Art of Sri Aurobindo,* New Delhi: S. Chand & Company, Ltd., 1979, p.117.
3. K.R. Srinivas Iyengar, *Indian Writing in English,* rpt.1984, pp.163.
4. Sri Auribindo, *The Future Poetry and Letters on Poetry Literature and Art,* p.285.

Bibliography

Abercombie, Lascelles, *The Idea of Great Poetry,* London: Martin Secker Ltd., 1925.

Andreach, Robert J., *Studies in Structure,* Fordham: University Press, 1964.

Bachelard, Gaston, *The Psychoanalysis of Fire,* London: Routledge & Kegan Paul, 1964.

Baldwin, Eaton Gratia, *The New Beatrice: Or the Virtue that Counsels,* New York: Columbia University Press, 1928.

Basler, Roy P., *Sex, Symbolism and Psychology in Literature,* New Brunswick: Routgers University Press, 1968.

Beach, Joseph Warren, *Obsessive images: Symbolism in Poetry of the 1930s and 1940s,* Minneapolis: University of Minnesota Press, 1960.

Beebe, Maurice, ed. *Literary Symbolism: An Introduction to the Interpretation of Literature,* San Francisco: Wordsworth Publishing Company Inc., 1960.

Benizer, James, *Images of Eternity,* London: Southern Illionois University Press, Simons Inc., 1968.

Bevan, Edwyn, *Symbolism and Belief,* London: Allen Unwin, 1938.

Bible. *The Holy Bible,* New Jersey: International Society, 1984.

Bodkin, Maud, *Archetypal Pattern in Poetry,* Oxford Paperback, London: Oxford University Press, 1971.

Bose, Abhinash Chandra, *Three Mystic Poets,* Kothapur: School and College Bookstall, 1945.

Bowra, C.M., *The Heritage of Symbolism,* London: Macmillan Co.Ltd., 1959.

Brookington, Alfred Allen, *Mysticism and Poetry,* London: Chapman & Hall Ltd., 1934.

Brooks, Cleanth, Warren, Robert P., et al. *An Approach to Literature,* New York: Appleton Century Crofts, Inc., 3rd. rpt.1952.

Cassirer, Ernst, *Language and Myth*, tr. by Susane K. Langer, New York: Dover, 1946.

_______________, *The Philosophy of Symbolic Forms*, tr. by Ralph Manheim, New Haven: Yale University Press, 1957.

Chadwick, Charles, *Symbolism*, London: Methuen Co. Ltd., 1971.

Chand, Rishab, "The Dawn", *Srinivantu*, ed. N.K.Gupta, Calcutta, vol.I. XIX, No.1 (Feb.1971).

Chaudhuri, Haridas and Frederic Spiegelberg, ed. *The Integral Philosophy of Sri Aurobindo*, London: George Allen & Unwin, 1960.

Chincholkar, L.G., *A Critical Study of Sri Aurobindo*, Nagpur: L.G.G. Chincholkar, 1966.

Cirlot, J. E., *A Dictionary of Symbols*, tr. from Spanish by Jack Sage, London: Routledge & Kegan Paul, 1962.

Cooper, J.C., *An Illustrated Encyclopedia of Traditional Symbols*, Thames and Hodson, 1978.

Coulton, G.G., *Medieval Faith and Symbolism*, New York: Harper and Brothers, 1958.

Crane, R.S., *The Language of Criticism and the Structure of Poetry*, Canada: University of Toronto Press, 1971.

Cornell, Kenneth, *The Symbolist Movement*, New Haven: Yale University Press, 1952.

Dante, Alighieri, *The Divine Comedy-I, Hell.* tr. by Dorothy L., Sayers, Middlesex: Penguin Books Ltd., 1978.

_______________, *The Divine Comedy-II, Purgatory*, tr. by Dorothy L., Sayers, Middlesex: Penguin Books Ltd., 1977.

_______________, *The Divine Comedy-III, Paradise*, tr. by Dorothy L. Sayers and Raynolds Barbara, Middlesex: Penguin Books Ltd., 1976.

Dell, W.S. & Baynes, C. F., *Modern Man in Search of His Soul*, New York, 1934.

Diwakar, R.R., *Mahayogi*, Bombay: Bhartiya Vidya Bhavan, 1954.

Eliade, Mircea, *Images and Symbols*, tr. by Philip Mairer, New York: Sheed and Ward, 1969.

Fedder, Lillian, *Ancient Myth in Modern Poetry*, Princeton, N.J.: Princeton University Press, 1971.

Fiedelson, Charles, Jr. *Symbolism and American Literature*, University of Chicago Press, 1955.

Flanders, Dunbar, *Symbolism in Medieval Thought and its Consummation in the Divine Comedy*, New York: Russell and Russell, 1961.

Fletcher, Angus, *Allegory: The Theory of Symbolic Mode*, New York: Columbia University Press, 1921.

Fletcher, Jefferson Butler, *Symbolism of Divine Comedy*, New York: Columbia University Press, 1921.

_______________, *Dante*, Indiana: University of Notre Dame Press, 1965.

Freccero, John, ed. *Dante: A Collection of Critical Essays*, Englewood Cliffs, N.J.: Princeton-Hall, Inc., 1965.

Frye, Northrop, *Anatomy of Criticism*, Princeton, N.J.: Princeton University Press, 1971.

_______________ "Symbolism", *Princeton Encyclopaedia of Poetry and Poetics*, ed., Alex Preminger, London: The Macmillan Press Ltd., 1975.

Ghose, Lotika, "The Poetry of Sri Aurobindo" *Sri Aurobindo Mandir Annual*, Calcutta, No.8, (1949).

Ghose, Sisir Kumar, *The Poetry of Sri Aurobindo: A Short Survey*, Calcutta: Chatuskona Pvt. Ltd., 1969.

Gokak, V.K., *Sri Aurobindo: Seer Poet*, New Delhi: Abhinav Publications, 1973.

_______________, *An Integral View of Poetry*, New Delhi: Abhinav Publications, 1975.

_______________, and Reddy M., ed. *The Flame of Truth*, Hyderabad: Institute of Human Studies, 1968.

Goodman, Nelson, *Language of Art: An Approach to a Theory of Symbols*, London: Oxford University Press, 1969.

Green, David, ed. *The Winged Word*, New Delhi: Macmillan, 1979.

Gupta, Nolini Kanta, *Collected Works of Nolini Kanta Gupta*, Pondicherry: Sri Aurobindo Ashram Trust, Vol. I to VII, 1978.

_______________, *Poets and mystics*, Madras: Sri Aurobindo Library, 1951.

_______________, "Savitri: An Editorial Commentary", *The Advent*, ed. N.K. Gupta, Pondicherry, February 1947.

Gupta, Rameswar, *Eternity in Words: Sri Aurobindo's Savitri*, Bombay: Chetana Prakasan, 1969.

Hawkes, Terence, *Metaphor*, London: Methuen Co. Ltd., 1972.

Hollander, Robert, *Allegory in Dante's Comedies*, New Jersey: Princeton University Press, 1969.

Hungerland, Isabel C., *Poetic Discourse*, Berkeley and Los Angeles: University of California Press, 1958.

Huta, *About Savitri*, Pondicherry: Sri Aurobindo Ashram, 1972.

_______________ , *Meditations on Savitri,* Pondicherry: Sri Aurobindo Ashram, 1962.

Iyengar, K.R.Srniva, *Indian Writing in English,* Bombay: Asia Publishing House, 2nd ed., 1973.

_______________ , *Dawn to Greater Dawn,* Simla: Indian Institute of Advanced Study, 1975.

_______________ , "A Note on Thought the Paraclete", *Srivantu,* ed. N.K.Gupta, vol.xx. No.4. November 1978.

_______________ , "The First Canto of Sri Aurobindo's Savitri", *Mother India,* ed. K.D.Sethna, Pondicherry: Sri Aurobindo Ashram, Sept. 1969.

_______________ , "Some Notes on English Mystical Poetry", *Mother India,* ed. K.D. Sethna, Pondicherry, No.13 (1949).

_______________ , "Romanticism, Symbolism and Mysticism", *Mother India,* ed. K.D. Sethna, Pondicherry, No.13 (1949).

Jacobs, Garry, *Guide to Sri Aurobindo's Savitri,* Vol.I. Pondicherry: Dipti Publications, 1973.

Jacobi, Jolanda, *Complex, Archetype, Symbol in the Psychology of C.G.Jung,* tr. from German by Ralph Manliam, London: Routledge, 1959.

James, William, *The Varieties of Religious Experience: A Study in Human Nature,* London: Longmans, Green & Co. 37th impt. 1928.

Khana, R.N., "A Study of Simile in Sri Aurobindo's Savitri", *Mother India,* ed. K.D.Sethna, Pondicherry, Semt. 1968.

Knight, G. Wilson, *The Wheel of Fire,* London: Methuen & Co. Ltd., 1954.

Knight, L.C.and Cotle, Basil, *Metaphor and Symbol,* London: Butler Worths Scientific Publications, 1060.

Kotky, P.C., *Indo-English Poetry,* Gauhati: Gauhati University Press, 1969.

Krishna Sarma, S., *Seed of Grandeur,* Viayawada: Kamala Publications, 1972.

Krishna Sastry, L.S., "Two Poems of Sri Aurobindo", *Banasthali Patrika,* July,1969.

Leach, Marian., ed. *Standard Dictionary of Folklore, Mythology and Legends,* London, 1975.

Langley, G.H., *Sri Aurobindo: Indian Poet, Philosopher and Mystic,* London: David Marlowe, 1969.

Lehman, A.G., *The Symbolist Aesthetic in France (1885-1895),* Oxford: Basil Blackwell, 1968.

Lewis, C.D., *The Poetic Image,* London: Jonathan Cape, 1947.

Lodge, David, ed. *20th Century Criticism*, London: Longman Group, Ltd., 1972.

Macdonnel, A.A., *A Vedic Reader for Students*, London: Oxford University Press, 1917.

Macfie, G.M., *Myths and Legends of India*, Edinburgh, T & T, 1942.

MacLeish, Archibald. *Poetry and Experience*, Middlesex: Penguin Books, 1960.

Maritain, Jacques and Raissa, *The Situation of Poetry*, New York: Kraus Reprint Co., 1968.

May, Rollo, *Symbolism in Religion and Literature*, New York: George Braziller, 1960.

Mehta, Rohit, *The Dialogue with Death*, Ahmedabad: Navjivan Press, 1972.

Members of Oxford Dante Society, *Centenary Essays on Dante*, Oxford: Clarendon Press, 1965.

Mishra, Nanda Kishore and Tripathy Sakita, *A Critical Response to Indian English Literatire*, New Delhi: Atlantice Publishers, 2002.

Modi, Rajani Kanta, "Poetic Imagery in Savitri", *Mother India*, K.D. Sethna, ed. No. 23,1950.

Moore, Edward, *Studies in Dante*, Oxford: Clarendon Press, 1916.

Naik, M.K., ed. *Indian Response to Poetry in English*, Madras: Macmillan & Co. ltd., 1970.

_______________, *Aspects of Indian Writing in English*, Delhi: Macmialln & Co. 1979.

Nandakumar, Prema, *A Study of Savitri*, Pondicherry: Sri Aurobindo Ashram Press, 1962.

_______________, *Dante and Sri Aurobindo*, Madras: Affiliated East-west Press, 1981.

Osgood, Charles Grosvenor, *Poetry as a Means of Grace*, London: Princeton University Press, 1964.

Pandit, M.P., *Key to Vedic Symbolism*, Pondicherry: Sri Aurobindo Ashram Press, 1971.

_______________, *Readings in Savitri*, Vol.I to X, Pondicherry: Sri Aurobindo Ashram.

Pearson, Nathaniel, *Sri Aurobindo and the Soul Quest of Man*, London: Allen & Unwin, 1952.

Perkins, David, *The Quest for Permanence: The Symbolism of Wordsworth, Shelley, and Keats*, Massachusetts: Harvard Univ. Press, 1959.

Piper, Raymond, *The Hungry Eye*, California, 1955.

_______________, "Sri Aurobindo's Savitri", *Mother India*, ed. K.D. Sethna, No.10 (Dec. 1958).

Prasad, S.K., *The Literary Criticism of Sri Aurobindo*, Patna: Bharati Bhavan, 1974.

Preminger, Alex, ed. *Princeton Encyclopaedia of Poetry and Poetics*, London: The Macmillan Press Ltd., 1975.

Purani, A.B. *Savitri: An Approach and a Study*, Pondicherry: Sri Aurobindo Press, 1970.

Reddy, Madhusudan, ed. *Towards Eternity*, Hyderabad: Institute of Human Studies, 1972.

Rehder, Helmut, ed. *Literary Symbolism:A Symposium*, Austin and London: University of Texas Press, 1965.

Santayana, George, *Three Philosophical Poets*, Cambridge: Harvard University Press, 1910.

Saunders, William, "The Collected Poems and Plays of Sri Aurobindo," *Golden Dawn*. Baroda: Souvenir, Sri Aurobindo Society, Feb.1978.

Sayers, Dorothy L., *Further Papers on Dante*, London: Methuen , 1957.

Seetaraman, M.V., "Dual Being", *The Advent*, ed. N.K. Gupta, Pondicherry, No.4 (November 1959).

Sethna, K.D., *The Poetic Genius of Sri Aurobindo*, Pondicherry: Sri Aurobindo Ashram Press, 1970.

______________, *Sri Aurobindo: The Poet*, Pondicherry: Sri Aurobindo International Centre of Education, 1970.

______________, "Agni in the Rig-Veda and Aswapathy in Savitri", *Mother India*, Pondicherry, Special Issue, No.8 (15 August 1982).

Singleton, Charles, *Dante Studies-2: Journey to Beatrice*, Cambridge : Harvard University Press, 1958.

Spurgeon, Caroline E., *Mysticism in English Literature*, Cambridge University Press, 1913.

Sri Aurobindo, *Collected Poems*, Pondicherry: Sri Aurobindo Ashram Press, 1969.

______________, *Essays on the Gita*, Pondicherry: Sri Aurobindo Ashram Press, 1970.

______________, *Hymn to Mystic Fire*, Pondicherry: Sri Aurobindo Ashram Press, 1971.

______________, *Letters on Yoga*, Birth Centenary Library Vol. Pondicherry: Sri Aurobindo Ashram Press, 1971.

______________, *Life Divine*, Pondicherry: Sri Aurobindo Ashram Trust, Bk.I & II, 1977.

______________, *On Himself*, Pondicherry: Sri Aurobindo Ashram Press, 1972.

______________, *Savitri: A Legend and a Symbol,* Pondicherry: Sri Aurobindo Press,4th Imprint., 1977.

______________, *Synthesis of Yoga,* Pondicherry: Sri Aurobindo Ashram Press, 1970.

______________, *The Foundation of Indian Culture,* Pondicherry: Sri Aurobindo Ashram Press, 1980.

______________, *The Future Poetry and Letters on Poetry, Literature and Art,* Ponicherry: Sri Aurobindo Press, 1972.

______________, *The Human Cycle,* American Edition, 1950.

______________, *The Ideal of Human Unity,* American Edition. 1950.

______________, *The Mother,* Pondicherry: Sri Aurobindo Press, 1969.

______________, *The Secret of the Vedas,* Pondicherry: Sri Aurobindo Ashram Press, Birth Centenary Library Vol. X, 1972.

______________, *The Upanishads,* Pondicherry: Sri Aurobindo Birth Centenary, Vol. XII, Sri Aurobindo Ashram Press, 1972.

______________, *Vyasa and Valmiki,* Pondicherry: Sri Aurobindo Ashram Press, 1964.

Sri Krishna Prem, "Savitri", *Srinvantu,* ed. N.K. Gupta, Vol. xx. No.4. Nov.1972.

Sullivan, J. P., ed. *Ezra Pound,* Middlesex, England: Penguin Books, 1975.

Symons, Arthur, *The Symbolist Movement in Literature,* London: Archibald Constable & Co. Ltd., 1908.

Thompson, David, *Dante's Epic Journey,* Baltimore and London: John Hopkins University Press, 1974.

Tindall, W. York, *The Literary Symbol,* Bloomington: Indiana Univ. Press, 1955.

Urban, Wilber Marshall, *Language and Reality: The Philosophy of Language and the Principles of Symbolism,* Part III, London: George Allen and Unwin Ltd., 1952.

Vickey, J.B., ed. *Myth and Literature,* Lincoln: University of Nebraska Press, 1966.

Vries , Ad de, *Dictionary of Symbols and Imagery,* London: North Hall Co. 1974.

Webster's Third International Dictionary, Chicago:Encyclopedia. Inc. Vol.III, 1976.

Weinberg, Bernard, *The Limits of Symbolism:Studies in Five Modern French Poets,* Chicago: University of Chicago Press, 1966.

William, Charles, *The Figure of Beatrice,* London: Faber & Faber Ltd., 1943.

Willis, Roy, ed. *The Interpretation of Symbolism*, London: Malaby Press, 1975.

Wilson, Colin, *Poetry and Mysticism*, London: Hutchinson & Co. Ltd., 1970.

Wilson, Edmund, *Axel's Castle*, New York: Charles Scribner's Sons, 1950.

Wimsatt, Jr., William, K. & Brooks, Cleanth, *Literary Criticism: A Short Survey*. New Delhi: Oxford and I.B.H. Publishing Co., 1970.

Yeats, W.B., *Essays*, London: Macmillan, 1924.

Zimmer, Heinrich, *Myths and Symbols in Asian Art and Civilisation*, ed. Joseph Cambell, New York: Pantheon Books Inc.,1953.

Index